UNORGANIZED WOMEN

PITTSBURGH SERIES IN COMPOSITION, LITERACY, AND CULTURE

David Bartholomae and Jean Ferguson Carr, Editors

UNORGANIZED WOMEN

REPETITIVE RHETORICAL LABOR AND LOW-WAGE WORKERS, 1834–1937

JANE GREER

UNIVERSITY OF PITTSBURGH PRESS

Published by the University of Pittsburgh Press, Pittsburgh, Pa., 15260

Manufactured in the United States of America
Printed on acid-free paper
10 9 8 7 6 5 4 3 2 1

Cataloging-in-Publication data is available from the Library of Congress

ISBN 13: 978-0-8229-4755-4
ISBN 10: 0-8229-4755-2

Cover photo: Factory Floor at the Donnelly Garment Co. Image Courtesy of State Historical Society of Missouri, Kansas City Research Center.
Cover design: Melissa Dias-Mandoly

In memory of my mom,
Lucille Booth Greer

CONTENTS

ACKNOWLEDGMENTS

Mary Heaton Vorse, a labor journalist of the early twentieth century, famously noted that "the art of writing is the art of applying the seat of the pants to the seat of the chair." Though the writing of this book has for too long had me applying the seat of my pants to the seat of my desk chair, the support of brilliant, generous friends and family has ensured that I was never working on my own. Abby Dubisar, Liz Tasker-Davis, and Lisa Shaver have read (and reread) every page of this book in five-page chunks for our monthly writing group meetings over the past several years. Their wisdom and insights have profoundly shaped my thinking. They have helped me see where I was misstepping and always encouraged me to keep working, keep writing. I am especially grateful to Lisa for reading a draft of my full manuscript at a crucial moment and for reassuring me—with her characteristic wry wit—that I had indeed written a book and not merely produced a collection of pages where some interesting ideas collided.

At the University of Missouri, Kansas City, English department chairs Jeff Rydberg-Cox, Virginia Blanton, Jennifer Phegley, and Laurie Ellinghausen have, through the years, helped create collegial, conducive working conditions for faculty, allowing my colleagues and me to follow our research interests and to bring our creativity and passion to the classroom. I am especially grateful to Jeff for introducing me to some of the research tools of the digital humanities and for patiently answering all my questions. I have also had the great good fortune to work with Sherry Neuerburg and Audrey Lester, both in the English department and now as important partners in UMKC's undergraduate research program. Thank you both for being brilliant problem-solvers, savvy tacticians, and lovely human beings. Two extraordinary women in academic leadership—Linda Edwards, dean emerita of the School of Education, and Cindy Pemberton, deputy provost emerita—have been important, inspiring mentors for me. I am a better faculty member, academic administrator, and, most importantly, a better person because of them.

The incomparable Stuart Hinds and the entire staff at the Dr. Kenneth J. LaBudde Special Collections and UMKC's University Libraries have supported my work and the research and writing of this book in countless ways. Stuart's encyclopedic knowledge of Kansas City history and of archives and repositories scattered across the region is exceeded only by his bounteous goodwill and good humor. Brenda Dingley pointed me in the right direction more than once as I tracked down obscure sources, and Anthony LaBat provided crucial digital services with great efficiency as I was wrapping up my work on this book. At the State Historical Society of Missouri Kansas City Research Center, Lucinda Adams and Whitney Heinzmann arranged for collections to be available for me in the reading room for extended periods of time, alerted me to new acquisitions, and were ready listeners when I most wanted to share documents and discoveries that intrigued me. Every researcher should be so fortunate to work with such knowledgeable, efficient, attentive, and engaging archivists. I am also grateful for the timely assistance of Melissa Holland and Steven Calco at Cornell University's Kheel Center for Labor-Management Documentation and Archives as well as the assistance of expert staff at the Special Collections Research Center at the University of Kentucky Libraries and the Schlesinger Library at the Radcliffe Institute, Harvard University.

My research and writing is always intertwined with my teaching, and I am grateful for so many important conversations with Melanie Burdick, Antonio Byrd, Sheila Honig, Paul Hanstedt, and Laura Taylor about teaching writing, researching writing, and being writers. I am also deeply appreciative for the fellowship and inspiration of Laurie Grobman, Joyce Kinkead, Jessie Moore, Doug Downs, Dominic Dellicarpini, Jenn Fishman, and the community of scholars and teachers who are committed to helping undergraduate students participate in the research conversations of our field.

I have benefited from the financial support of the University of Missouri Research Board, which provided grant funding to support my initial trips to archival repositories across the country. A faculty research grant from UMKC's Women's and Gender Studies program provided additional support at a critical stage during my revisions. Portions of chapter 3 originally appeared in "Expanding Working-Class Rhetorical Traditions: The Moonlight Schools and Alternative Solidarities among Appalachian Women, 1911–1920," which was published in *College English*, vol. 77, no. 3, 2015, pp. 216–35. (Copyright 2015 by the National Council of Teachers of English. Reprinted with permission.)

While writing this book, three canine companions have kept me afloat—Lizzie, Maggie, and Bessie. Doggie snores resonating from underneath my desk and long walks through our Brookside neighborhood have always helped me untangle snags in my thinking and made sure I stayed focused on what really matters most in life. Each one of them has stolen her own special piece of my heart and paradoxically made what was left behind a little bigger.

To my husband, Neil, thank you for making me more adventurous, more flexible, more willing to listen to other people's perspectives. Your confidence in me, your patience, and your support made this book possible. Saying yes to a second first date with you is one of the best decisions I have ever made. I am deeply appreciative as well to all the Tenbrooks, Natoniewskis, Wellens, Rosses, Cyrs, Andersons, Pauls, and Garrisons who have made me feel welcome in their family and have been so gracious in their hospitality. To my own extended family—Booths, Wittels, Greers, and all the rest—thank you for your love and for always reminding me that the world is much bigger than academia and that there is much wisdom to be found in spaces beyond the classroom and the library.

This book is dedicated to the memory of my mom. I will never be able to express fully how grateful I am to have been raised up by a woman of such quiet strength and courage. There is some work words just can't do, no matter how many times you repeat them.

UNORGANIZED WOMEN

INTRODUCTION

WORKING WOMEN, WORKING WORDS

Having raised eight children on a mountaintop farm in West Virginia, Myrtle Tenney Booth, my grandma, was one of the hardest-working women I have ever known. At age thirteen, Grandma left school to nurse her mother through a serious illness. As a fifteen-year-old, she worked as a cook in a camp for railroad workers in Mock Hollow, and four years later, she was sorting tin plate at the Weirton Steel Mill in Clarksburg. At age twenty-one, she married my grandpa, who had saved enough money from his wages as a sawmill worker to buy a sixty-seven-acre farm up the road from Pickens. For the next forty-six years, Grandma made cheese, gathered eggs, chopped wood, butchered hogs, canned peaches, nursed sick children, pieced quilts, and coped with the unending cycle of chores that are part of raising a large family on a small farm.

In my earliest memories, Grandma is already an old woman who can barely hobble to the woodshed for kindling or wring a chicken's neck with her gnarled fingers. Her body told the tale of her lifetime of labor, and I learned the value of work in her kitchen and on her farm. She was too busy to chatter much with children, but in the countless grown-up conversations floating over my head, I heard women praised for being good workers. You could be pretty, slim, or even smart, but a worthy woman was one who knew how to work.

Despite her deep investment in the dignity of work—no matter how mundane, how messy—my grandmother never aligned herself with organized labor. As a young girl working to feed railroad workers while they laid and maintained the track that helped move timber and coal out of the mountains, Grandma would not have been a potential union member. Men employed by the Baltimore & Ohio Railroad in the early decades of the twentieth century had a proud tradition of organized labor activism dating back to the Great Railroad Strike of 1877, but Grandma was not employed by the railroad. Instead, she had a more informal employment arrangement with the woman who ran the camp where railroad workers were housed and fed. While working long hours as a tin plate sorter in a steel mill, Grandma undertook dangerous and difficult tasks. According to Louis C. Martin, "Women in the assorting room used knives to pry apart sheets [of tin plate] that were partly welded together in stacks" (497). They would then inspect the tin-coated sheets of steel and pack them for shipping. Deemed "unskilled labor," such work was hazardous, monotonous, and poorly remunerated. While her employment as a tin plate sorter was precipitated by economic necessity, Grandma also recognized that her sojourn in the industrial workforce would likely be brief. Like many, though certainly not all, young white women in her circumstances, her experience as an industrial laborer ended with her marriage, and she had little time to develop an opinion on Weirton Steel's labor practices and its efforts to forestall unionization.

Once my grandparents settled on their own small subsistence farm, the idea of organized labor seemed even less relevant to Grandma's working life. While tending a garden and raising livestock to sustain her growing family, my grandma had few, if any, opportunities to consider the possibility of formal organizational strategies that might have allowed Appalachian families to band together to gain a greater measure of control over their often precarious economic lives. Instead, like the generations of farm women who preceded her, Grandma relied as best she could on her own resources and the support of family and friends. When times were good she took advantage of opportunities to trade the cheese and butter she made to neighbors in exchange for goods and services her family needed, and she drastically cut household expenses when times were bad. She spent long hours preparing meals in the kitchen and making sure the farmhouse was a clean, comfortable space for her family, but her workspace expanded to the barn where cows needed to be milked and pigs needed to be fed when my grandpa found it necessary to work for wages off the farm at nearby strip mines or on road-building projects sponsored by the Works Progress Administration (WPA) during the 1930s. She took great pride in the fact that she was able to serve as a cook at the local one-room schoolhouse and provide a hot meal to all the children in her rural community on the limited funding provided by the state school board, yet she also accepted the fact that her own children—including my mother—would need to leave home to earn their own living before they turned sixteen.

Despite their hard work, my grandma and the generations of low-wage white women workers who, like her, were not affiliated with labor organizations have received scant attention from feminist rhetoricians. We know little about how they described themselves as workers within their communities or the discursive strategies they used to document their labor. The less formal types of collective activity they chose to pursue to gain a greater measure of control over their economic lives remain hidden from our view, and the rhetorical labor that allowed them to build a sense of common cause and community has yet to be accounted for in histories of women's rhetoric. *Unorganized Women* addresses these omissions and enriches feminist histories of rhetoric by making space for the voices of low-wage white women workers who were not part of the organized labor movement.

I offer here four historical case studies of such unorganized women workers—the "mill girls" of Lowell, Massachusetts, who used the *Lowell Offering* (1840–1845) as a vehicle to share their lives and labors with a wider audience;[1] domestic workers in Boston who were hailed by the Women's Educational and Industrial Union (WEIU) through its Domestic Reform League and other initiatives designed to solve the "servant problem" in the final decades of the nineteenth century; Appalachian farm women who participated in the Moonlight Schools founded in Rowan County, Kentucky, by Cora Wilson Stewart in 1911; and the seamstresses who worked at Kansas City's Donnelly Garment Company (DGC) and spurned the overtures of the International Ladies' Garment Workers' Union (ILGWU) in the 1930s. All these women workers undertook significant forms of rhetorical labor. By composing essays, stories, poetry, petitions, and letters, they crafted public representations of themselves as workers and as women. They constructed new communication channels or co-opted existing ones, such as periodicals, employment records, and legal documents, in order to generate and circulate information they found immediately useful. They recognized the need to address a range of audiences that included their employers and coworkers, family members, philanthropists, educators, government officials, members of the judiciary, union officials, cultural tastemakers, and more. They resisted the inscription of their lives and labor into broader economic and cultural narratives they did not find productive, including well-worn plots about the deleterious impact of industrial labor on white women's moral standing and about the promise of scientific advancements in housekeeping and agriculture to improve the lives of rural families and to usher their communities into the modern era. They engaged in a range of often unrecognized collective endeavors as they sought to gain greater control in their working lives and improve their financial circumstances and their communities. And at times, they created or reinforced discursive bulwarks that perpetuated white supremacy and preserved the modicum of social and economic privilege they enjoyed as low-wage white women at the expense of Black women workers and recent immigrants. The lives and rhetorical labor of these unorganized working women are the focus of this book.

WHY THESE WORKING WOMEN?

The white women featured in this book earned their livings in a variety of occupational spaces and undertook diverse forms of labor—weaving cloth on power looms; cooking and cleaning in the homes of well-to-do families; working with livestock, raising crops, and feeding their own families on subsistence farms; and participating in the mass production of women's apparel. I refer to all these women as "low-wage" workers in recognition of the fact that economic precarity was a critical concern in their lives, whether they were paid to work on a factory floor or in someone else's home, or even if they didn't necessarily earn wages on a regular basis and instead bartered or traded goods in a rural economy. As low-wage workers, the women whose lives and labors are the focus of my attention netted minimal remuneration for tackling a variety of physically draining, mentally demanding jobs, and the money they earned or other resources they garnered were critical for their survival as well as the survival of their families. And like so many other people with limited financial resources, the low-wage women workers who animate the pages of this book also have in common the experience of producing considerable social consternation among the members of the cultural and economic elite, who have debated their moral standing, castigated their work habits, lamented their seeming failures to integrate themselves productively into the national economy, and questioned their decisions about how best to manage their working lives.

Dividing economically imperiled women into granular categories based on the type of work they perform or the sources of their income can occlude common obstacles they confront in seeking to provide for themselves and their families as well as the range of strategies they have deployed in seeking to improve their work lives. As economist Michael Zweig has argued, drawing sharp distinctions among people with few financial resources and limited control over their economic lives will do little to advance social equality or lead to a sustainable future (78–79, 92). In this book, I thus bring together a range of white women workers under the term "low-wage," and I am able to document a wide spectrum of collective activities and alliance-building strategies that have appealed to them: participating in textual communities of writers and editors; engaging with philanthropists and educational reformers; fostering their own workplace-based identities and coalitions. My title, *Unorganized Women*, signals that the women under study here were not part of the organized labor movement while also inviting fresh consideration of the often unrecognized ways low-wage workers have come together to advance their economic interests.

I begin with the Lowell mill girls as my first historical case study because they were one of the earliest groups of industrial women workers in the United States who experimented with varied forms of collective action in the 1830s and early 1840s. I end with the DGC workers and their resistance to the ILGWU in the 1930s because they present a particularly knotty set of questions about low-wage women workers and their responses to organized labor. As I discuss in greater detail later in this introduction, the mill girls of Lowell and the DGC workers bookend a critical century—from the 1830s through the 1930s—in which women who earned their livings in the industrial workforce had a particularly fraught relationship with organized labor movements. During this time period, assumptions about the primacy of white men as wage earners for their families shaped the practices and policies of unions, workers' associations, and other labor organizations, leaving many low-wage women workers looking for other ways to gain a measure of control over their economic lives. Investigating the rhetorical labor that seemed efficacious to the women who contributed to the *Lowell Offering* and the women employed at the DGC affords feminist rhetoricians an opportunity to develop a more finely textured sense of how low-wage white women workers have sought to exercise power in industrial workplaces.

The two middle chapters of *Unorganized Women* move beyond the factory floor to bring forward questions about how white women who earned their livings in other spaces have grappled with workplace exploitation and financial precarity. The circumstances of women who were employed as household workers in Boston and women who lived and worked on subsistence farms in Appalachia did not lend themselves to typical forms of labor organizing. These low-wage women workers were, however, encouraged to engage in other forms of affiliative behavior and collective activity by philanthropic organizations and educational activists. Both historically and in the present moment, vast numbers of women have earned their livings as household workers and on farms. Placing such women workers alongside women working in industrial settings yields a fuller and more nuanced accounting of the varied forms that workers' activism can take.

Moving from industrial to domestic to agricultural workspaces also affords me the opportunity to study various forms of rhetorical labor—the publication of a periodical; the use of business genres including contracts and employment records; letters directed to a variety of audiences; and petitions and testimonials. Documenting the wide range of rhetorical labor in which white women have been engaged in the past makes it possible to trace a richer array of connections to the rhetorical labor of contemporary women workers and to better appreciate the sorts of collective activities that seem most efficacious in the twenty-first century, both in the United States and around the globe. These are connections and questions I explore in the afterword to this volume.

The four historical case studies that comprise this book focus on workspaces dominated by white women. This may seem curious given that more than two decades ago historian Sharon Harley and the Black Women and Work Collective excoriated scholars working in labor history, Black studies, and women's studies, noting that they had "focused on black men and white women as workers, thereby continuing to slight black women's work" (xvii). In the late twentieth century, Harley, Tera W. Hunter, Jacqueline Jones, Dolores E. Janiewski, Kibibi Voloria C. Mack, and other historians had begun engaging in pioneering work that addressed this slight. They undertook critical research projects centered on the experiences of Black women and their labors. In doing so, they laid the groundwork for a burgeoning of vital scholarship in the twenty-first century on Black women workers in a variety of contexts, including domestic labor; industrial settings; service industries; food production; occupations deemed criminal, such as sex work and numbers running; and the prison-industrial complex (Green; Branch; Sharpless; Nadasen; LeFlouria; Blair; Gray; Harris).

By focusing on white women workers in this book, my intention is not to recenter or reassert their experiences as normative or to occlude the work experiences of women of color. Instead, my goal in selecting the four workplaces that are featured in this book is to bring forward the range of ways in which white women who grappled with financial precarity have sought to shore up their place in the labor pool and in the civic life of the nation through particular forms of rhetorical labor. Their rhetorical labor frequently involved the marginalization and oppression of Black women workers and immigrants. By attending to such patterns of privilege and oppression, I answer labor historian Dana Frank's call for greater exploration of white supremacy and for research that "situate[s] white working-class women within a racialized nation" (81). Racism and nationalism have shaped the economic landscape of the United States, and white women have historically had access to occupations unavailable to women of color. They have also been paid higher wages for performing the same labor and enjoyed greater job security than Black women. And though economically impoverished, low-wage white women have had access to property and assets through their relationships to white men (e.g., fathers, brothers, boyfriends, husbands, and sons)—property and assets that were not equally available to Black families and other people of color. It is important to acknowledge that all too often the white women workers featured in this book deepened divides based on race and birthplace. They engaged in rhetorical labor that forestalled their association with women of color and newly arrived immigrants, associations they believed would undermine their economic prospects and their sociocultural status.

Throughout *Unorganized Women*, I argue that careful attention to ingenious, persistent rhetorical labors of white women workers as well as to their divisive discursive moves holds out the promise of imagining new kinds of coalitions among workers in the future. Though their rhetorical labor includes much that is disturbing, the women working in the Lowell textile mills, domestic servants in Boston, Appalachian farm women in the early twentieth century, and the DGC seamstresses who resisted the ILGWU in the 1930s merit a place in histories of rhetoric as we seek to develop richer understandings of the past and to imagine a future filled with greater economic justice for all.

WORKING WOMEN'S RHETORICS: PAST AND PRESENT

The twenty-first century has seen numerous calls for rhetoricians to pay greater attention to women's work-related rhetorics. Michelle C. Smith notes that "studies of gendered labor help feminist rhetoricians to move beyond a sometimes limiting preconception with civic and political rhetorics" (144). And writing with Sarah Hallenbeck, Smith cogently argues that "workplaces, work tasks, and work arrangements are . . . sites where gender and work themselves are rhetorically contested and constructed." Hallenbeck and Smith go on to note that "workplaces and professions are often key axes in the maintenance or disruption of gendered, raced, classed, and ability-based differences" (201). Observing that labor historians have long "meditated on women's historical relationship to work," Jessica Enoch similarly points out that "feminist rhetoricians have only just begun to consider the question of how their scholarly perspectives and investments might add substance and perspective to this conversation" (*Domestic Occupations* 19). Through her study of women's workplaces and related spaces, including schoolrooms, domestic science laboratories, and childcare centers, Enoch deftly reveals how the spatial rhetorics of home and domesticity have historically enabled middle-class white women to take on new kinds of work.

When feminist rhetoricians have focused their attention on the work-related rhetorics of women with limited economic resources, they have often gravitated toward the discursive innovations and accomplishments of women labor leaders and activists, including Nannie Helen Burroughs (Popp and Phillips-Cunningham), Dolores Huerta (Sowards), Rose Cohen and Elizabeth Hasanovitz (Goldman), Elizabeth Gurley Flynn (Tonn), Emma Goldman (Solomon), Mary Harris "Mother" Jones (Tonn; Waggoner), Meridel Le Sueur (Boehnlein), Leonora O'Reilly (Triece), Rose Schneiderman (Glascott; Kvidera), Theresa Malkiel (Kvidera), Rosina Corrothers Tucker (Chateauvert), and Marian Wharton (Allen). Research on labor schools, such as the Brookwood Labor College and Bryn Mawr Summer School for Women Workers, and on the educational programs sponsored by unions, such as the ILGWU, has helped to amplify the voices of rank-and-file workers that might never have been entered into the historical record if they had not contributed an article to a school newspaper or composed an autobiographical essay for a class assignment (Kates; Hollis; Wan, *Producing Good Citizens*).

Doubly marginalized by both class and gender, women labor leaders and the workers they sought to mobilize challenged idealized notions of female behavior through their rhetorical performances. They marched on picket lines and delivered speeches at mass meetings. They authored textbooks and other pedagogical materials that interrogated the investment of the economically elite in definitions of standard English and opted instead to validate working-class vernaculars. They forged strategic alliances with men in the labor movement when it suited their purposes, and they took up the pen to ensure that their lives and work were made visible in union newspapers and bulletins. As Anne F. Mattina summarizes, "In the evolution of feminist rhetorical criticism, analysis of working-class rebels adds nuance to our understanding of women's persuasive practices. . . . Freed from the constraints of middle-class 'ladyhood,' they demonstrated their dissatisfaction with the status quo not by adapting to those confines but by shouting, signing, and pushing back against them with all of their might" (66). Mattina's description of the working-class women rebels who have become part of our rhetorical histories aligns with William DeGenaro's perspective that working-class rhetorics "agitate and antagonize" and are defined by "a certain consciousness—an awareness that class (and, by extension, class division and class conflict) exists" (6). To be a working-class rhetor is to be consciously engaged in the struggle between labor and capital, between the economically elite and those who struggle to make ends meet.

Such a definition of working-class rhetoric, however, excludes many low-wage white women, including women like my grandma, from our rhetorical histories. While keenly aware of economic inequalities, many low-wage women have not always engaged in class-conscious "agitation and antagonism." Low-wage women who gained visibility through unions and workers' rights organizations were actually atypical in the nineteenth and early twentieth centuries. Labor historian Alice Kessler-Harris estimates that "something like 3.3 percent of the women who were engaged in industrial occupations in 1900 were organized into trade unions . . . [and] a reasonable estimate might place 6.6 percent of wage-earning women in trade unions by 1920" (*Out to Work* 152). The vast majority of women working in low-wage jobs in the time period covered by this study were not able to insist on the importance of their labor or advocate for their economic needs via the mechanisms of organized labor.

While labor unions have been essential for securing workers' rights, many labor organizations born in the second half of the nineteenth century, like the Knights of Labor and the American Federation of Labor (AFL), were steeped in racist and patriarchal values. While there are notable examples of interracial organizing in specific industries or geographic regions in the late nineteenth and early twentieth centuries, "most craft unions were openly racist, excluding Black members either formally or by custom" (Goldfield 5).[2] Black men were perceived as a threat to a white man's right to a fair wage that would allow him to support his family. Similarly, women workers were viewed by the white men who ran unions as well as rank-and-file members as imperiling the relationship between white masculinity and economic power. For white women, their most important jobs were presumed to be as wives and mothers in their own homes. Union publications, including the AFL journal, *American Federationist*, "romanticized women's jobs at home, extolling the virtues of refined and moral mothers, of good cooking, and even of beautiful needlework" (Kessler-Harris, *Out to Work* 154). For Black women, racist assumptions about their intelligence, work ethic, and moral character ensured they were largely "concentrated at the bottom of the economic ladder" and were viewed as "the most disposable segment of the American labor force" (Harley, Rusan Wilson, and Wilson Logan 4). Men involved in the labor movement thus had no qualms about excluding women by holding meetings in saloons late in the evening, charging initiation fees and union dues beyond the means of women who were paid lower wages, and mocking women who spoke publicly about the need for workplace reform (Kessler-Harris, *Out to Work* 158).

White women who did join unions and had the temerity to aspire to leadership roles often found themselves closed out of critical positions. Labor historian Philip S. Foner observes that even in industries where women dominated the rank-and-file membership, such as garment manufacturing, "men still monopolized all union offices, and male chauvinism expressed itself in a variety of other ways" (*Women and the American Labor Movement* 390). Rose Pesotta's experience with the ILGWU serves as an example. As a seamstress, she joined the union in 1914 and became one of its most effective organizers, rising to the rank of vice president by the mid-1930s. But Pesotta resigned from the union when ILGWU president David Dubinsky denied her request for more autonomy in running a local in Los Angeles. Pesotta had built strong working relationships with the Latina women who comprised most of the local's membership. In a scathing letter to Dubinsky, Pesotta noted that the "men to whom I have been so useful" did not seem "to recognize the fact that I was competent" (Laslett 36). Pesotta's experiences were not unique. Writing more broadly about the labor movement in the first half of the twentieth century, Foner observes that when local women organizers were about to lead a walk-out or strike, national union officials would typically send in men to direct the action (*Women and the American Labor Movement* 390).

In the early decades of the twentieth century, unions and labor organizations aggressively pursued important financial benefits for men (e.g., wage scales, seniority rights, pensions, life insurance policies), while the needs of women were often defined in terms of sociability—lunch/coffee breaks, recreational opportunities, employer-sponsored social services (Kessler-Harris, *In Pursuit* 46–47). When the financial crisis of the 1930s forced legislators and government leaders to craft policies for unemployment insurance and other social safety nets, the labor movement resisted entitlement programs that would undermine the dignity and self-sufficiency of working men. Due in part to the influence of labor leaders, social security and unemployment insurance were linked to one's participation in the waged workforce, thus preserving patriarchal conceptions of masculinity and the status of men as breadwinners while effectively sidelining women (Kessler-Harris, *In Pursuit* 68, 84). As Kessler-Harris notes, programs like Aid to Dependent Children and Maternal and Infant Healthcare, which served as safety nets for women, were based on need and were thus stigmatized as welfare, while a working man could accept a social security check with honor because it was based on his years of paid labor (*In Pursuit* 66).

As World War II saw the entrance of women into industries traditionally dominated by men, women's relationships with labor unions became more complex. Kessler-Harris has noted that some unions, such as the International Boilermakers, Iron Shipbuilders, Welders and Helpers, remained highly resistant to women's membership on any terms, even as the war necessitated an increasing number of women working in these industries. Other unions welcomed women workers during the war but continued to treat them as second-class members and sidestepped their demands for equal pay, equitable job classifications, and seniority rights as well as their calls for unions to address issues like childcare and maternity leave. There is no doubt, though, that women's union membership increased dramatically during World War II. According to economist

Gladys Dickson, only eight hundred thousand wage-earning women were unionized when the war began, making up just 9.4 percent of organized workers. By war's end, more than three million women were union members, or 22 percent of trade union membership (cited in Kessler-Harris, *Out to Work* 291). Though many women left the workforce as men were demobilized from the armed forces in the mid-1940s, the next three decades would see a dramatic rise in women's participation in the waged workforce. By 1975, women would comprise 40 percent of wage-earning workers in the United States (Kessler-Harris, *Out to Work* 301), and these demographic changes were accompanied by alterations in the gendered imagination surrounding women, work, and their roles within labor organizations (Kessler-Harris, *In Pursuit* 205–6).

Stretching from the 1830s through the 1930s, *Unorganized Women* thus focuses on a critical span of one hundred years in which traditional labor organizations presented complex opportunities to women workers. Most unions were deeply invested in racist and patriarchal conceptions about the centrality of white men as wage earners and as leaders in the labor movement and about the marginality of women in the workforce.

In addition to the patriarchal norms and white supremacy that governed labor unions in the time period under study here, the nature of the work performed by many women in this time period did not lend itself to formal organization. Domestic service was by far the most common occupation for women working outside their own home in the late nineteenth century. Historian David M. Katzman has documented that "in 1870, one-half of all women wage earners in the United States had been domestic servants" (53), and according to Lucy Maynard Salmon, the census of 1890 revealed that "one and a half million persons are actively engaged [in domestic service], to whom employers pay annually at the lowest rough estimate in cash wages more than $218,000,000" (3). As individuals employed in private homes, domestic employees had limited opportunities to find common cause with other household workers.

The few organized labor actions undertaken by domestic workers in the late nineteenth century were led by Black laundresses in the South who lived with their own families, picking up soiled garments and household linens from their employers on Monday; washing, drying, and pressing the laundry in their own homes throughout the week; and returning clean clothes and linen to their employers at week's end. Tera W. Hunter has documented strikes by washerwomen in the nineteenth century in a number of southern cities, including Atlanta, Georgia; Jackson, Mississippi; and Galveston, Texas. These were, though, largely isolated events. As Hunter notes, "domestic workers rarely organized strikes" ("Domination and Resistance" 206).

Similarly, the 53 percent of American households that were engaged in agriculture in 1870, according to the United States census, would not have been sites for labor organization. Women who lived and worked on their families' farms often did not necessarily think of themselves as "wage earners," nor did they typically hold title to land or financial assets. Their work in kitchens, gardens, fields, barns, and other spaces created the conditions of survival for their families, rather than fungible goods. When their labor did produce a surplus, it often flowed into networks of barter and exchange among neighbors, rather than the marketplace. Though women living on small farms built and maintained long-standing networks of solidarity among families in their rural communities, such networks are not typically considered as a form of organized labor.

Despite many working women's seeming lack of access to, interest in, or frustration with formal labor organizations, this book demonstrates that low-wage white women were keenly aware of economic disparities and invested considerable energy in rhetorical labors that would help them achieve a measure of control over their work lives. Taken together, the historical case studies assembled here underscore the importance of deploying a nuanced, feminist understanding of class that expands beyond the labor movement and traditional notions of class consciousness. As sociologist Joan Acker observes in *Class Questions, Feminist Answers*, many feminist scholars have come to eschew well-established methods for defining class. Included among the approaches to class that many feminists find inadequate are Marxist perspectives that identify a foundational set of class relations rooted in capitalist structures; historical materialist approaches that focus on structural change resulting from class conflict; and Weberian theories of class that account for social status and prestige as well as financial resources and economic power (6). Such approaches to defining class, according to Acker, conceptualize "class and capitalism as gender- and race-neutral structures or processes, while implicitly modeling the class actor on a male worker or capitalist" (5). As Acker notes, "Class theories . . . often assume a generic 'worker' and 'manager' who, it turns out, is not so generic for he is white and male" (170). The work experiences of women and people of color and their abilities to access financial opportunities and accumulate economic resources are shaped by the gendering and racialization of their bodies. Understanding how such workers understand and respond to workplace exploitation, financial precarity, and economic oppression requires different ways of thinking about class.

To acknowledge the work experiences of women and the diversity of their economic lives, Acker defines class as the "practices and relationships that provide differential access to and control over the means of provisioning and survival" (68). Such a feminist definition of class creates space to acknowledge a wide range of both waged and unwaged labor; to trace how economic resources are distributed as well as produced; and to account for the broad web of intellectual and affective relationships in which workers, employers, the state, labor organizations, philanthropic social service providers, educators, cultural tastemakers, and others are all connected. Moreover, defining class as the "practices and relationships" that shape how people have differential access to the resources they need to survive and thrive makes possible a nuanced and intersectional understanding of class, gender, and racial processes that contrasts sharply with categorical approaches that assign individuals and families to theoretical or a priori class positions or identities and then correlates class with other variables (Acker 48). Working from the understanding of class that Acker offers makes it possible, for example, to interrogate how the DGC employees responded to their employer's gendered and racialized business practices that were designed to create a strong sense of workplace community for the white women who comprised the majority of the workforce. Nell Donnelly paid wages above the market average, offered a rich array of employee benefits, ensured that her factory was a safe, comfortable workspace, and maintained sharp distinctions between jobs for white women at the DGC and jobs for Black men and women who were employed only as janitors and maids at the company. Similarly, the *Country Life Readers* that Cora Wilson Stewart authored for families living on farms in Appalachia called rural women into particular relationships with consumer culture and the market economy. Such a move in Stewart's textbooks and in the broader country life movement of the early twentieth century helped to reinforce the mythology of the native-born, white yeoman farmer living on his own acreage with a wife and children and helped to eclipse both the presence of immigrants in many rural communities and the very different situations of Black farm families, many of whom were trapped in a system of sharecropping and tenant farming throughout much of the South. These types of material and representational practices create very different avenues to access "the means of provisioning and survival" among people with limited economic resources.

Investigating class as such ever-shifting "practices and relationships" requires scholars to focus their attention on the lived experiences of contemporary women and historically specific accounts of women's lives and labors in decades past. Attending to the concrete experiences of women in specific circumstances reveals the range of ways in which women have been able to pursue their material interests; how their work was been organized and what opportunities they have had to shape their labor; and what gendered and racialized images and stereotypes have informed their understandings of themselves and others as workers (Acker 68–69). The dynamic practices of low-wage white women workers and the web of relationships in which they are positioned are at the heart of *Unorganized Women* and my efforts to understand their rhetorical labors.

WORKING RELATIONSHIPS

Each of the upcoming chapters demonstrates that many white women workers were particularly concerned with their complex and contested relationships with women of a different economic status and of different races and ethnicities—not necessarily between labor and capital. As Michelle C. Smith has demonstrated in her study of utopian communities in the 1840s, gendered rhetorics of labor all too often "function to increase divides among women and preclude alliances on the basis of gender" (5). Some women, like those working in the textile mills of Lowell and farm women in Appalachia, responded to disparaging comparisons between themselves and women of more elite economic status that circulated widely in periodicals and textbooks. Taking their pens in hand, they worked to disrupt linkages between female citizenship and gentility and the consumption patterns of more economically privileged women. Other women, including domestic servants and the workers at the DGC, were more directly engaged with women employers who provoked a range of emotions, from frustration to admiration. To mediate their employment relationships and document their labor, these low-wage women workers produced texts in a wide variety of genres, such as letters, standard contracts, and employment records, that directly addressed the women who employed them.

Charlotte Hogg has rightly called for feminist historians to attend more closely to relationships among women's rhetorics across the ideological spectrum. For Hogg, exemplars of such relational studies include Erin Kempker's work on both women who opposed initiatives linked to second wave feminism and those who supported such initiatives. Hogg also points to the work of literary and rhetorical scholars, such as Theresa Gaul and Julie A. Bokser, who acknowledge, rather than sidestep or "*over*correct," stubborn elements of women's writing that may be difficult to assimilate into the ideological frameworks of contemporary feminist scholars (400, emphasis in original). As Hogg insightfully concludes, focusing on the "interplay" of diversely positioned women's rhetorics yields "more robust insights into both [conservative and feminist agendas] and more closely resembles the realities of our wider culture (400). Feminist rhetoricians have yet to pay close attention to the sometimes agonistic relationships between women whose relationships are defined by economic disparities. Studying the rhetorical performances that emerge from these vexed relationships among women with varied access to material resources usefully expands our understandings of the roles that affect plays in the workplace and challenges the adequacy of framing women's grasp of their economic agency in purely cognitive or intellectual terms.

While the low-wage white women workers in this study invested much of their rhetorical labor in defining and mediating their relationships with women who commanded more economic resources and social capital than they did, they were also deeply concerned about their relationships with Black women and people who had recently immigrated to the United States. White supremacy, enforced segregation, and nationalism dictated that the workspaces I study here were dominated by white women who considered themselves to be deeply rooted in America. As members of a racial majority, the women featured in this book enjoyed economic and social prerogatives accorded to them based on their skin color, and they often chose to remain silent about the exclusion and/or exploitation of Black women workers and other minorities. For example, the mill girls who contributed to the *Lowell Offering* rarely addressed slavery and the forced labor of Black people in the South in the pages of their periodical. Similarly, the white Appalachian women who attended the Moonlight Schools encountered textbooks and other pedagogical materials that defined the white farm family as normative, and there is a little evidence that they chose to use their expanded literacy skills and rhetorical repertoires to cross the color line as they wrote letters that reinforced their traditional networks of solidarity and support in their rural communities. Moreover, there is no archival evidence that they challenged the idea that their Black neighbors should attend segregated Moonlight Schools.

The silence of low-wage white women on issues of race would not surprise rhetoricians who have called attention to the need to study whiteness and white supremacy. Krista Ratcliffe has observed that "out of necessity, non-whites have been quite savvy in articulating the power, privilege, and violence of whiteness throughout US history. Out of privilege, many whites have refused to see it, let alone critique its dysfunctions" (103). Ratcliffe argues that "whiteness is a privileged norm split from other cultural categories in ways that render it invisible, hiding its violence behind parlor manners and polite language" (39). The dysfunction and violent invisibility of white supremacy is not, though, confined only to the parlor. Workplaces and spaces are crucial sites for studying how a wide range of rhetorical performances—not just polite language—creates and sustains white supremacy and structures relationships between women of different races, ethnicities, and nationalities. Interrogating how low-wage white women workers engage in rhetorical labor to structure their relationships to Black women workers and immigrants is a theme in each of the chapters to come, just as are the relationships low-wage white women create with economically elite and socially privileged women.

HERE WE GO AGAIN . . . AND AGAIN . . . AND AGAIN

Workers' activism and its associated rhetorical performances have often been defined by dramatic moments—strikes, sit-downs, walkouts, fiery speeches on factory floors. For example, Clara Lemlich is remembered for her impassioned speech at Cooper Union that helped spark the Uprising of the 20,000 in 1909. Mari Boor Tonn has productively analyzed how Mary Harris "Mother" Jones staged spectacular "pageants of poverty" as she advocated for workers' rights and child labor laws in the early twentieth century. Before she was martyred in the Gastonia Textile Strike of 1929, Ella May Wiggins, a single mother of five children, was known for drawing upon her maternal ethos as well as her talents as a balladeer as she ardently addressed her fellow workers about the importance of unions. As organizers and orators, such women labor leaders seized kairotic moments to deliver noteworthy performances. Their original speeches, pageants, and songs were immediately consequential for the movements they helped to lead, and they reached even wider audiences as their rhetorical performances were reported in the media.

But the women workers under study here made no such speeches, organized no pageants, and performed no original songs for enraptured audiences. Instead, they relied on the cumulative force of a wide variety of iterative rhetorical activities—the publication of a periodical to sustain a relationship between author and audience through repeated interactions over time; the use of unvarying, standardized language in employment documents; the everyday circulation of letters to family and friends that reinforce long-standing community norms; and the collective stockpiling of shared workplace experiences in order to achieve evidentiary heft. Their efforts bring to mind Kenneth Burke's admonition that "we must think of rhetoric not in terms of some one particular address, but as the general *body of identifications* that owe their convincingness much more to trivial repetition and dull daily reinforcement than to exceptional rhetorical skill" (26, emphasis in original). Sidestepping the lure of exceptional rhetorical performances and focusing instead on the power of "trivial repetition and dull daily reinforcement" allows feminist historians to expand our view beyond well-known women labor leaders and activists and provides us with a point of entry for analyzing the rhetorical lives of a wider range of women workers.

Closely attending to the seemingly inconsequential, iterative texts produced by white women workers also adds texture to our understanding of the nature of repetition and its rhetorical functions. To date, discussions of repetition have centered on pedagogy, style, and, more recently, digital media. Rote learning—repeating after a teacher or copying material from an authoritative text—has typically been castigated as ineffective, even cruel, pedagogy. Debra Hawhee has, though, recuperated repetition as a central focus of rhetorical education and athletic training for the Sophists. She notes that Isocrates stressed that one's ability to respond appropriately to others can be developed only through "repeated encounters with difference: different opponents, different subject matter, different times and places" (152). The mill girls of Lowell knew this lesson well. The pages of the *Lowell Offering* are filled with countless articles, stories, poems, and editorials that challenged the journalists, religious leaders, wealthy women, and other cultural tastemakers who castigated women laboring in industrial settings. Through their repeated efforts to defend themselves and their labor in the mills, the contributors to the *Offering* honed their rhetorical skills.

In terms of style and figures of speech, the list of rhetorical strategies that involve repetition is extensive—alliteration, assonance, anadiplosis, anaphora, epistrophe, mesarchia, expolitio, palilogia, traductio, to name just a few (Burton). From the exact duplication of letters and sounds, to the repetition of words, phrases, and clauses, to the reiteration of ideas in new words, repetition draws upon the power of patterns for making meaning and building relationships. But how far can a text vary from the original and still be considered a repetition? Linguist Barbara Johnstone posits that the answer lies in audience perception and whether readers/listeners "can identify something as being 'another one of those'" (3). Johnstone goes on to note that "repetition of particular words is the easiest kind to identify, and there is more difference of opinion about whether to use [the] term in cases of pragmatic repetition such as paraphrasing, in which there really is nothing palpable that's the same" (3–4). Repetition's range is on full display in the four historical case studies that make up *Unorganized Women*. The exact duplication of words and sentences is what makes the standardized contracts signed by domestic workers and written records of their employment histories rhetorically powerful, but it is the variation found in the letters penned by women workers at the Donnelly Garment Company that helps to establish their ethos as they address common themes, such as their knowledge of the labor market, their sense of agency as wage earners, and their affectionate loyalty for their charismatic employer, Nell Donnelly Reed. By thus investigating the range of forms repetition can take and how it functions in particular contexts, I productively disrupt simplistic understandings of repetition as banal, unimaginative, and tedious.

I share this goal with many scholars who focus their attention on the (re)circulation of images and words through digital media. Laurie E. Gries's award-winning 2015 study of the "Obama Hope" poster, *Still Life with Rhetoric*, provides a powerful methodology—"iconographic tracking"—for studying the repetition (and variation) of images across time and space. Similarly, researchers who study memes often focus on how images and ideas are replicated and distributed at lightning speed around the globe (e.g., Jenkins; D. Johnson). In such studies, geographic and chronologic mobility tend to be privileged. The immediate circulation and uptake of the image/text/idea by diverse, digitally sophisticated audiences is of greater interest than the long-standing forms and functions of iterative texts within more local communities by people presumed to be working with their hands rather than their heads.

The women under study here were rooted in particular workspaces—the mills of Lowell, the middle- and upper-class homes of Boston; the farms of Appalachia; and Kansas City's Donnelly Garment Company—at particular moments of economic upheaval. Undertaking tedious tasks that imperiled their bodily well-being, these women workers also found themselves subjected to questions about their mental capacities and the sophistication of their judgment. Mike Rose has documented how this tendency to make assumptions about the intellectual abilities of people who undertake physically demanding jobs remains all too common in the twenty-first century. He calls for a greater recognition of the intelligence of workers and of the "various ways—even as work threatens body and dignity—people tend to seek agency and meaning within the constraints placed upon them" (xxviii). *Unorganized Women* is an attempt to answer Rose's call. Inquiring deeply into the local, historical contexts in which low-wage white women were situated and studying the iterative texts they produced reveal they constructed public representations of their lives and labors, rewrote their relationships with their employers, reinforced long-standing traditions and economic relationships in their communities, and resisted narratives about their work lives that they felt were inaccurate. All by saying the same thing, again, and again, and again.

WORKING BITS AND PIECES INTO NARRATIVES: A COLLECTIVE CASE STUDY FROM THE ARCHIVES

As with any historically marginalized group of people, the voices of low-wage white women are difficult to locate in the archives. Jonathan Buehl, Tamar Chute, and Anne Fields have made clear that "archives are repositories of records, but they are also repositories 'of record' and thus sites of memory and power. . . . We must be mindful that archives, like universities, are often 'insides' defined by what (and who) is 'outside'" (298). Saidiya Hartman also eloquently argues that historians interested in marginalized populations must "grapple with the power and authority of the archive and the limits it sets on what can be known, whose perspective matters, and who is endowed with the gravity and authority of historical actor" (xiii). Low-wage women workers of all races are rarely considered historical actors and are typically seen as outsiders. For too long their work and their words were not deemed worthy of attention by libraries, archives, museums, and other cultural institutions that take as their mission the preservation of the nation's heritage. But with careful, creative, and persistent effort, archival possibilities emerge. Repositories and records that were never intended as official spaces and places for documenting the repetitive rhetorical labor of low-wage women workers can be identified, though my process of locating such archives did not involve a straightforward, unerring research trajectory.

The influence of my grandmother and other women in my family spurred my abiding interest in how white women who face economic challenges have described their working lives and engaged in a range of collective activities. This attunement to and curiosity about the voices of white working women positioned me to locate the historical documents and materials that are the basis of this book in a variety of sometimes unforeseen ways. Like many of the scholars who chronicle their research experiences in Maureen Daly Goggin and Peter N. Goggin's *Serendipity in Rhetoric, Writing, and Literacy Research* (2018), I have learned, "through practice, through living on the edge of ignorance, [to] expect to find the unexpected . . . [and] to stay open to possibilities" (Goggin and Goggin 3). A willingness to dwell with my own ignorance while also remaining hopeful about the possibilities of unpredictable and seemingly fortuitous research opportunities ultimately afforded me fruitful occasions for engaging with the literacy practices and rhetorical performances of low-wage white women workers, even in archival spaces that were not designed to preserve their voices.

On a long-ago road trip through New England and the maritime provinces of Canada with my mom to celebrate the end of my first year as an assistant professor, we made an unplanned stop at the Lowell National Historical Park. There I was introduced to one of first populations of white women factory workers in the United States and how they used the publication of a periodical to establish their place in the civic life of the nation. My ears were still ringing from the deafening clatter of the looms in the weave room at the Boott Cotton Mills Museum while I browsed the books on display in the visitor center and purchased a copy of Benita Eisler's slim anthology of articles excerpted from the *Lowell Offering*. Outstanding interlibrary loan specialists at my university then helped me acquire microfilm of a full run of all issues of the *Lowell Offering*, which allowed me to develop a richer, more textured understanding of the rhetorical labor undertaken by the *Offering*'s contributors than I might have envisioned if I had restricted my investigation to the materials that Eisler excerpted from the periodical.

Anne Ruggles Gere's magisterial volume on women's clubs, *Intimate Practices: Literacy and Cultural Work in US Women's Clubs, 1880–1920*, introduced me to the Women's Educational and Industrial Union of Boston as a "cross-class" organization whose leaders devoted "considerable attention to the problems working women faced" (76). Gere's meticulous endnotes revealed that the WEIU papers were housed in Boston-area repositories, and at the Schlesinger Library I found annual reports, research studies, publicity materials, and organizational records that were intended to document the organization's considerable accomplishments and civic contributions. But in those same documents I also found evidence of how domestic workers enlisted the organization's resources to gain a greater measure of control over their economic lives at the turn of the twentieth century.

Another unexpected discovery came when I was browsing the stacks of my university library, and I ran my finger across the spine of Willie Nelms's biography of Cora Wilson Stewart, the founder of the Moonlight Schools. Nelms's work pointed me toward the University of Kentucky, where Stewart's papers are preserved. Stewart was eighty years old when the university contacted her about acquiring her papers, and, filled with pride, she assembled the materials that now stand as the central archive of the Moonlight Schools (Baldwin 3–4). Her collected papers fill close to seventy boxes and serve as a remarkable resource for researchers interested in her lifelong career as an educator. But scattered throughout the materials are letters from some of the students who attended the Moonlight Schools, and these missives afforded me new possibilities for investigating the rhetorical labor of women living on small farms in Appalachia.

And I first learned of the Donnelly Garment Company at a fundraising event for my university library—the featured speaker was Terence Michael O'Malley. He was promoting his just-completed documentary and accompanying book on the DGC's charismatic founder, Nell Donnelly Reed, who also happened to be his great, great aunt. While chatting with O'Malley as I purchased a copy of his book and a DVD of his documentary, I learned of the cache of letters written by DGC employees that could be found in the archives of James A. Reed, who was a US senator from 1911 to 1929. Nell Donnelly had taken Reed as her second husband in 1933, and the former senator served as one of the DGC's attorneys in the company's battle against the ILGWU and its organizing efforts. Fortuitously, James A. Reed's papers are stored at the Kansas City Research Center of the State Historical Society of Missouri, just across the street from my campus office. The scope and content description at the beginning of the finding aid for Reed's papers explains that "the bulk of the collection consists of correspondence, both personal and professional. Many letters are from admirers and critics on a variety of topics such as economic conditions, Prohibition, agricultural policy, the New Deal, judicial reform, and other political subjects." The description goes on to mention Reed's work as an attorney handling legal work for the Newman and Royal Theatres in Kansas City, an interstate railroad case, and a patent case for Universal Oil. Only when I scrolled through the entire forty-page finding aid—with its inventories of fifty-nine document boxes, two flat boxes of clippings, and three boxes of phonographic recordings—did I spot Box 34 and the perfunctory notation "Copies of letters by Donnelly Garment Co. employees, July 1937." Reed's voluminous collected papers serve to endow him with the "gravity and authority of historical actor" (Hartman xiii), but the briefly noted contents of Box 34 afforded me the opportunity to endow a group of garment workers from the 1930s with their own gravity and authority as historical actors.

Unorganized Women is thus crafted from my engagement with archives and other sources that I was fortunate to encounter at sometimes unexpected moments. The diversity of archives and sources that I draw upon in *Unorganized Women* has necessitated that in each chapter I deploy specific analytic methods and theoretical frameworks informed by the work of scholars in a variety of research areas. In chapter 1, I am indebted to the research and theoretical frameworks generated by scholars working in the interdisciplinary field of periodical studies. James Mussell, Margaret Beetham, and Fionnuala Dillane have all usefully theorized the repetitive nature of readers' encounters with journals, magazines, and other recurrent texts as well as about authors' efforts to capitalize on the serial nature of such publications. In chapter 2, sociologist Dorothy E. Smith's theorization of "documentary reality" informs my focus on the network of genres—circulars, contracts, receipts, employment records, diplomas—that domestic workers navigated in seeking to gain a greater measure of control over their work lives. In chapter 3, the work of educational historians provides me with strategies for interrogating pedagogical materials that addressed Appalachia farm women as well as their responses. Jennie L. Vaughn's conception of a "living archive" that enhances researchers' interpretation of traditional archival sources plays a key role in helping me extend my analysis of epistolary artifacts contained in Stewart's archives. And in chapter 4, the short letters composed by the DGC workers lend themselves to the digital tools and forms of computational analysis associated with the digital humanities. Throughout *Unorganized Women*, I strive to articulate my own work processes as an archival researcher and historical scholar. Jessica Enoch has argued that when historians detail their research methods, "we attain a clearer sense of what . . . [they] are and are not doing when they compose their narratives. And, through this atomistic view, we have the opportunity to assess the practices that open up and close down historiographic possibilities, learning more about the methodological thruways and roadblocks that allow for and prevent alternative histories to be composed" ("Changing Research Methods" 49). In detailing my methods and the theoretical frameworks that inform each chapter, I hope I have contributed to the creation of a wider, smoother research path for other scholars interested in working women and feminist rhetorical studies, a path that can lead us all to more nuanced understandings of our shared past and better prospects for great economic justice in the future.

Taken collectively, the four chapters in this book stand as an argument for the methodological value of the collective case study (Stake 237–38). As a research method, the singular case study privileges concrete details over abstract theory and "afford[s] researchers opportunities to explore or describe a phenomenon in context using a variety of data sources" (Baxter and Jack 544). Ideal for asking *how* and *why* questions, the case study and other forms of qualitative research are rooted in a constructivist paradigm that "recognizes the importance of the subjective human creation of meaning but doesn't reject outright some notion of objectivity" (Miller and Crabtree 10). The dynamic tensions between the multiple perspectives of varied stakeholders and between subjective perception and objective reality provide the inquiry's energy. Indeed, each of the chapters to follow functions as a singular historical case study. I work to contextualize the circumstances under which my subjects labored, and I draw upon archival data sources that include periodicals, autobiographies/memoirs, organizational records, pedagogical materials, transcripts from legal proceedings, oral histories, letters, and other materials. These varied sources have enriched and complicated my arguments about why these low-wage white women were seemingly unorganized and how they labored with language to claim a measure of control over their economic lives.

When aligned, the four individual case studies assembled in this book reveal noteworthy consistencies and common patterns in how low-wage white women have helped construct and respond to the complex web of class relations and practices in which they were "enmeshed" (Acker 47). In particular, they have sought to assert control over public representations of their lives and labors, using a variety of genres and addressing a range of audiences. In doing so, they have consistently challenged the invisibility that Barbara Ehrenreich deems an unfortunate condition of the lives of women working in low-wage jobs (216). Moreover, their rhetorical labor was often invested in defining their relationships to other women, including well-to-do or middle-class women who were held up as models of feminine virtue; women who were minoritized based on race, ethnicity, or place of birth; and women whose views differed from their own about how best to gain power in the workplace. Rather than a teleological narrative of women's economic progress and empowerment over the course of a century, this collective case study speaks to the enduring obstacles that low-wage white women workers have faced and their persistent ingenuity in striving to engage in collective activity they find meaningful and efficacious.

Chapter 1, "Weaving New Identities: Mill Girls and the *Lowell Offering*, 1834–1845," demonstrates how some of the young white women employed in the nation's textile mills in the 1840s capitalized on the rhetorical affordances of the periodical and the power of often repeated cultural commonplaces to sidestep the criticism generated by mill girls' early strikes and walkouts in the 1830s. By publishing poems, narratives, and essays that affirmed their commitment to widely shared values, editor Harriet Farley and the textual community of mill girls who published in the *Offering* seized control of their public image as working women and countered arguments that women working in industrial settings were a threat to the health and welfare of the nation. The *Offering*'s contributors also opted to remain largely silent in the pages of their periodical about the enslaved women in southern states who picked the raw cotton that was spun into thread and then woven into cloth in the Lowell mills. Focused on their own precarious status as industrial workers, the mill girls were unable or unwilling to acknowledge how their ability to earn a living was predicated on the labor of enslaved human beings. As conditions in the mills deteriorated, some mill workers opted to align themselves with the Lowell Female Labor Reform Association (LFLRA), which published the *Voice of Industry* in partnership with the New England Workingmen's Association. Farley and the women workers who maintained their affiliation with the *Offering* forswore the more agonist approach of Sarah Bagley, who edited the *Voice of Industry*, but they still saw their work as contributing to campaign for workers' rights, rather than competing with the LFLRA.

Chapter 2, "Service(able) Rhetorics: Repetition, Standardization, and Household Workers, 1877–1902," shows how women who earned their livings as domestic workers responded to the possibility that routine, standardized documents—contracts, account books, receipts, employment records—might give them a greater measure of control over their working lives. The WEIU, founded in Boston in 1877 to promote cross-class alliances, advocated for such repetitive rhetorical performances through its Committee on Protection, Domestic Reform League, and School of Housekeeping, initiatives that were all designed to address the vexed relationship between well-to-do women and the household workers who prepared their meals and cleaned their homes. Capable of transforming often complex relationships and shifting realities into seemingly stable textual artifacts that could be referenced by a range of readers, such documents gave household workers some measure of control over representations of their labor and their working lives. For women with only rudimentary reading and writing skills, and for those less familiar with the English language as spoken in the United States, the sort of documentary systems advocated by the WEIU could be efficacious, allowing them to gain a greater measure of control over their working lives. The rhetorical labor of documentation and systematization did little, however, to foster collective activities among household workers, even though archival traces suggest women who attended the WEIU's School of Housekeeping deeply desired a sense of common cause and community with their fellow workers. Ultimately, domestic workers' most impactful rhetorical labor may have been their refusal to participate in initiatives that did not serve their needs and desires.

Like domestic workers employed in private homes, women living on subsistence farms in Appalachia in the early twentieth century were a group of workers whose circumstances made them unamenable to traditional forms of labor organization. Chapter 3, "Revisiting *Imitatio,* Reinforcing Neighborly Networks of Solidarity: Appalachian Farm Women and the Moonlight Schools, 1911–1920," shows how women living and working in rural communities responded to opportunities to acquire basic literacy skills and expand their rhetorical repertoires at the Moonlight Schools, which were founded by Cora Wilson Stewart in Rowan County, Kentucky, and quickly spread across the nation. Grounded in *imitatio*, a pedagogy of repetition, Stewart's educational program was specifically designed for rural residents. Stewart both celebrated agrarian lifestyles and traditions and urged farm families to engage in new economic activities and formally organized community activities. Though segregated

Moonlight Schools separately served both Black and white students, the visual rhetoric of Stewart's textbooks focused on white farm families, and like the broader country life movement, the Moonlight Schools did not address challenges of Black families trapped in racialized systems of sharecropping and tenant farming. Archived copies of students' letters reveal, though, the iterative nature of rural women's epistolary efforts. Typically brief, the letters repeat expressions of affection and gratitude that served to reinforce the networks of family and friends that have long sustained farm women and their communities. There is little evidence that increased access to rhetorical education realigned rural women with the "modern" white housewife who was held up as an aspirational model in Stewart's textbooks or to form the sorts of formal organizations that many rural reformers advocated for in the early decades of the twentieth century.

Chapter 4, "Piecework: Rhetorical Accrual at the Donnelly Garment Company, 1933–1937," examines the repetitive rhetorical labor of women workers at the DGC in Kansas City as they aligned themselves with Nell Donnelly Reed, the founder and president of the company, and resisted the unionization efforts of the ILGWU in the 1930s. This chapter centers on more than seven hundred letters written by DGC employees in 1937. My close reading of these letters and other DGC-related documents is supplemented with the practice of "distant reading" enabled by tools from digital humanities. My analysis reveals that many of the women workers at the DGC factory were not opposed to labor unions in general, nor were they dupes who failed to recognize "their own self-interest" (Ancel). Instead, they were pragmatic women, capable of reading the material realities of their working lives and of inscripting those realities in repetitious texts that they hoped would function as a persuasive body of evidence to justify their rejection of the ILGWU. In a process I name as "rhetorical accrual," the women workers consistently offered their assessments of the local labor market and repeatedly asserted that their membership in the DGC's workplace community was deeply satisfying in both financial and emotional terms. While the voices of the majority of DGC employees suggest that they were able to use repetition to craft a workplace identity they found as comfortable and practical as the garments they stitched, both the powers and limits of rhetorical accrual come into view most sharply when I turn to the voices of Black workers at the DGC, whose job opportunities were limited to custodial roles at the factory, and to the voices of the limited number of women workers who publicly declared their interest in the ILGWU's overtures.

In this volume's afterword, I connect lessons from this collective case study of low-wage white women workers in decades past with current and future forms of workplace solidarity and collective activism that serve women with few economic resources. As sociologist Bent Flyvbjerg argues, narratives, such as those that emerge from historical case studies, "not only give meaningful form to experiences we have already lived through. They also provide us a forward glance, helping us to anticipate situations even before we encounter them, allowing us to envision alternative futures" (138). With the ever-widening income gap of the twenty-first century, the movement of labor and capital around the globe, new work arrangements (e.g., the "gig" economy, outsourcing), and ongoing threats to the viability of traditional labor unions, visions of richer, more sustainable futures for low-wage women workers, and all people, are very much in need.

CHAPTER 1

WEAVING NEW IDENTITIES

Mill Girls and the *Lowell Offering*, 1834–1845

In the winter of 1834, the mill girls who doffed bobbins, tended looms, and sized fabric at the textile mills in Lowell, Massachusetts, learned that their wages were going to be reduced by an unspecified amount on the first of March. Responding to broadsides that announced the reduction in general terms, the women workers began meeting during their dinner breaks and circulating petitions that declared their intention to quit their jobs if the reductions were enacted. In early February, one of the women leading the efforts was fired, and approximately one-sixth of all the factory operatives "turned out" of the mills in support of their coworker (Dublin, *Women at Work* 90–91). They marched through the city's streets, and as the *Boston Evening Transcript* reported, "One of the leaders mounted a pump and made a flaming Mary Woolstoncroft [*sic*] speech on the rights of women." The newspaper went on to conclude that the entire affair was "not altogether to the credit of Yankee girls" ("Turn Out at Lowell").

Not only were the women workers castigated for publicly protesting the proposed wage cuts in February 1834, but they were also unsuccessful in their attempt to shut down the mills and force the textile magnates to acknowledge their claims for better treatment. Within a week of the turnout, the mills were again running at near capacity. Most of the strikers returned to work, and those who did not were easily replaced (Dublin, *Women at Work* 92). Two years later, in October 1836, the women workers would again march out of the mills to protest an increase in the fees they paid to lodge and dine at company-owned boardinghouses (Ware 275). Thomas Dublin reports that at least two of the mills in Lowell did back down and chose not to deduct the increased fees from their workers' wages, but this modest success must be partially credited to the economic conditions of late 1836 (*Women at Work* 99–100). With robust demand for their product, the mill owners were running their factories at capacity and could not recruit additional women willing to engage in industrial labor. In her memoir of life as a mill girl, Harriet Hanson Robinson notes, though, that ultimately "this strike did no good" as "wages became more and more reduced" over time, and she recalled that the public speeches delivered by the factory operatives had once again caused "surprise and consternation" (51, 52).

Like many women in the early nineteenth century, the women working in Lowell's mills found that addressing public audiences was a complex, difficult endeavor. Impassioned speeches in the public square and marches through the streets did not yield the desired outcomes for workers and instead created opportunities for critics who wished to impugn their character.[1]

In 1840, some of the women working in the mills opted to undertake a different form of rhetorical labor to shape public representations of their lives as industrial workers and to make their voices heard in discussions about the conditions in mills and boardinghouses. They brought forward the *Lowell Offering*, a monthly periodical filled with poems, short stories, and essays they had written.

The October 1840 issue of the *Lowell Offering* proclaimed the periodical's purposes: "The objects of the publication are, to encourage the cultivation of talent; to preserve such articles as are deemed most worthy of preservation; and to correct an erroneous idea which generally prevails in relation to the intelligence of persons employed in the Mills" (16). The opening editorial continues: "An opinion extensively prevails, not merely beyond the limits of Massachusetts, that the Manufacturing city of Lowell is a nucleus of depravity and ignorance. . . . We have this to testify however, that they who know the least of the people of Lowell, including the Factory Operatives, entertain the most unworthy and unjust opinions of them. Close personal observation has satisfied us, that in respect of morality and intelligence, they will not suffer in comparison with the inhabitants of any part of moral and enlightened New England" ("Editorial Corner" 16). While their labor produced countless yards of cloth, the young white women who first entered the industrial workforce in the United States were also well aware that their working lives and their early experiments with collective labor activism troubled the social fabric of the nation.

Women's labor (e.g., spinning yarn, weaving cloth, churning butter, making soap and candles, preparing home remedies, and raising produce) had been an integral part of the agrarian economy of colonial New England. In the early years of the Republic, though, the United States needed to develop a more balanced and diversified economy, including manufacturing. Adapting technology developed in England, entrepreneurs in the United States invested in textile mills that could house hundreds of power looms. Young white women from rural communi-

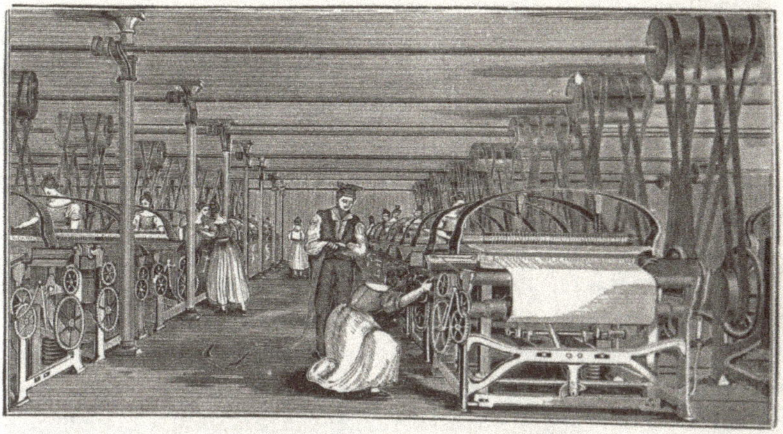

POWER LOOM WEAVING EARLY IN THE CENTURY.
(From an old print.)

1.1. "Power Loom Weaving." From *Illustrated History of Lowell and Vicinity*, Courier-Citizen Co., 1897. Image courtesy of LaBudde Special Collections, UMKC University Libraries.

ties provided the necessary labor for these early New England factories. Thomas Dublin observes that "poverty itself did not drive rural daughters to enter the mills, as millhands came from middling farm families. These were larger families, however, and a lack of future prospects in static or even declining farm communities undoubtedly played a role in women's choices" (*Transforming Women's Work* 105). Noting that factory operatives were often eldest daughters and that they entered the mills between the ages of fifteen and nineteen, Dublin concludes that living space may have become uncomfortably tight in the homes of large families as children entered their teen years and that the unpaid, household labor of a nearly adult daughter was easily replaced as younger siblings began to take on chores (*Transforming Women's Work* 104).

While white women from the most economically precarious farm families across New England could avail themselves of the employment opportunities presented to them by Lowell's mills, there was a "conspicuous absence of black female workers in the newly formed factories," which "reflected the racial animosity toward black females of both white employers and their workers" (Harley 6). Betsey Guppy Chamberlain, who came to Lowell in 1831 as a thirty-three-year-old widow, stands as the only documented example to date of a woman of Native American descent working in the mills. According to Judith A. Ranta, Chamberlain's ancestry "almost certainly derives from a tribe of the Algonkian Confederacy" (7), and contemporary descendants of the Guppy family maintain their family has roots among the Abenaki of New Hampshire (9). In "brief biographies" of sixteen of her coworkers and fellow contributors to the *Offering*, Robinson notes that Chamberlain "had inherited Indian blood, and was proud of it. She had long, straight black hair, and walked very erect, with great freedom of movement" (86). Chamberlain is the only factory operative whose racial heritage and physical presence (e.g., gait and bodily carriage) are exoticized by Robinson, thus underscoring the overwhelming whiteness of the mill girls.

To attract this racially homogenous group of white women workers, textile corporations built boardinghouses in communities like Lowell. Reputable matrons were employed to supervise the young women, and Caroline F. Ware notes that "the girls lived under regulations strict enough to satisfy even the puritan Yankee farmers" (65). Company regulations prohibited alcohol and "games of hazard" and mandated that employees attend religious services. During their six-day workweek, women employed in the mills in the 1830s and early 1840s labored for twelve to thirteen hours a day, earning on average a little more than three dollars a week in 1836 (Dublin, *Women at Work* 80, 185). Fees for room and board in the company-owned boardinghouses were deducted from these wages. By 1840, more than eight thousand young white women were living and working in Lowell (Dublin, "Women, Work, and Protest" 99).

Acutely aware of the cultural anxiety that surrounded their status as industrial workers and potential labor activists, some of the young women who worked in Lowell's textile mills recognized the need to disrupt simplistic assumptions that linked factory work and labor activism with questionable behavior and moral degradation. Contributing stories, essays, and poems to a periodical that billed itself as "written, edited and published by female operatives employed in the mills" would serve as an alternate to marching in the streets and making public speeches as they sought to gain greater leverage over their economic lives. Through such rhetorical labor, the mill girls of Lowell addressed a broad audience as they sought to weave new identities for themselves as women workers and shape their public image.

This chapter begins with a brief history of the *Offering* and its reception. I then argue that the mill girls astutely yoked the rhetorical affordances of the periodical as a genre defined by repetition with the argumentative force of durable cultural commonplaces. In doing so, they produced a nuanced discourse through which they might shape public perceptions of their identities as white women working in an industrial setting. Moreover, their repetitive rhetorical labor served as means by which they could control how their relationships would be defined both to the ladies of leisure, who were becoming the de facto model for female citizenship in the United States, and to enslaved Black people, who produced the bales of cotton that served as the raw material for the textiles produced at Lowell. Though the textual community of writers and editors who produce a periodical is not often viewed as a labor organization, the *Offering* allowed the mill girls to address a wide range of stakeholders about their lives as workers.

HISTORY AND RECEPTION OF THE *LOWELL OFFERING*

The Reverend Abel C. Thomas is credited with first suggesting to some of the mill girls that they publish the best manuscripts that had been shared at an improvement circle that had long been meeting at his Second Universalist Church in Lowell.[2] In his autobiography, Thomas recalled the purpose of the improvement circle: "Improvement in composition was the principle aim, and whosoever felt disposed, was invited to furnish original articles. These were corrected by the Pastors . . . and publicly read at the meetings, with suggestive comments, to large assemblies. By this process, surprising advancement was visible among those who persevered, and several persons of extraordinary talent were discovered, mostly females. Why should we not make a selection of the best articles, and present them to the public in print?" (266). Mill girl Harriot F. Curtis was more imaginative in her description of the improvement circles in the March 1841 issue of the *Lowell Offering*. Signing her essay only as "C," Curtis likens participating in an improvement circle to attending a pleasant summer picnic, and all were expected to contribute their writerly efforts to the feast.[3] She writes, "Though I cannot furnish the rich viands, and delicious fruits, that many others do, I can at least prepare a loaf of plain bread, which, though it may not be so palatable . . . may serve to give a better relish to the richer provision" (64). The quality and diversity of the compositions shared in the improvement circles are represented in the pages of the *Offering*, where readers found religious poetry, essays on science, pastoral reveries, and humorous short stories.

Thomas's editorial oversight shaped the early issues of the *Lowell Offering* until it merged with the *Operatives' Magazine*, a publication of textile workers' writing that grew out of a similar improvement circle that met at the First Congregational Church. Curtis, along with fellow mill girl Harriet Farley, then took over editorial duties. Farley penned most of the editorial columns that appeared in the *Offering* and became the public face of the magazine; Curtis served as a business agent for the magazine and traveled through New England seeking subscribers and patrons (Robinson 80).

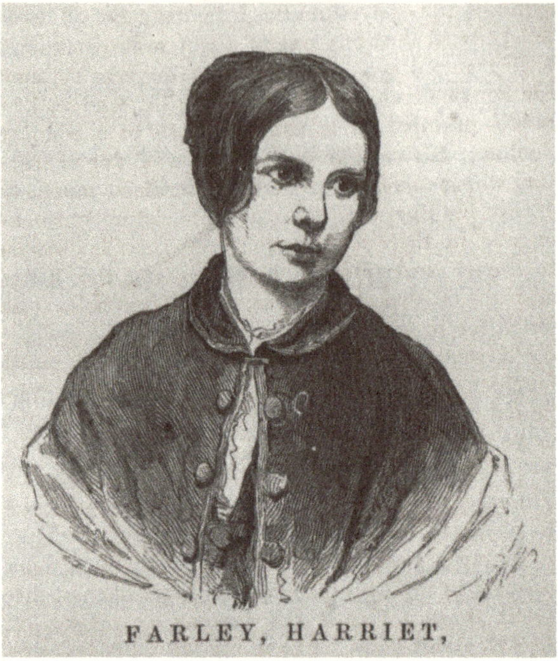

1.2. "Harriet Farley." From Sarah Josepha Hale's *Woman's Record: Or, Sketches of All Distinguished Women*, Harper Brothers, 1870. Image Courtesy of LaBudde Special Collections, UMKC University Libraries, UMKC.

The monthly magazine enjoyed immediate widespread acclaim. Editorials in newspapers like the *Pawtucket Gazette* and *Portland Transcript* offered glowing reviews, as did leading literary figures of the day, including Michel de Chevalier, Charles Dickens, and Harriet Martineau. Through her connections with British publisher Charles Knight, Martineau arranged for selections from the *Offering* to be reprinted as *Mind amongst the Spindles* (1844), penning an introductory letter for the volume that praised the mill girls for having "command of themselves and of their lot in life" (xxii). And when Nathaniel Hawthorne marshaled a fictive "Procession of Life" in his *Mosses from an Old Manse* (1846), he had those who share the "gifts of intellect" march together, declaring that the "factory girls from Lowell shall mate themselves with the pride of drawing-rooms and literary circles, the bluebells in fashion's nosegay, the Sapphos and Montagues and Nortons of the Age" (227).

As conditions in the mills continued to deteriorate in the 1840s, some of the factory operatives came to be less than satisfied with the *Offering* and its approach to representing their lives as working women. In 1844–1845, the Lowell Female Labor Reform Association (LFLRA) was formed and pursued a campaign to have the Massachusetts legislature pass laws protecting mill workers, including a ten-hour limit on the workday. Sarah Bagley, who had worked in the mills for six and a half years and had contributed several articles to the *Offering*, served as the LFLRA's president. She joined an editorial triumvirate to oversee the *Voice of Industry*, a joint publication of the LFLRA and the New England Workingmen's Association. Though the *Offering* ceased publication at the end of 1845, the *Voice*, with its more explicit calls for working women to engage in activism, was ultimately more short-lived than Farley's organ: it ceased publication in 1848 after a three-year run.

Focusing on more easily recognizable forms of labor activism, many historians and literary scholars have celebrated the *Voice of Industry* (Wan, "Republicanism") and narrowly categorized the *Lowell Offering* as a demure publication that was not sufficiently critical of the mill owners and was not vigorous enough in asserting the rights of women working in the mills (Boryczka). In one of the earliest histories of Lowell and its workforce, Hannah Josephson chastises *Offering* editor Harriet Farley for her "timid refinement" and "namby-pamby attitude" concerning issues of labor reform, and she charges Farley with a "failure to come to grips with the real concerns of the factory girls" (199). According to Thomas Dublin, the writers for the *Lowell Offering* were "loyalists, more interested in demonstrating their own upstanding morality than in pointing out the shortcomings of millowners and agents" (*Women at Work* 124). Kristie Hamilton suggests that writers for the *Offering* were invested "in asserting the already equal status of all virtuous individuals [and] were obliged to avoid details that would indicate that equal opportunity was not working." For Hamilton, the *Offering* thus becomes "a literature of inaction, since the only action deemed necessary in their bid for bourgeois approval was internal improvement, accomplished in part through the production and consumption of literature at one's leisure" (117). Such readings of the *Offering* too neatly sequester the magazine from histories of activism by working women and thus impoverish our sense of the diversity of their rhetorical labor as they advocated for themselves and staked their claims to a place in the civic life of the nation.

More recently, historians and literary scholars have begun to revisit the *Offering* in a more "complicated and ambivalent way," as Kathryn A. Cady has noted (28). Rather than generalizing about the *Offering*'s content and agenda over the hundreds of pages produced during its five-year publication history, Cady advocates for "exploring tensions within single *Offering* selections as well as among texts within the *Offering*" (28). Such a reading strategy allows Cady to pinpoint strategic silences in the magazine regarding the nineteenth-century marriage market and to use a single story, "Ann and Myself," to suggest the presence of women's same-sex love and "female masculinity" in the magazine's pages (36). Literary scholar Sylvia Jenkins Cook similarly narrows her focus to specific authors and their stories in the *Offering*. In building a case for the mill girls as "self-fashioning workingwomen," Cook centers her study on "a distinct minority of the *Lowell Offering*'s writers [who] were able to match the novelty of their new authorship with an accompanying range of innovative literary approaches . . . and [who] fashioned work that countered moral absolutism with humorous pragmatism and tempered poetic excess with graphic, detailed accounts of everyday experience" ("'Oh Dear!'" 233). Like Cady and Cook, I call for a more capacious understanding of the complexities of the *Offering*, an understanding that allows for the magazine to be positioned within histories of unorganized working women's rhetorics. More particularly, I argue that the *Offering* stands as a critical project of self-representation for white women workers in a time of social, cultural, and economic instability. I build my argument not by focusing on singular stories or an elite cadre of authors who contributed to the magazine; instead, I attend to how the genre of the periodical served as a vehicle for repeatedly circulating reassuring commonplaces about feminine behavior, even as the mill girls who wrote for the *Offering* subtly advanced more disruptive arguments calling for fair wages and safe working conditions. Such arguments were coupled with the mill girls' repeated rhetorical labor to define their relationships with ladies of leisure and with enslaved Black women.

MAGAZINES AND MILL GIRLS: THE RHETORICAL AFFORDANCES OF THE PERIODICAL FOR THE NATION'S EARLIEST INDUSTRIAL WORKERS

Ephemeral texts, including tracts, newspapers, magazines, and other periodicals, were widely available and very popular with the young women working in the mills. One of the American Tract Society's colporteurs anticipated a profitable 1840 trip to Lowell to sell his wares: he wrote to his superiors that his visit would be "peculiarly auspicious" and that he reasonably hoped to sell one thousand tracts within a few days (quoted in McCauley 14–15, n. 1). Secular publishers also recognized that Lowell's population of literate, wage-earning women made it a lucrative market for selling periodicals. Elfrieda B. McCauley reports that between 1825 and 1840 no less than twenty journals were launched in Lowell, and at least nine were specifically directed to women readers (276). In addition to these local publications, widely circulating periodicals like the *Boston Daily Times*, *Blackwood's Magazine*, *Westminster Review*, *Edinburgh Review*, *North American Review*, *Godey's Lady's Book*, *Graham's Magazine*, and the *Liberator* were available in the boardinghouses, and issues were passed around among the mill girls (Robinson 56; L. Larcom 232, 240).

As inexpensive, disposable texts, periodicals and newspapers were particularly suited to the material circumstances of the mill girls' working lives. In her memoir of life in the mills, Lucy Larcom acknowledges that "the printed regulations forbade us to bring books into the mill, so I made my window-seat into a small library of poetry, pasting its side all over with newspaper clippings" (175–76). Periodicals were also ideal for allowing factory operatives to maintain their connections with their distant loved ones. Many women workers made it "their habit, after reading their copies, to send them by mail or stage-coach to their widely scattered homes, where they were read all over a village or neighborhood; and thus was current literature introduced into by and lonely places" (Robinson 56). Because periodicals were compatible with working conditions in the mills and could be widely shared, mill girls were avid consumers of periodicals, and with the *Lowell Offering*, they became producers of a periodical.

As a genre, periodicals depend on routine and repetition. A periodical reaches readers at regular intervals; its design is typically consistent across issues; and readers can expect to find the same features and columns in each issue, such as an opening letter or introduction from the editor, or a section of readers' letters. As literary historian James Mussell notes, "The repetition of formal features (typeface, layout, tone) within an issue and between issues (plus the structure of departments and so on) provides each magazine with an identity that surpasses its partial representation in any particular article or issue" ("Repetition" 348). Beyond its formal features, consistent content and a recognizable editorial stance that is reinforced in each issue defines the periodical's audience and allows it to build and sustain its relationship with readers. "The periodical . . . may offer its readers scope to construct their own version of the text by selective reading," as Margaret Beetham explains, "but against that flexibility has to be put the tendency in the form to close off alternative readings by creating a dominant position from which to read, a position which is maintained with more or less consistency across the single number and between numbers" (99). This regularity that is endemic to the genre of the periodical functions as a powerful rhetorical tool, advancing arguments through repetition.

Because periodicals construct a textual world that becomes familiar to readers through repeated acts of writing, editing, purchasing, and reading, it also becomes possible to introduce new ideas with minimal disruption. Mussell notes that periodicals can transform "the new into the familiar, where difference becomes variation" and "the new . . .

[is] accommodated within existing bodies of knowledge" ("Cohering Knowledge" 101). To be sure, an item appearing in a periodical that constitutes too much of a break with readers' expectations may produce a strong reaction. Fionnuala Dillane argues that "it is the contrast between anticipated repetition and actual swerve from the expected that creates affective intensity" (12). As a periodical, the *Lowell Offering* afforded mill girls a sustained opportunity to repeat familiar commonplaces, thus reassuring readers of their commitment to widely shared cultural values. The reiteration of these familiar commonplaces over months and across multiple issues of the magazine, though, also functioned to heighten the evocative force of the demands for equitable wages and safe working conditions that appeared in the *Offering*, when the mill girls chose to swerve away from the expectations they had created for readers.

"THE UNCOMMON WORK" OF COMMONPLACES

Like periodicals, commonplaces derive their power from repetition and variation. Seanna Sumalee Oakley observes that commonplaces, ranging from Aristotle's twenty-eight common topoi to the kinds of platitudes and proverbs that served as topics for composition exercises in nineteenth-century schools, may be "dismissed as trite or revered as truth," but they "populate our conversations. . . . [and] they are durable" (35). Reflecting the enduring wisdom of a community and deriving much of their power from repetition and (re)circulation, commonplaces stand as highly regarded resources for making arguments. But as Richard McKeon has argued, the rhetorical power of commonplaces is paradoxical. Even as they allow rhetors to access traditional ways of making arguments, commonplaces are tools for invention as "the certainties of the familiar are brought into contact with the transformations of innovation" ("Creativity" 208). In other words, when a speaker or writer invokes oft-repeated commonplaces, they are reinforcing widely shared cultural wisdom and can then leverage their alignment with established values to make more innovative, perhaps disruptive, claims. Elizabeth Kimball has similarly argued that "commonplaces do uncommon work" as they "effect both continuity and change" (374, 376). Kimball draws these conclusions based on an analysis of how Quaker advocates for higher education in the nineteenth century marshaled faith-based commonplaces about the value of moral and practical education for all while simultaneously advancing new positions about the value of an elite liberal education. As Kimball states, "Commonplaces work as bricks in the road of change: they are familiar and solid and beneath our feet, but lead us to new places" (385). By yoking the power of durable commonplaces with the repetitive rhetorical affordances of a monthly periodical, the mill girls who contributed to the *Lowell Offering* labored to construct a public representation of themselves as women working in an industrial setting. In reading the *Offering* through its entire five-year run, a set of commonplaces emerges—the importance of Christian devotion, the restorative powers of nature, and the virtues of domesticity—that the mill girls deployed to accommodate audience expectations and reassure readers, even as these commonplaces made way for them to call for equitable wages and safe working conditions.

CHRISTIAN DEVOTION

Christian commonplaces surface throughout the *Offering* and can be found in a variety of genres, including poems, essays, and fiction. By aligning themselves with widely shared and durable values of the wider community, the mill girls affirmed their status as virtuous young women. For example, the first issue of the *Offering* in October 1840 included Ellen's poem "Divine Love," which concluded with the following two stanzas:

> But God hath sent his Son to men,
> To lead them to their home above,
> That heaven and earth may strike again
> The harp of everlasting love.
>
> O let this Love our souls inspire,
> This love unchanging, boundless, free;
> And while we wonder and admire,
> The praise, O lord, we give to Thee. (12)

With this apostrophic stanza celebrating God's love, Ellen demonstrates her commitment to Christian values.

An essay titled "Forgiveness" published in 1841 stands as a similar endorsement of Christian doctrine. In her opening paragraph, the writer, Eveleen, laments that all around her she sees "strife, contention, and the spirit of revenge which pervade all ranks of society!" (29). She then offers a concrete example in the story of two brothers from a country town who "had been at variance . . . for some trifling cause" (30). When even a deathbed plea for reconciliation from one brother fails to soften the heart of his estranged sibling, Eveleen notes, "O, how different was this man's spirit from the spirit of the meek and lowly Jesus" (30). In the remainder of the essay, Eveleen traces Jesus's earthly pilgrimage, citing his forbearance and mercy to those who persecuted him. In concluding the essay, Eveleen calls readers to join her in contemplating the lessons of Christ: "May we all strive to cultivate the mild and gentle spirit of forgiveness which characterized our Saviour while on earth" (31). The pious tone of the *Lowell Offering* that was established in its first issues remained consistent through every issue, and in 1845, the magazine published religious poems such as "The Visions of Life" and "They That Seek Me Early Shall Find Me"; theological essays with titles like "Kindness," "Is There a God?" (a question vehemently answered in the affirmative), and "The Old Village Church"; and several installments of an allegory titled "Truth's Pilgrimage," which follows a heavenly spirit dubbed "Truth" making an earthly journey and encountering all forms of humankind. This drumbeat of commonplace attitudes about Christian devotion in the pages of the *Lowell Offering* allowed the mill girls to align themselves with the dominant value system of New England, even as the material circumstances of their lives raised complex new questions about white women's roles in society.

In 1841, the *Offering* even featured engravings of Lowell's churches, including the First Universalist Church, the Appleton Street Congregational Church, the First Freewill Baptist Church, the Methodist Church on Hurd Street, and the Roman Catholic Church. Functioning as visual commonplaces, these images further impressed on the magazine's readers that religion loomed large in the lives of women working in the mills. Moreover, by including a range of churches, the *Offering* avoided participating in unnecessary sectarian conflicts. The appearance of engravings of Lowell's churches provided the *Offering* with a nonsectarian religious imprimatur that would have helped to deflect any criticisms about the mill girls.

In addition to texts that took up explicitly religious topics or quoted Christian scripture, secular stories and poems published in the *Lowell Offering* also upheld commonplace moral standards. Villainy is punished, virtue is rewarded, and the repentance of sinners is celebrated by the entire community. For example, the June 1843 issue featured a story by Annaline titled "The Wanderer," in which a mother, who exemplifies "every grace and virtue desirable," is betrayed by her son, Charles, who takes to the sea against her wishes (194). The violent weather, bodily illnesses, and other deprivations that Charles endures while sailing the South Pacific seem appropriate punishment for his filial disobedience. Ultimately, a much wiser Charles returns to his family home, where "the meeting between him and his mother was mingled with grief and joy; and they all forgave him readily his misdemeanor, and welcomed him home with gladness" (198). By publishing such stories in the *Lowell Offering*, the mill girls were able to establish that industrial labor need not be detrimental to the morals of young white women. "The Wanderer" and the many similar stories that appeared in the *Offering* illustrate the importance of accepting the benevolence of parental authority and the unpleasant consequences of rebellion. Though presented as family dramas, these stories reinforce commonplace attitudes about ethical behavior. In conjunction with the texts on overtly Christian themes, such stories were a rhetorically astute means by which the mill girls could repeatedly link themselves to well-established values in nineteenth-century America.

The repetition of Christian commonplaces and traditional religious themes in the *Offering* may seem less than radical to twenty-first-century readers interested in women's labor activism. Lisa J. Shaver has, though, demonstrated that religion and women's activism were often complexly intertwined in the early nineteenth century, and she counsels feminist rhetoricians of "the precarious nature of attempts to separate them" (131). Writing more specifically about the temperance movement, Carol Mattingly has noted that early temperance workers often lectured in churches in order to forestall opponents who would attack them for speaking publicly to mixed audiences. As Mattingly suggests, "Activity given religious sanction could hardly be condemned" (21). Focused on Black women's activism in the nineteenth century, Shirley Wilson Logan observes that "the church served a central role in black women's racial uplift work" (156). Like the activists studied by Shaver, Mattingly, and Wilson Logan, the mill girls who contributed to the *Offering* recognized the value of linking their faith commitments with their persistent efforts to represent themselves as women workers to wider publics.[4]

CELEBRATING NATURE

Along with religiosity, the sublime beauty of the natural world is a recurring commonplace throughout the *Offering*'s run. Environmental historian Chad Montrie reads the mill girls' reveries about nature's beauty as a nostalgic longing for the more direct, albeit utilitarian, relationship with the natural world that they enjoyed in their rural homes as well as a critique of the working conditions of industrial capitalism. Montrie overlooks, though, the precarious status that white women working in newly established factories occupied in antebellum America, and he fails to recognize that an appreciation of nature was a commonplace by which individuals could establish their commitment to the value system that governed nineteenth-century communities in the United States. According to S. Michael Halloran, descriptions of picturesque scenery were an important form of epideictic rhetoric in the young nation. Citing the literary works by Nathaniel Hawthorne, Henry David Thoreau, William Cullen Bryant, and Henry Wadsworth Longfellow and paintings by Thomas Cole, Frederic Church, and others, Halloran argues that the prevalence of picturesque scenery in the works of American writers and visual artists of the early nineteenth century played a role in establishing a sense of nationhood. While tapping into the tide of romanticism that had swept through Europe, Americans' descriptions of the landscape and the beauties of nature focused more particularly on the unique qualities of the untamed wilderness and situated mythologized versions of Native Americans, early colonists, and Revolutionary War heroes within the arcadian splendor of the North American continent (236–37). By appropriating such cultural commonplaces, a rhetor in the early nineteenth century could gain respect and a sympathetic hearing from fellow community members.

The preponderance of texts in the *Lowell Offering* that offered picturesque descriptions of New England's hardwood forests, brooks and rivers, bounteous orchards, early spring blossoms, and seaside cliffs suggests that the factory operatives became well aware of the long-standing rhetorical power of commonplaces about the restorative power of nature. Writing as "Abigail," Abby D. Turner published "A Merrimack Reverie" in the December 1840 issue of the *Offering*. The essay serves as a representative example of the mill girls' writing about nature. As she glances at the river flowing past her window, Abigail decides to take a mental voyage. She sails upstream to "Lake Winnipisseogee," which she appreciates for its "beautiful, sparkling" waters, its "numerous islands of various magnitude," and "its shores indented with many miniature bays and harbors" (29). When Abigail then retraces her watery route, she passes through Pawtucket Falls, affording her an opportunity to admire "the wonderful works of art in dams, and canals, to raise, receive and carry the water through almost every part of the city, and then causing it to put in motion such a vast quantity of machinery, by which thousands of persons are profitably employed" (29). Abigail goes on to note, though, that "while our admiration is deeply excited by the contemplation of all these noble works of art, . . . we cannot but be forcibly struck with their inferiority, when compared with the sublime scenes of nature" (29). Though she diplomatically recognizes that the built environment has an aesthetic of its own, she reiterates commonplace conceptions of the natural landscape as the work of the "great Architect" (29). Like the more well-known writers analyzed by Halloran, Abigail's ability to compose a picturesque description of the natural landscape is positioned as a reflection of the noble content of her own character. And by reiterating for readers that she values the visual wonders of nature she has witnessed, Abigail signals her belief that she and her audience share an admiration for the ennobling North American landscape.

Complementing texts, like Abigail's, that described specific scenes in nature were numerous essays in the *Lowell Offering* on the general theme of nature as a tutor of the finest sensibilities. In February 1841, Emeline Larcom, writing as "Agnes," argued that "to be insensible to the charms of nature, is to treat with indifference the goodness of Him whose will it is that all his intelligent offspring should be happy, in the highest possible degree; and who has therefore not only placed us in a world of beauty, but has given us the faculties necessary for its enjoyment" (42). In February 1843, S. J. H. published "The Silent Expressions of Nature," querying: "Shall we not then, as we contemplate the silent course of nature, list to the voice which speaks in her works, and borrowing the language of poesy say, each to his own heart?" (102). And in May 1844, Jane Sarah Welch (J. S. W.) reminded readers of the *Offering* that "Earth Speaks In Many Voices," noting that the most powerful lessons of mortality can be learned by contemplating the passing seasons, the oceans, and the mountains (157–58). By repeating such commonplaces about the North American continent's unique natural bounty, the mill girls reminded their audience that industrial labor had not made them coarse or brutish. Despite their long hours in the mills, they were still capable of appreciating the sublime grandeur of the natural world and its instructive moral lessons.

DOMESTIC VIRTUE

Perhaps most surprisingly, the *Offering* reiterated and repeated cultural commonplaces about domestic virtue, despite the crowded boardinghouses, clattering looms, and long hours of factory labor that dominated the lives of the mill girls. Readers who picked up the first issue of the *Offering* in October 1840 found Josephine L. Baker's essay on "Woman's Proper Sphere." Identifying herself only as "B" in the pages of the *Offering*, Baker queries why a woman would want to "leave the pleasant duties that await her at her own fireside, for others which require the daring and bold spirit, and more enduring frame of man to execute?" (3). Over the course of seven well-developed paragraphs, she reasons that women sacrifice their holy ability to "elevate" and "ennoble" when they step outside the domestic sphere, and she cautions that women who resign their sacred trust open themselves to the "poisoned arrows of slander" (3). Baker concludes her argument by invoking Felicia Hemans's "The Switzer's Wife," a poetic approbation of domestic devotion. While expressing sentiments that Barbara Welter would characterize as a nineteenth-century "cult of true womanhood," it is striking that this essay was penned by a woman who has stepped beyond "her own fireside" to labor in the mills of Lowell. Unlike Hemans's heroine, Baker has "[gone] forth to join in the strifes and contentions of the world" as a factory worker, and the material circumstances of her life would seem to belie the attitudes expressed in "Woman's Proper Sphere." Baker's essay is not, however, atypical of the texts published in the *Lowell Offering.* The magazine repeatedly included texts that affirmed commonplaces about the merits of hearth and home, even though such domestic ideals seem far removed from the mill girls' industrial labors.

In 1841, "Adelaide," or Lydia Sears Hall, penned a poem reminding a young bride that her place is within the home and that "cheerful toil" and "grateful love" will "mark the spot / Where thou art mistress, friend and wife" (282). In December 1842, readers of the *Offering* encountered a poem titled "The Young Wife" and its eponymous protagonist, who fears that as her beauty wanes her husband will no longer love her and that their marriage will deteriorate into an empty exchange of courtesies over the breakfast table. When her husband becomes ill, though, the young wife discovers within herself untapped reserves of spiritual fortitude and compassion. The author, Harriot F. Curtis, writing under the pen name "Grace," describes how the young wife nurses her husband back to health and then, upon giving birth, discovers that her husband's feelings for her have only ripened and matured. She is beloved for her inner beauty, and as a stalwart wife and devoted mother, she merits her husband's sincerest affections (51–54). Like countless other contributors to the *Offering*, Curtis invokes the commonplace power of domestic virtue and thus aligns herself and her coworkers with the cultural norms that shaped the lives of people living in nineteenth-century New England.

As a rhetorical strategy, the reiteration of commonplaces about Christianity, nature, and domesticity in the pages of a magazine that readers could interact with on a regular basis served as an important means by which the mill girls could defuse attacks on their character, like those leveled against them when they engaged in more confrontational forms of labor activism in the 1830s. Rather than calling attention to the ways in which their working lives might challenge the idea that white women could best exercise their noble influences when ensconced in a domestic sanctuary, they used the affordances of the *Offering* as a periodical to affirm the durable commonplaces of their community. By repeating such commonplaces within the pages of the *Offering*, the mill girls established common ground on which to regularly meet their readers.

DISRUPTING THE COMMONPLACE AND CALLING FOR CHANGE

What is noteworthy about the mill girls' iterative affirmation of cultural commonplaces throughout the five-year run of the *Offering* is that these commonplaces appeared alongside more radical texts in which the mill girls insisted upon fair wages and resolutely argued for safe working conditions. Swerving from durable commonplaces to more disruptive calls for equitable treatment allowed the mill girls to enhance the emotional impact or "affective intensity" of their arguments as they worked to manufacture a positive public image of themselves (Dillane 12).

As early as February 1841, the magazine chastised the mill owners for the fees charged in the corporate hospital, noting that the weekly rate of three dollars "would greatly diminish, if not wholly absorb the savings" of an operative coping with an extended illness ("Plan for Mutual Relief" 48). In subsequent issues, the *Offering* called for the mill owners to establish bathing rooms for the factory operatives, to provide better ventilation in company-owned boardinghouses, to reduce the number of hours in each workday, and to cease paying male supervisors on a premium system that rewarded them for pushing the operatives to speed up their work. As the March 1841 edition of the *Offering* proclaimed, "Property owners, whether of real estate or investments in the mills, have an abiding interest, not merely in knowing the truth, so far as the condition and prospects of our population are concerned, but in every means employed to secure exemption from the evils of the British manufacturing districts" ("Permanency of the *Offering*" np). And the May 1845 issue of the *Offering* featured Josephine L. Baker's "A Second Peep at Factory Life," which allowed readers to eavesdrop on a group of mill girls as the factory bell rang releasing them for their midday meal. Writing as J. L. B., Baker describes the operatives' "earnest gestures and clouded brows" as the following dialogue unfolds:

> "Well, I do think it is too bad," exclaims one.
>
> "So do I," says another. This cutting down wages *is not* what they cry it up to be. I wonder how they'd like to work as hard as we do, digging and drudging day after day, from morning till night, and then, every two or three years, have their wages reduced. I rather guess it wouldn't set very well."
>
> "And, besides this, who ever heard, of such a thing as their being raised again," says the first speaker, "I confess that I never did, so long as I've worked in the mill, and that's been these ten years." (98, emphasis in original)

These disruptive calls for fair labor practices become more emotionally powerful and less threatening because they are embedded among stories, poems, and essays that affirmed commonplace arguments about religiosity, nature, and domesticity that appeared regularly in the *Offering*.

The mill girls also used the flexibility of fiction to comment on the darker side of employment in the mills while still reinforcing commonplace arguments about religious devotion. Jane Sarah Welch (J. S. W) titled her 1844 story "The Mother and Daughter." The narrative describes a young woman, Anna, working in the mills of Lowell so that her family can afford to educate a younger brother. Tragically, Anna dies in a factory fire on the very day she announces to her fellow workers that she will end her participation in the industrial workforce and return to her rural home. The story's final paragraphs emphasize the importance of submission to divine providence: Anna has a comforting dream of her mother as she is overcome by the "noxious vapor" in the factory, and upon learning of the tragedy, Anna's mother "repined not, though her heart was riven with anguish," and "she meekly bowed to the will of HIM who prepared the bitter cup" (128). Though the story ends with the mother's obedient resignation to the Lord's will, the narrative itself is not quite so tractable. Earlier in the story, the author makes clear that men working as supervisors had allayed operatives' fears when the flames initially broke out and then failed to evacuate the mill, even though "one flight of stairs was already nearly consumed" by flames (127). Though buried in the middle of the story, the supervisors' disregard for the workers' safety paints a disturbing portrait of the increasingly strained relationships between the women workers and their employers.

One of Harriet Farley's most poignant editorials perhaps best demonstrates her keen awareness of how she might best blend commonplace arguments that would reach readers on a regular schedule through the magazine with more disruptive calls for the equitable treatment of women workers. In the column, she addresses the suicides of two female operatives, one in Lowell and one in another nearby manufacturing town. Though not personally acquainted with either of the tragic young women, Farley empathetically attempts to describe the circumstances that might lead a mill girl to take such a drastic step:

> She rose at early dawn, and toiled till night. Day after day brought the same wearisome round of duties; and, as she looked forward, she saw no prospect of a brighter future. It would take long years to procure an independence by her slight savings, and mayhap, with her sinking energies, she hardly gained a maintenance. Her spirits were gone, but life remained; and vitality seemed fixed upon her as a curse. The physical laws of her nature had not been violated, and nature still resisted the spirit's call for death. Perhaps it was frenzy, perhaps despondency, but—the rest is a short item in the common newspaper. ("Editorial—The Suicide" 213)

Farley then addresses readers who might feign surprise that Lowell is not an industrial paradise and that the population of workers who produce the *Offering* is indeed engaged in difficult industrial labor. She writes,

"We have not thought it necessary to state, or rather to constantly reiterate that our life was a toilsome one—for we supposed that would be universally understood, after we had stated how many hours in a day we tended our machines. We have not thought a constant repetition of the fact necessary, that our life was one of confinement" ("Editorial—The Suicide" 214). Rather than continually presenting readers with the aspects of women's industrial labor that were most difficult and novel in the early decades of the nineteenth century, Farley chose to reassuringly repeat what was most conventional and commonplace about the mill girls' lives in Lowell. The less traditional, more difficult, and dangerous aspects of mill girls' lives were shared less frequently, but when such experiences were presented in the periodical, they had greater affective intensity. The pages of the *Offering* thus served as "the place in which the certainties of the familiar are brought into contact with the transformations of innovation" (McKeon, "Creativity" 208). Through such repetitive rhetorical labor, the mill girls of Lowell could weave a public identity for themselves as white women workers. In doing so, though, they also had to distinguish themselves from ladies of leisure as well as from enslaved Black women. Again, repetition would serve as a useful rhetorical tool.

CRITIQUES OF LADIES OF LEISURE

For the mill girls of Lowell, the elevation of "she who sits at ease in her parlor" was a significant impediment to their efforts to manufacture a new identity for themselves as women workers.[5] It is thus the lady of leisure who is subjected to the strongest, most consistent criticism in the pages of the *Offering*. The censure of the leisured woman is apparent in even the earliest issues of the magazine. Publishing under just her first name, Betsey Guppy's "Recollections of an Old Maid" appeared in October 1840:

> There was but one young lady in our village:—I mean by this, that there was but one young female who did no work. The word *lady* has now a very indefinite signification. It means, sometimes, merely a female; sometimes, a female distinguished from most of her sex by elegance of mind, or appearance; and sometimes again, one whose claims to distinction are those of birth or wealth. But those of every class and character who can contrive to worry away their lives without being of any benefit to "that vulgar herd," the world in general, have a great desire to appropriate this cognomen to themselves; and as people are apt to designate others by the names which they assume, so those are often called ladies (*par excellence*) who do no work. (5, emphasis in original)

Cognizant of the power of language to shape perceptions, Betsey bristles as the term "lady" is applied to women "who do no work." She also astutely recognizes that the tendency to deem the general populace a "vulgar herd" allows such ladies to "worry away their lives without being of any benefit to . . . the world in general." By imputing a disdain for the "vulgar herd" to "ladies," Betsey suggests that wealth and leisure make one blind to the useful labor accomplished by others.

Two months later, when S. G. B. (Sarah Bagley) opened a December 1840 essay on the "Pleasures of Factory Life" with a conversational gambit steeped in irony, the editors wanted to make sure the criticism she directed against "ladies" was clearly recognized. Bagley's essay begins "Pleasures, did you say? What! pleasures in *factory* life! From many scenes with which I have become acquainted, I should judge that the pleasures of factory life were like 'Angels visits, few and far between'—said a lady whom fortune had placed above labor." The editors then inserted their own comment in brackets: "[Indolence, or idleness, is not *above* labor, but *below* it.]" (25, emphasis in original). Bagley's essay then rebuts the charges of the leisured women who mistakenly assume that factory work is degrading. She notes that mill girls often use their wages to assist aged and infirm parents, thus earning "the confidence and respect of those with whom we are associated" (25). Recognizing that their public identities as white working women were deeply entangled with the public identities of women with more economic resources, Bagley and the editors attempted to strip idle, wealthy women of their status as respectable and realign that term with wage-earning white women who placed themselves and their limited financial resources in the service of others.

In addition to frequent expository writing that explicitly censured leisured women, the mill girls who contributed to the *Lowell Offering* also used fiction to chastise their well-heeled sisters. Many issues of the periodical feature stories in which an economically privileged young woman suddenly finds that her circumstances have changed and that she must learn to earn her own living. One such story is "Disasters Overcome," published in July 1842 by a mill girl identified only as "F." In this story, wealthy friends Sophia and Amy discover that their fathers' mutual business interests have failed. While Amy can only weep, the more serious Sophia enters the mills to discharge her father's debt, and she earns the respect of her coworkers, her minister, and the pupils she voluntarily teaches in a Sabbath school. Such fictional reversals of fortune were common in the *Offering* and were a significant component of the mill girls' attempts to challenge the social supremacy of economically privileged women. These types of stories call attention to the risks of the marketplace, the ephemerality of social status, and the dangers of believing that personal worth is defined by material possessions. Appearing in nearly every issue of the magazine, such stories worked collectively to persuade through their repetition.

SILENT ON SLAVERY

While the contributors to the *Offering* repeatedly critiqued ladies of leisure, they maintained a sustained silence on the lives of enslaved Black women in the South. The mill girls understood that linking their struggles for public recognition with abolitionist efforts to end slavery would undermine their most immediate goal of shaping a positive representation of themselves as dignified laborers. Robinson recalls that the mill girls who walked off the job in October 1836 sang a parody of the popular song "I Won't Be a Nun":

> Oh! isn't it a pity, such a pretty girl as I—
> Should be sent to the factory to pine away and die?
> Oh! I cannot be a slave,
> I will not be a slave,
> For I'm so fond of liberty
> That I cannot be a slave. (51)

Though this strike song suggests that degradation of factory conditions would transform the mill girls' existence into a life of bondage, it also emphasizes that the factory operatives have the power to resist any attempts to enslave them. By the 1840s, the mill girls who contributed to the *Lowell Offering* would largely avoid the topic of slavery altogether.

Like other northern workers in antebellum America, the *Offering*'s contributors were extremely uncomfortable with comparisons between themselves and enslaved people. Historian David Roediger argues that in the decades after the American Revolution, white workers in the North "made independence a powerful masculine personal ideal" and "responded to a fear of dependency on wage labor and to the necessities of capitalist work discipline" through a process of racial othering (13). Black laboring bodies became associated with a host of negative attributes, and for white workers, any comparison to enslaved Black people "violated at once their republican pride and their sense of whiteness," according to Roediger (86). For working women, like those in Lowell, comparisons to enslaved Black women carried added complications. In the nineteenth century, Black women's bodies were often associated with licentiousness and depravity, and Black women were stereotyped "because of their roles as 'breeders' and rape victims during slavery" (Royster 181). Roediger surmises that "factory women who rejected the term [slave] knew this, and knew that slavery implied sexual exploitation as well" (85). As women working outside the home under the supervision of male overseers, the mill girls were sensitive to ways in which their own sexual propriety was at times questioned. The mill girls who contributed to the *Offering* thus rarely addressed the issue of slavery directly in the pages of their periodical.

The few references to slavery that do appear in the pages of the *Offering* neither call attention to the injustices endured by enslaved Black people nor point out the differences between the work for wages undertaken by the mill girls and the forced labor of enslaved human beings. Instead, the scattered references to slavery in the *Offering* largely function as part of the mill girls' project of critiquing leisured women. As discussed earlier in this chapter, the mill girls who contributed to the *Offering* depict leisured women as being incapable of understanding and assessing the value of work. Wrongly released from their obligation to engage in productive labor, wealthy women could draw only uninformed and inappropriate comparisons between enslaved people and the mill girls. For example, in a July 1841 story by Ethelinda, a tactless and ignorant young woman named Caroline, suggests at a party that mill girls are "driven like slaves, to and from their work, for fourteen hours in each day, and dare not disobey the calls of the factory bell. If they had the means of improvement, they have not the time; and it must be that they are quite as ignorant as the southern slaves, and as little fitted for society" (142). Attending the party is the wealthy hostess's cousin, who happens to work as a factory operative. The mill girl eloquently rebuts the thoughtless and cruel remarks, and the other party guests quickly realize that "even one who 'had to work for a living,' could by her conversation add much to the enjoyment of 'good society'" (142). The privileged Caroline is thus silenced and can draw no more odious comparisons between mill girls and enslaved Black women. Similarly, in an 1844 dialogue titled "Factory Labor" and composed by W. J. S., another snobbish young woman from a well-to-do family queries a mill girl about her decision to return to Lowell after a vacation, suggesting that "to be called and to be dismissed by the ringing of a bell, savors of compulsion and slavery." The mill girl responds energetically: "Our engagements are *voluntarily* entered into with our employers, with the understanding that they may be dissolved at our pleasure. However derogatory to our dignity and liberty you may consider factory labor, there is not a tinge of slavery existing in it" (199, emphasis in original). The wealthy young woman can make no reply to such an eloquent argument, and the issue of slavery makes no further appearance in the story. Placing misguided comparisons between wage labor and chattel slavery in the mouths of leisured women allowed the mill girls to articulate the crucial ways in which they distinguished themselves from enslaved Black people while also substantiating their repeated claims that exempting genteel ladies from productive work warped their understanding of the value of labor.

One of few mentions of free Blacks in the *Lowell Offering* comes in an 1843 story titled "The White Dress; or, Village Aristocracy." This complex story participates in the periodical's project of critiquing leisured women while also suggesting to readers that a woman's worth to a community lies in the work she accomplishes, regardless of race. Harriot F. Curtis, writing under the pen name "Kate," describes the "good village of Clairbury" where a clique of families, including the Crawsons, have begun to imagine themselves the elite of the community (169). When a local merchant offers for sale just six patterns of the newest, most fashionable dress style, the Crawson daughters purchase three for themselves and plan to alert two of their well-to-do friends of the availability of the highly desirable patterns. On departing from the shop, the eldest Miss Crawson admonishes the clerk, "Don't sell the other pattern to any common girl." Appalled by such elitism, the clerk immediately proceeds to the house of Aunt Ruth, "an orderly, active, neat negro—a widow, and the nurse of all the babies 'round about'" (170). He offers the pattern to Ruth's three "neat, tidy daughters," who were "the best *help* in the country," and he singles out the middle daughter, her mother's namesake, as "the most genteel and elegantly formed female in the country of any color; and withal a good and virtuous girl" (170, emphasis in original).

In her description of this family, Kate highlights that Aunt Ruth is "the nurse of all the babies 'round about,'" and she deliberately emphasizes that Ruth's daughters are "the best *help* in the country." By designating Ruth's daughters as "*help*," Kate marks them as different than servants, a term that was sometimes used in the South as a euphemism for slavery and that in the second half of the nineteenth century came to be associated with a distinctly un-American social caste system (Dudden 5–6; Sutherland 125–26). The term "help" or "hired girl" generally referred to young women employed in rural households to assist in producing goods for market (e.g., textiles, dairy products). A hired girl worked alongside her employer, both performing the same or similar tasks (Dudden 12–14). Young women who worked as help in small, rural communities were usually treated with the dignity accorded to the daughters of small producers in a preindustrial society, even though they worked outside the homes of their own families. Because of their tangible contributions to the economic lives of rural families and communities, help could be easily accommodated within the image of working women to which the mill girls were committed. By making clear that Ruth's daughters are "the best *help* in the country," Kate draws a sharp distinction between them and enslaved Black women, and she emphasizes that Ruth and her daughters are valued members of their community. Not surprisingly, Kate concludes her story with the humiliation of the Misses Crawson, who are flabbergasted when the Black women arrive in church looking particularly stunning in the latest fashion. Kate thus joins other contributors to the *Lowell Offering* who critique leisured women by showing that they are incapable of understanding the value of work and its relationship to character. She even goes a step further by demonstrating that the value of work is not determined by the color of one's skin. By making visible the ways in which Aunt Ruth and her daughters enrich their community, Kate constructs a more fully egalitarian vision of antebellum life. In the pages of the *Lowell Offering*, "The White Dress" is, however, unique. Its portrayal of free Blacks as valued workers and contributors to their community highlights the absence of any sustained conversation about the forced labor undertaken by the majority of Black people in the United States who were held in bondage.

The *Lowell Offering*'s relative silence on the issue of slavery is particularly striking given that the mill girls spent their days working with the cotton produced by slave labor, and as Sylvia Jenkins Cook has noted, the mill girls' labor returned to the South as rough cotton cloth used to create garments for enslaved people. Such cloth became "commonly known . . . as lowell cloth, lowel, or lowells. Eventually 'lowells' became a synonym for slave clothing even when the cloth was spun and woven on plantations rather than at New England mills" (Cook, *Clothed* 10). Moreover, there is ample evidence that many mill girls did participate in the abolitionist movement. According to Edward Magdol, "Working-class women, although nonvoters, contributed to the immense antislavery endeavor. Most of them were operatives—weavers, spinners, dyers, and others—in woolen and cotton mills" (70). In Lowell specifically, Magdol has documented that more than 200 of 1,409 signers (16.8%) of an 1836 antislavery petition were mill girls; he concludes, "This is significant evidence of working-class participation in the antislavery movement" (70). The *Liberator* circulated in the operatives' boardinghouses (Robinson 56), and the *Offering*'s editors listed among their more famous subscribers the names of many antislavery activists, including Elizabeth Peabody, Emma Willard, Harriet Martineau, William Ellery Channing, and John Greenleaf Whittier (Husband 14). As women who worked for wages, the *Offering*'s contributors determined, though, that the sustained presence of Black people in the pages of their periodical would constitute too great a rhetorical risk. Comparisons between factory work and chattel slavery could only undermine the mill girls' attempts to create and manage their own public identity. The *Lowell Offering* thus maintains a concerted silence on the issue of slavery. As Cheryl Glenn has noted, silence can be a rhetorical tactic that carries its own meaning: "Like the zero in mathematics, silence is an absence with a function" (263).

But the *Offering* also stands as the mill girls' calculated attempt to intervene in these processes of social change and to control their public image as white workers. Astute rhetors, the *Offering*'s editors and contributors yoked the repetitive power of the periodical as a genre with the durable power of cultural commonplaces. Such continuity made it possible for the mill girls to issue repeated calls for fair wages and safe working conditions in ways that may have garnered a more friendly hearing from the wider public, and it afforded the mill girls opportunities to establish their own position in complex webs of class relationships among white women. Punctuating these strategic repetitions were sustained silences that marked the mill girls' awareness of their own precarious status and their unwillingness to assume the rhetorical risk of aligning their waged labor with chattel slavery. In short, the mill girls who contributed to the *Offering* constructed a reiterative model of public engagement that they hoped their allies would find engaging and their critics disarming.

COMPLEMENTARY, NOT COMBATIVE: A CAPACIOUS APPROACH TO LABOR REFORM

The textual community of contributors to the *Offering* addressed a broad audience, worked to construct a public image of themselves as workers, and expressed their opinions about their working conditions; they did so by tapping into the rhetorical affordances of the periodical as a genre and by using cultural commonplaces as "bricks in the road of change" that would be "familiar and solid" beneath readers' feet but would lead them to accept new ideas about white working women laboring in industrial settings and their rights as workers (Kimball 385). Such rhetorical labor by white women workers has typically been overlooked or even denigrated by activists committed to more traditional forms of labor organization and activism. Such was the case in Lowell when the LFLRA emerged in December 1844.

Eloquent and outspoken, LFLRA president Sarah Bagley was profoundly dissatisfied with the persuasive tactics of the *Offering*. Bagley had been an early contributor to the *Offering*, but in speeches she delivered throughout New England and in articles she published in Lowell's newspapers she began to decry Farley's editorial strategies. Bagley argued that Farley opted not to publish material that critiqued conditions in the mills or argued for higher wages, and she suggested that the *Offer-*

ing did not represent the views of the majority of the women workers in Lowell. Amelia Sargent, another member of the LFLRA, characterized Farley as an editor who had "walked all around the truth, and that at a very respectful distance too."

Despite the imputations leveled against both her editorial work and her integrity, Farley did not respond in kind or seek to draw sharp distinctions between the rhetorical labor of the *Offering*'s contributors and the LFLRA's agenda. Instead, she advanced the idea that the activism of the women working in the mills might take a number of complementary forms. Farley used her first editorial column of 1845 simply to restate her editorial stance and her openness to publishing work by mill girls that critiqued their working conditions, life in the company-owned boardinghouses, and the mill owners. She noted that she had "published all the fault-finding communications which have been sent to us, . . . expressed our readiness to receive more, and . . . even desired our contributors to write freely their own views of the wants, evils and temptations to which they and their companions are subjected" ("Editorial—The Aim" 22). Four months later, Farley praised Bagley and members of the LFLRA who had presented a petition advocating for a ten-hour workday to the Massachusetts legislature. Though Bagley was "plied . . . with questions intended to embarrass her" when she gave testimony before the legislature's Committee on Manufactures (Josephson 258), Farley declared in her April 1845 editorial that the members of the LFLRA had been "proper and dignified" in presenting their case to elected officials, and she was "surprised that they effected nothing" ("Editorial, Report of the Committee" 96). Farley offered her most explicit articulation of a multifaceted and collaborative approach to labor activism in the summer of 1845, when Bagley aired her complaints about Farley and the *Offering* in the pages of Lowell's newspapers. Writing in response, Farley noted: "I had ever before considered Miss B. and myself upon one side of that great question—what are the rights and capacities of the laborer?" (qtd. in Foner, *Factory Girls* 64–65). Farley went on to suggest that the cause of labor reform should transcend differences: "The Labor Question is the great Reform taper of the day. William Ellery Channing, Lydia Maria Child, and many others, work upon the same side with Geo. Ripley, Michael Walsh, and Sarah Bagley. In each of these I find something in which I can and must sympathize, though they are widely different" (qtd. in Foner, *Factory Girls* 65). Tolerant of different approaches to workers' activism, Farley expresses here that gains for low-wage women workers can be pursued in a variety of ways. She demonstrates a capacious understanding of the agency of white women workers and the diverse ways in which they seek to gain greater leverage over their economic lives.

"THE DAY OF SMALL THINGS"

The *Lowell Offering* has too often been dismissed as conservative and castigated for failing to boldly challenge the "lords of the loom." Such superficial appraisals fail to appreciate the complex rhetorical challenges faced by America's first population of white women working in factories and how the partial failures of their earliest walkouts and marches in the 1830s laid the groundwork for the less adversarial rhetorical labor of the *Offering* in the 1840s with its repetition of cultural commonplaces.

Quick dismissals of the *Offering* also leave unchallenged modern historiographic biases. Feminist rhetoricians and other scholars have long focused on the more overtly militant resistance of marginalized populations and more formally organized women workers. Simplistic dichotomies are easily drawn between the savvy, vocal woman worker who marches defiantly on the picket line or shouts from the podium with an upraised fist and the naive woman worker who is manipulated by her employer into shoring up an oppressive system through her own conciliatory or accommodating discursive performances. Recognizing the dangers of such binary conceptions of women and their ideological positions, Charlotte Hogg urges feminist rhetoricians to explore the messy realities and relationships between women and their diverse rhetorical performances. For Hogg, acknowledging the "interplay" of women rhetors who pursued different strategies and exercised different forms of agency can yield more "robust insights" (400). Both Sarah Bagley and the members of the LFLRA and Harriet Farley and the contributors to the *Offering* were committed to pursuing greater economic agency for themselves and their coworkers. Farley believed the efforts of the contributors to the *Offering* could coexist and complement the efforts of the LFLRA, while Bagley did not.

In a March 1844 essay, *Offering* contributor Mary Anne Spaulding (M. A.) reflected on the improvement circles and rhetorical labor of many of the women in the mills who published in the periodical. Spaulding explained her philosophy of "small things," perhaps providing a window into how the differences in Farley's and Bagley's approaches to labor activism were viewed by at least some of their fellow workers. Spaulding wrote, "The tiny stream, that steals its way down from the mountain's side, and winds silently through the vale below, dwindles into insignificance beside the broad deep bosom of the mighty river; and yet the little stream scatters many a blessing in its path, as it goes onward bathing the spotless cheek of the lily, washing the roots of the daisy on its banks, and tinging the meadow with a more vivid green" (114–15). Connecting her fellow *Offering* contributors to this small stream,

Spaulding notes, "True, we are but a band of feeble sisters, pursuing our way in obscurity, and making our efforts in silence, but who shall despise 'the day of small things'?" (114). The mill girls' repetitious rhetorical labor in the *Offering* may be a small thing when compared to the "broad deep bosom of the mighty river" of organized labor and unions. The factory operatives affiliated with the *Lowell Offering* did not forestall the degradation of working conditions in the mills or the decline of wages, and in the pages of their periodical, they remained silent on the southern system of slavery that produced the bales of cotton delivered to northern mills. But when included as part of our histories of working women's rhetorics, they remind us of women's long-standing engagement with diverse techniques of rhetorical (as well as industrial) production. Feminist rhetoricians might well reconsider legacies of unorganized women workers, like those who contributed to the *Offering*, and honor the ways in which they, too, have scattered many complex blessings in our path.

CHAPTER 2

SERVICE(ABLE) RHETORICS

Repetition, Standardization, and Household Workers, 1877–1902

In 1870, 50 percent of working women in the United States had been employed as domestic workers at some point in their occupational history (Katzman 53). Over the next forty years, the number of women earning their living through paid household labor would nearly double, rising from just more than 960,000 to nearly 1,830,000 (46). As urban areas of the Northeast continued to grow and the South began to rebuild its economic infrastructure after the Civil War, the demand for household employees expanded rapidly in the final decades of the nineteenth century. Employing domestic workers increasingly served as a status marker for members of the elite classes and for families aspiring to upward mobility, and the observance of genteel domestic decorum depended on the daily work performed by maids, cooks, and laundresses.

While the demand for household workers was high, domestic positions were often the least attractive employment opportunity among women who needed to earn a living. According to historian David M. Katzman, household work prior to 1920 predominantly involved a "live in" arrangement (87) and residing in the home of an employer was an isolating experience.[1]

Such an arrangement limited a working woman's ability to maintain connections with her own family and friends and made her particularly vulnerable to economic exploitation and physical violence at the hands of any member of her employer's household. Moreover, a domestic employee had little control over her work life. She could be called at all hours of the day or night to prepare and serve a meal, to attend to an ill member of her employer's family, to launder the linen of newly arrived guests, or to clean up any unexpected mess.

Domestic service positions were thus most likely to be filled by women with the fewest financial and social resources. Since girls presumably learned essential housekeeping skills—cooking, cleaning, laundry, mending—at an early age in their own homes, it was assumed they could easily transfer their domestic abilities into an employer's home.

As Lucy Maynard Salmon noted in her 1897 study of domestic workers, "household employments and service are still generally considered occupations that any one can 'pick up'" (112). In northeastern cities in the late nineteenth century, domestic workers were often white women who had recently immigrated to the United States from Europe; in the South, racist education and employment practices meant that most Black women had few job opportunities other than domestic work (Katzman 44–94; Dudden 60–65; Nadasen 10).[2]

The high demand for domestic workers coupled with the fact that they were among the most marginalized of wage earners meant that well-to-do women who hired domestic workers often expressed their frustration with the less privileged working women with whom they cohabitated. They devoted much ink and energy to lamenting "the servant problem." For example, an unsigned article in the *Continental Monthly* in 1864 summarized the "chief evils" of domestic workers as "ignorance, wastefulness, untidiness, pertinence, or downright impudence, and what is called 'independence,' a term which all housekeepers thoroughly understand" ("Our Domestic Affairs" 243–44). Similarly, Patience Price's "The Revolt in the Kitchen: A Lesson for Housekeepers," published in *Godey's Lady's Book and Magazine* in 1868, positioned elite women and domestic employees as "natural enemies" (142). In *The Servant Girl Question* (1881), Harriet Prescott Spofford acknowledged that the cultural, ethnic, and racial identities of domestic workers were often confounding for the genteel white women who employed them. Spofford noted, "It is not upon nationality nor upon religion that that trouble hinges altogether, though these things have very much to do with it." Using stereotypical names for domestic workers (e.g., Bridget for an Irish immigrant, Dinah for a Black woman), Spofford continued voicing the concerns of economically privileged women who employed domestic workers:

> You may think, for instance, that nothing could be worse than your Irish girl, till you get an African one; the Swede who takes the latter's place is only good while she is fresh—she needs to be in the country but six months before she knows all the "tricks and manners;" the sprightliness of the French maid is as aggravating in its own way, and stolidity of the German makes you long for the blarneying tongue of Bridget once again. It is true that Bridget's masses upset the whole household arrangements, but so do Dinah's praise-meetings, for the matter of that; and you feel that it would be better for you and Fifine together if her masses did too; while if, in disgust with the whole sisterhood of them, you at last secure an American, her familiarity makes you wish you could do the work yourself. (17–18)

Doing the work themselves was not an option many well-to-do women seriously considered. Instead, many genteel women deployed the rhetorical tools available to them to shape public understandings of household workers and how their seemingly unsatisfactory work habits threatened the domestic well-being of the home and the nation.

While women who employed domestic workers were able to widely circulate their sense of "the servant problem," the voices of household workers are more difficult to discern. Indeed, there is no parallel discussion in nineteenth-century books and periodicals in which domestic workers articulated their concerns about "the employer problem" and the difficulties of their working situations. Historian Premilla Nadasen has noted that household workers are seldom recognized "as agents of history." She goes on to observe that they typically "exist on the sidelines, serve as a backdrop for the stories of others, or, when they are cast as the main actors, give voice to victimization and oppression" (2). It has perhaps been too easy to accept claims like those made by Lillian Pettingill, a college-educated journalist who decided to enter domestic service to discover why women preferred to work in factories and shops rather than become household employees. In her foreword to *Toilers of the Home* (1903), Pettingill wrote of a friend who earned her living as a domestic worker: "Gretchen cannot tell me, and I am likely to wait long before one of her class pictures to the public the conditions of their industrial life. Neither pen nor brush, scrub-brush excepted, has so far been effective in their hands" (vii). While devoting fourteen hours or more a day to cooking, sweeping, scrubbing, dusting, laundering, and ironing, domestic workers at the turn of the twentieth century would seemingly have had little time or energy to take up more than a scrub brush.

Lack of access to educational opportunities also put the author's pen and the artist's paintbrush beyond the grasp of most women who earned their livings through domestic work. More than seven hundred household workers responded to a survey that was part of Salmon's study, and many cited their lack of education as a reason for going into domestic service. "I went into housework because I was not educated enough for other work," noted one woman. Another woman responded to Salmon's queries: "I haven't education enough to do anything else" (113). Once engaged as a domestic worker, a woman typically found herself closed off from any further schooling, and many household workers voiced their dissatisfactions with how their jobs precluded them from taking advantage of opportunities for intellectual advancement. One of Salmon's respondents noted that "a young woman doing housework is shut out from all society, nor can she make any plans for pleasure or study, for her time is not her own," and another succinctly noted that "domestics never have a chance to go to school or study" (154). The ringing of the factory bell marked the boundary between hours of labor and the hours when women working in the Lowell mills could attend lectures, avail themselves of lending libraries, and participate in improvement circles, but household workers did not have such a clearly defined workday.

Compounding the problem, well-to-do women who employed household workers were often indifferent, if not outright opposed, to any educational aspirations their employees might harbor. In 1900, Mary Dewson conducted a study of the social conditions of domestic work for the Massachusetts Bureau of Labor, and over 80 percent of the employers who responded to her survey indicated that their household employees had no desire for additional education. Dewson surmised, though, that this indifference to educational opportunities attributed to domestic workers was likely due to lack of support from their employers: "In many cases, no doubt, an expression upon this point [a desire for education] has never been invited [by employers], and if not invited would not be likely to be expressed" (Massachusetts Bureau of Labor 10). If many well-to-do women seemed merely uninterested in supporting educational opportunities for domestic workers, others were overtly hostile to the intellectual aspirations of those they employed to do household labor. Some genteel women even advocated abolishing the public schools above the primary grades on the ground that too many young girls were educated above their station. Writing in the *Galaxy* in 1872, Grace A. Ellis conjectured that "our common school, grammar school, and high school system is every day fitting fewer and fewer persons to make good and faithful servants" (353), and Salmon reported that one of the well-to-do mistresses who responded to her survey announced that she would "not engage women [as servants] who have been beyond the third reader and the multiplication table" (179). Though a genteel woman might refer to her maid as "a shocking dunce" or lament that "her *dullness* is so provoking!," individual employers were generally not supportive of their servants' desires for further schooling (Dudden 204, emphasis in original).

Not only did most household workers lack the time, educational resources, and support to write extensively about their lives and labors and thus gain a measure of control over their public image, but the conditions of their employment also created obstacles to any kind of organized or collective efforts to gain a greater agency over their economic lives. Working in private homes, they did not have access to the same sense of shared identity or common cause that women working in factories or shops developed. Domestic workers commonly faced a "certain amount of regulation . . . in regard to the number and character of visitors received" at their employers' homes (Salmon 152), and the capriciousness of employers regarding working hours and days off also made it difficult for many household workers to regularly attend religious services, meetings organized by social service groups, or even gatherings with friends. Clubs and other collective activities among domestic servants thus tended to be "very short-lived" in the late nineteenth century (Murolo 19). An individual household worker might express dissatisfaction with the terms of her employment in a variety of ways, including slowing down the pace at which she worked, spoiling dinner, scorching linen as she ironed, breaking household articles as she dusted, or simply quitting. But collective action among household workers was uncommon.[3]

Recognizing the circumstances that both limited domestic workers' opportunities to control their public image through their own writing and made organizing domestic workers particularly challenging, this chapter focuses on how they used standardized documents, such as written contracts, receipts, employment records, and diplomas, to represent themselves and their labor and gain a measure of control over their working lives. Such documents are certainly far removed from the *Lowell Offering* with its essays, poems, and stories that allowed the mill girls to reiterate cultural commonplaces and shape their public identity as working women. But the diversity of ways in which low-wage women workers earn their livings necessitates an expansive appreciation of the discursive tools that they might take to hand. As a form of repetitious rhetorical labor, the use of standardized work documents seemed one of the most promising ways household workers might gain a greater level of economic agency in the decades just before and after the turn of the twentieth century.

More particularly, this chapter turns to the archives of the Women's Educational and Industrial Union (WEIU) of Boston to investigate how household workers responded to suggestions about documenting their labor to gain a greater measure of control in their relationships with the women who employed them. A progressive philanthropic club that sought to promote cross-class collaboration among women, the WEIU launched three initiatives—the Committee on Protection, the Domestic Reform League, and the School of Housekeeping—that attempted to address the needs of local women who earned their livings through household labor and the women who employed them. Each of these initiatives sought to remedy the so-called servant problem and empower household workers by promoting forms of rhetorical labor that relied on the power of standardization and repetition. Domestic workers' responses to these initiatives varied as they weighed the amount of time and energy required for their participation and gauged the effectiveness of standardized documents as a form of repetitive rhetorical labor that could improve their working lives.

After offering a brief overview of the WEIU and its mission, I theorize the rhetorical function of repetition within documentary systems of standardization that the WEIU advocated. I turn then to the work of the WEIU's Committee on Protection, its Domestic Reform League, and its School of Housekeeping, focusing on the particular repetitious rhetorical labor associated with each initiative. My analysis reveals how household workers took up the repetitive rhetorical labor of standardized documents as a way to broker a new power relationship with their employers and how they responded to the WEIU's alternatives to the affectively oriented "*parlor* traditions of rhetoric" (N. Johnson 2, emphasis in original) that genteel women had long used to manage their households. As JoAnne Yates has cogently documented, a wide range of American businesses were embracing standardization in the later decades of the nineteenth century as their enterprises became more complex and geographically dispersed. To streamline communication and increase efficiencies, documents such as time sheets, schedules, training manuals, and standard operating procedures became part of workers' lives. Women earning their livings as household workers had a chance through the WEIU to experiment with how standard contracts, receipts, employment records, and other highly formalized texts might also transform their fraught relationships with the women who employed them. Evidence suggests that household workers recognized both the powers and limitations of the repetitive rhetorical labor advocated by the WEIU, making strategic decisions about when to accept the advice and opportunities offered by the organization and when to decline to participate in the organization's initiatives.

THE WEIU: AN ORGANIZATION FOR BOTH "HEAD WORKERS AND HAND WORKERS"

The WEIU was founded in 1877 by Dr. Harriet Clisby, a Boston physician. Clisby described her original vision of the organization in her unpublished autobiography: "For many years I had dreamed the ideal dream of seeing *at work* an Institution wherein the *needs* of *all classes* of women would be met and which should be held together by the bonds of a love whose effects would be shown in *mutual service* and healthy co-operative activities. I had seen and felt the loneliness, the poverty, the dreadful *apartness* caused by class feeling" (107, emphasis in original). Guided by this vision, the WEIU sponsored a wide range of programs for women in the final decades of the nineteenth century: public lectures on Goethe and Italian art, classes in stenography and dressmaking, a lunchroom where working women could purchase a reasonably priced meal and avoid the cheap eateries of rougher reputation where men tended to congregate, and a consignment shop where women could earn a small income by selling handicrafts or homemade foodstuffs. With its focus on meeting the needs of a wide range of women, the WEIU was able to attract twelve hundred members in just its first decade of existence (Deutsch, *Women and the City* 146).

As historian Sarah Deutsch has noted, many WEIU members were women who worked; she points out that several of the club's early leaders were "women who had already broken bounds by joining the professions or having a public writing and speaking career" ("Learning to Talk" 388). Along with Clisby, physicians Arvilla B. Haynes and Mercy B. Jackson were instrumental in founding the WEIU, and early membership rosters were composed of progressive women who had served as teachers at the Concord School, studied under Margaret Fuller Ossoli, worked at Brook Farm, moved within the circles of prominent transcendentalists, or were active in the abolitionist cause. These women included Julia Ward Howe, Ednah Dow Cheney, Abby May, Abby Morton Diaz, and Mary Livermore (Deutsch, "Learning to Talk" 388, n. 33). Though the majority of WEIU members came from Boston's WASP-ish Back Bay, its ranks became more diverse as the organization moved toward the twentieth century, with prominent Jewish, Irish, and Black women stepping into leadership roles. Alice Goldmark Brandeis, Mary Kenney O'Sullivan, and Josephine St. Pierre Ruffin all served as WEIU officers (389).

In addition to the fact that many of the organization's early leaders had themselves moved well beyond the domestic sphere, the WEIU is notable for its emphasis on validating women's work. While the mill girls of Lowell had struggled some forty years earlier with an emerging caste system that positioned "ladies" above those who toiled outside the home for their daily bread, the WEIU sought to elevate labor by linking wealthier women with their working sisters. Rather than upholding a normative definition of womanhood based on the genteel homemaker, the WEIU opted for a more expansive vision of a woman's potential to contribute to her community by working outside the home. For WEIU members, financially secure women who chose to work cast a protective shadow over low-wage women workers who were so often excoriated in the press for failing to conform to the dictates of white, middle-class domestic life. Mrs. S. E. Eaton, who helped lead the WEIU's Industries Committee, pointed this out in her 1882 report on the organization's consignment shop: "Every woman of wealth or position who does *any* work, and more especially work for sale, does so much toward elevating labor. Again, her work was accepted under the same conditions as the poorest consigners or the humblest work. Thus was she doing much to break down the dividing lines of society, and make labor honorable" (37, emphasis in original). In her presidential address at the WEIU's annual meeting in 1887, Abby Morton Diaz struck a similar note when she reminded the assembled women of the value the organization placed on the diverse abilities of its membership: "We appreciate the gifts, the learning, the culture, the advantages of wealth. But we appreciate also the business ability of our business people and the self-supporting independence of the workers, whether head workers or hand workers" (8). Whether wealthy women who devoted their "learning" and "culture" to the common good or women who toiled with head or hand to earn their daily bread—the WEIU professed to value the labor of all women.

Domestic workers, however, presented a special challenge to the WEIU's vision of itself as an egalitarian organization that validated women and the varied work they accomplished. Organizations like the WEIU were dependent on the leadership of elite, educated women who could choose to devote their time and energy to social interests and charitable organizations, rather than cleaning their homes or preparing their families' meals. Moreover, as Deutsch argues, genteel women could point to their skillful management of homes and household workers as warrant for their involvement in more public arenas (*Women and the City* 5). But in the highly charged space of the home, encounters between economically privileged women and the domestic workers they employed were fraught.

Nan Johnson has charted how women in postbellum America were encouraged to rule domestic spaces through an emotionally laden "parlor rhetoric" that emphasized feminine self-sacrifice, beneficence, and moral rectitude. Johnson's reading of postbellum parlor rhetoric extends the work of Barbara Ryan, who has put forward an instructive portrait of how antebellum sentimental literature variously lectured both northern housekeepers and southern enslavers on the importance of standing in loco parentis to both free household workers who earned wages and to enslaved Black workers who were forced to undertake domestic labor in the homes of white people (6–10). According to Ryan, the ideal mistress most often portrayed in sentimental literature would be interested in the welfare of anyone working in her home, not just in overseeing their performance of household duties. She was responsible for providing domestic workers, free or enslaved, with moral instruction and for promoting their happiness. In return, she could expect both competent service and affectionate loyalty from her "family" of domestic workers.

For wage-earning household workers, though, the parlor—and the dining room, kitchen, and laundry—were workplaces, not family spaces. Domestic workers needed rhetorical skills that would allow them to successfully negotiate these complexly layered locations. Through the WEIU, household workers encountered an alternative to parlor rhetorics that might move them from a presumed familial relationship to a business relationship with their employers. The organization promoted a program of standard business practices that relied on repetitive rhetorical labor in order to afford household workers a greater measure of control over their individual economic lives and a way to manage their fraught relationships with their employers. In doing so, household workers were participating in trends of documentation and systematization that were becoming widespread in a variety of commercial enterprises.

SYSTEMATIZATION AND DOCUMENTATION: THE ROLE OF REPETITION

As the United States became a fully industrialized nation over the course of the nineteenth century, methods for storing, retrieving, and communicating both schooled knowledge and practical "know-how" became essential to individual commercial enterprises and the nation's economy as a whole (Anderson and Bowman 16). JoAnne Yates has noted that commercial enterprises in the early nineteenth century were largely family owned and carried out their business activities within a local community. Face-to-face communication and individualized personal letters addressing unique situations served the needs of business owners and customers. As entrepreneurs expanded their operations and organized into corporations, they began employing greater numbers of workers and serving a greater number of geographically distant customers. New systems of communication were needed for these new commercial circumstances. According to Yates, between 1850 and 1920, "the informal and primarily oral mode of interaction gave way to a complex and extensive formal communication system depending heavily on written documents of various sorts" (xv). To manage their increasingly complex operations, business enterprises, such as the railroads, brass manufacturers, and chemical companies in Yates' study, began creating complex networks of documents—standardized schedules, training manuals, written orders, time sheets, employment records, and reports as well as elaborate filing systems to contain such texts and make them easily accessible.

Sociologist Dorothy E. Smith provides further insight into how such a "documentary reality" functions and the important role that repetition plays in such a system. Smith observes that organizational documents serve to name, assemble, and analyze events and the human beings involved in them into forms that can be repeated again and again (257). For Smith, systems of documentation create "a complementary organization of knowers. A factual organization aims not precisely at a plurality but at an open-ended more-than-one. It is not just between us, it is the same for anyone. Although 'facts' may be restricted in their circulation to specific groups or statuses, they are constituted as the same on each occasion of their telling or reading. They would be the same to anyone else. . . . This 'sameness' is a product of a social organization in which the knower may treat her knowledge as what is or could be known by anyone else" (259). In other words, the documentation of a standard operating procedure (SOP), for example, ensures that all employees have access to the same description of tasks to be accomplished. The written text of the SOP repeats itself for each reader, ensuring that what one employee knows about the required actions is the same as what every other employee knows as well as what the employer knows.

The repetition inherent in such texts can have a powerful stabilizing effect. Authority resides on the page, rather than in the informal, ephemeral oral exchanges between human beings. The unchanging text can be consulted by disparate readers at different points in time and in different locations. This stabilizing effect is compounded as texts multiply and cohere into intricate systems of documentation. A document outlining an SOP may be referenced in a personnel evaluation in terms of whether an individual employee meets performance expectations, and one employee's performance evaluation can be compared to dozens, hundreds, or even thousands of other employees' performance evaluations because it repeats the same generic features and formats information in identical ways.

The iterative nature of textual encounters in such documentary systems also functions to minimize the literacy skills and interpretive sophistication required of participants within the system. An employee with minimal skills in reading printed English can discern what they need to accomplish on the job because each day's work order is identical to the previous day's work order, except perhaps for the variations in the quantities of X and Y widgets that need to be produced. A frontline supervisor can quickly complete employee evaluations because each evaluation follows the same repetitive format—the supervisor need only fill in the number of times an employee is absent or the production rate of pieceworkers, for example. These kinds of routine, repetitive rhetorical performances lower the cognitive demands of the communication process, and people willing to inhabit, even temporarily, the positions affixed for them in such work-a-day documents can enjoy tangible, economic benefits. The time card an employee signs at the end of each week serves as evidence of the hours they worked should an employer dispute the amount of the employee's paycheck; a standard certificate or diploma from a training program allows a job applicant to quickly signal the skills they bring to a potential employer; routine written instructions provide daily guidance for employees and can be used as a checklist to assert that a job has been completed.

It may be surprising to think about these kinds of documentary systems, which are most often associated with large industrial workplaces, making their way into more intimate domestic spaces in the nineteenth century, but the WEIU advocated just such a documentary network of repetitive texts—standard contracts, receipts, employment records, and diplomas—as a way to mediate between household workers and the women who employed them. Such standard, seemingly objective documents might serve as a way to help economically privileged women manage their relationships with domestic workers of different races and nationalities, women whom Harriet Spofford had dismissively deemed Bridgets, Dinahs, and Fifines. For women who worked as domestic servants in Boston in the later decades of the nineteenth century, the repetitive rhetorical labor of such a documentary system might afford them greater control over their isolated work lives.

Such documentary systems and the repetition that serves as their foundation also have considerable limitations, though. Eugene Matusov and John St. Julien point to how documentary systems do not acknowledge nuanced contextual elements in which such repetitive communicative transactions may be situated or the individuality of participants in such a system. They argue that people too easily become no more than the paper on which their lives are inscribed. According to Matusov and St. Julien: "The (incorrect) underlying assumption of a bureaucratic system is that the meaning of the text is in the text itself and can be revealed through an intertextual analysis without consulting the extratextual reality of socially active goals- and values-driven subjects" (214). In her analysis of "documentary reality," Smith demonstrates just how people's lives are flattened and oversimplified by routine and seemingly objective systems of record keeping through close readings of documents ranging from the records of a probation officer to birth certificates to medical records. Emotion, deeply felt human relationships, individuality, structural inequalities, racism, and other factors do not enter into the seemingly objective rendering of facts that such documentary systems repeat and repeat again. Smith concludes, "Knowledge must appear in an administratively recognizable and standardized form capable of yielding sense to the standard procedures for reading it and on the standard occasions of its reading" (265). This flattening of people's identities and lived experiences into standardized, repetitive documents also does little to create spaces for common cause and collective activities, limitations domestic workers no doubt recognized.

While household workers may have been keenly aware of their lack of formal education and lamented the limited opportunities available to them for intellectual advancement, they were more than capable of assessing how language practices assigned them to particular identities and oversimplified their lived experiences. For example, domestic workers recognized that the term "servant" itself carried with it connotations of social inferiority, making them vulnerable to ridicule. Many household workers thus bristled at being designated a "servant"; Salmon lists a selection of the responses she received to a survey question about the term:

> "I fairly hate the word 'servant.'"
>
> "I don't like to be called a 'menial.'"
>
> "American girls don't like the name 'servants.'"
>
> "I know many nice girls who would do housework, but they prefer doing almost anything else rather than be called 'servants.'"
>
> "I don't know why we should be called 'servants' any more than other people." (155)

Women employed as household workers also resented being addressed by their first names. As Salmon notes, "A second mark of social inferiority is the use of the Christian name in address. It may seem a very trifling matter, yet the fact again remains that domestic employees are the only class of workers, except day laborers, who are thus addressed (156). Drawing upon her contact with women seeking jobs as household workers through intelligence offices or employment bureaus, Frances Kellor quotes one young woman who remarked, "Of course when I am with a mistress and she knows me, I am glad to be called Mary, but why should every mistress do it before she even engages us, and why should it be done in such a way that the iceman and grocer's boy and every Tom, Dick, and Harry always calls us that? I am Mary to every guest in the house and every stranger who appears at the kitchen door; in fact, how can I respect myself when no one else shows me any!" (10). Domestic workers thus attuned to the nuanced exercise of power through language would also have recognized both the benefits and limitations of having their work lives conscripted by new discursive practices as the nineteenth century came to a close. As will be seen in the next section, domestic workers made discerning judgments in response to the repetitive rhetorical labor the WEIU advocated through its program of standardized documentation.

STANDARDIZING SERVICE: THE WEIU AND DOCUMENTATION

The elite women who served as the WEIU's leaders were not among the first or only women to advocate for using standard written documents to mediate the troubled relationship between domestic workers and their employers. In the 1862 edition of *Miss Beecher's Domestic Receipt Book*, Catharine Beecher lauded the efforts of an "accomplished housekeeper" who systematically "arranges the work for each domestic, and writes it on a large card, which is suspended in the kitchen for guidance and reference" (247). Similarly, Catherine Owen encouraged "progressive housekeepers" to "have a list of the weekly duties of each servant, which you read to her when engaged; have a copy of this list for each. . . . Write the list in the order in which you wish the work done" (118). In using its organizational resources to advocate such forms of standardized documentation, the WEIU gave credence to the idea that particular repetitive rhetorical labor could improve the working lives of domestic employees and solve the "servant problem" for middle- and upper-class women. Over the course of thirty years, the WEIU pursued this goal in a variety of ways.

The Committee on Protection

> We listen to constant disputes between mistress and maid concerning domestic service, till we feel ashamed of both. Our whole business has become petty in the details at issue and in the amounts of money received. . . . Every one knows how that service ranges from happy serving to tortuous and torturing ways. There are rights for both housekeeper and servant. We must ignore neither the technical and moral rights of the employer, nor make our clients, the employees, feel that discontent on their part releases them from fulfillment of duties which are disagreeable. Because a mistress is exacting, a servant's carelessness or sudden leaving of a place is not justified. But the mistress may often learn, if she will, from her domestic troubles that the imperfections of her household are due to herself. (35–36)

So wrote Kate Gannett Wells in 1888 as she summarized the activities of the WEIU's Committee on Protection (also known as the Protective Committee) in the organization's annual report. As one of the earliest committees provided for in the WEIU's constitution, the Committee on Protection was charged "to commend the legal and social rights of women to public attention, and endeavor to awaken a sentiment which shall be a sufficient guarantee that no wrong shall be unredressed and no right disregarded" (Donham 7). And the Protective Committee was the first site within the WEIU where a discourse began to emerge about the value of printed documents in mediating relationships between domestic workers and the women who employed them.

In describing the committee's activities in the WEIU's first annual report in 1879, Charlotte Redfern announced that "on Wednesdays and Saturdays, from three to five o'clock, we [committee members] are present at the Union Rooms to receive complaints" (21). As Wells would lament in her report for the committee ten years later, "We listen to constant disputes between mistress and maid," and virtually every other report from the Protective Committee similarly announces that disputes regarding domestic service predominated ("Report from the Protective Committee . . . 1888" 35–36). In 1889, the committee members reported, "We wish to emphasize our difficulties in regard to domestic service, for claims for such unpaid work constitute a large part of our business" (Wells, "Report from the Protective Committee . . . 1989" 36). In 1891, Julia A. Sprague authored the committee's annual report, noting that "domestic service complaints are the most numerous, and the most difficult to adjust" (42). In 1892, the committee similarly reported that "domestic service still presents the largest and the pettiest claims" (Wells, "Report of the Protective Committee . . . 1892" 48), and in 1901, the committee heard 173 cases, seventy-one of which involved household helpers (Morse 57–58).

Typical cases included a woman who sought seven dollars in payment for doing the laundry of a Harvard student, a domestic worker who continually allowed her employer to defer her payment until she was owed ninety-two dollars, and a woman who nursed her employer through a final illness only to be informed that her deceased patient's estate was bankrupt and that she would not be compensated for her services. Committee members would undertake an investigation of any complaint brought by a household worker to one of its Wednesday or Saturday afternoon sessions, and if the case merited it, the committee would seek appropriate redress, calling on the offending parties, sending letters, and turning to lawyers as a last resort.

Overwhelmed by the number of cases it was asked to adjudicate, the Committee on Protection began to seek other ways to deal with the exploitation experienced by household workers. One of the committee's first steps was to publish a circular to apprise household workers and those who employed them of their legal rights. Yates has noted that as businesses grew in size and complexity in the later part of the nineteenth century, they adopted "circulars" or "circular letters" as formal vehicles for downward communication from managers to employees (66–71). Duplicated and distributed in order to ensure consistency and compliance, such written circulars essentially repeated the same information to readers far and near. The WEIU's circular on domestic service covered such topics as agreement for wages, a week's trial, giving notice of intention to leave or dismiss, forfeiture of wages, breakage of articles, effects of compromise concerning wages, poor debtor processes, and the detention of servants' trunks and personal belongings. As a primer on mutual rights and responsibilities, this circular no doubt provided many household workers and their employers with useful information. Written in clear, simple language, the circular acknowledges that many household workers had little formal schooling and perhaps only a rudimentary knowledge of English. The circular's dispassionate, disembodied institutional tone also productively filtered out the overwrought language that the writers of sentimental literature and conduct books, such as Harriet Prescott Spofford and Patience Price, brought to bear upon "the servant problem."

Quickly, though, the members of the Committee on Protection decided that slightly more active and engaged rhetorical labor might better address the needs of domestic workers and their employers. The committee began to insist that written contracts be used to establish the terms of domestic service. Servants and their employers could negotiate and then affix their signatures to a document that specified wages, days off, and general household responsibilities.[4]

Traditionally, the oral agreements made between servants and their employers spelled out such particularities, but lacking the weight of a written text, oral contracts were easily broken. In her study of the notoriously corrupt intelligence offices that functioned as placement bureaus for domestic workers, Frances Kellor pointed to the unfavorable conditions in which many such oral contracts were formed between household workers and employers:

> The crowded waiting-rooms of many offices certainly have an influence upon the permanency of contracts, for in ninety per cent, they are publicly made. This means that it is in the presence of many curious, critical, and often railing listeners. Promises are made which are broken as soon as the girl is in her position. Many misunderstandings arise, due solely to the fact that each is trying to make a good impression before others. Mrs. A— does not wish Mrs. B—, sitting next to her, to know how little she pays a maid, so she offers a sum she cannot afford and later assures the girl it is a mistake; or she wishes her neighbor to believe she gives unusual privileges and makes an attractive proposal, which she later retrenches on all sides. A girl will often refuse to yield a minor point because she knows her listening "pals" will guy her, or accuse her of having a "weak back" or "broken spirit." The employer is thus tempted to make big promises, and the employee to make unreasonable demands, largely due to the desire to "show off" before these third parties. (64–65)

Lillian Pettingill, a college-educated woman who entered household service in order to better understand the "servant problem," quickly discovered how easily such oral contracts between employers and household workers could be violated. Despite an agreement to give the newly hired Pettingill Thursday afternoons off, one employer, Mrs. Scharff, did not hesitate to require that Pettingill forego her leisure time in order to oversee workmen performing minor repairs in the house. As Mrs. Scharff explained to her justifiably disgruntled employee, "this afternoon isn't due you—that is, I don't have to give it to you. I can make you take Sunday instead" (163). The intimate, face-to-face negotiation of oral contracts might have afforded household workers enough rhetorical space to assert themselves, but they were often subject to unilateral alterations and misinterpretations.

In her 1889 summary of the Protective Committee's activities, Wells expressed her frustration with the casual ways in which domestic workers and their employers arranged the terms of their working relationships, and she reiterated the organization's commitment to helping usher in the written contract as a solution:

> The very idea of a contract seems . . . foreign to employer and employé. Service is on the "do-as-I-please" principle. Some housekeepers act as if for $2.00 or $3.00 a week they had a right to seven days' unremitting labor. Some domestics behave as if they, in turn, should dictate what should be done and when. One is exacting, the other impertinent, and domestic peace and skilled intelligence are still the dream of weary mistress and careless maid. Until domestic service is recognized as a contract compelling mutual duties, there is little hope of any family millenniums. The petty quarrels that are brought to your Committee for settlement would never have arisen if each party had remembered that the requiring and rendering of a service was a matter of contract. Our very work seems degraded when two angry women dispute about half a dollar. We appreciate the purchasing power of fifty cents and endeavor to gain it for the girl, if convinced it belongs to her. But why should there be any doubt as to the sum for which she was engaged? Engagements should be made in writing, definitely. (36–37)

Writing for a wider audience in the *North American Review*, Wells made the same point when she identified "the want of written contract" as "the real issue in the 'servant-girl question'" (718).

To promote the use of written agreements, the WEIU created and distributed a standard contract that required domestic workers and employers only to fill in a weekly wage and job title and to affix their signatures. The "terms" of the standard contract repeat for each and every employer and employee that the first week is to be a trial week, after which termination of employment by either party must be preceded by a week's advance notice. Such a standard contract leaves out many of the vexing particulars that led Wells to acknowledge that domestic employment could range from "happy serving to tortuous and torturing ways." Moreover, the enforcement of these types of contracts would have required the use of attorneys and the judicial system, and the small sums involved if written contracts between domestic worker and employer were breached would have made litigation unlikely (Katzman 107). The power of such contracts was thus derived not from their link to the judicial system but instead from their ability as widely circulating discursive products to repeat the same information to an indeterminate number of working women and their employers, standardizing their relational expectations and the social roles they might inhabit. The preprinted contracts afforded domestic workers some measure of agency as they negotiated wages and made more formal agreements with their employers, extending the work begun with the Protective Committee's original circular in terms of using standardized documents and language to deliver the same message again and again.

In addition to its circular and standard contract, the Protective Committee also encouraged the use of account books by household employees and their employers to record the payment and receipt of wages. "If we could only impress upon each family the need of a record-book for wages just as much as a pass-book for the grocer, we should indeed, rejoice," explained Wells ("Report from the Protective Committee . . . 1889" 37). Julia M. Sprague picked up this refrain when she reported for the Protective Committee in 1891. She recommended to employers that they "be more systematic in payment of service, making a clear settlement with employees at the end of every month, or fortnight if they prefer, but having a set time, recording the payment in an account book in the presence of the servant, and encouraging her to do the same, much trouble would be avoided, by such a business-like method" (42). The routine of regularly recording the payment and receipt of wages first establishes and then continually reinforces the norms of the relationship between employer and employee while also creating systematic documentation that any third party, such as the members of the Protective Committee, might consult to mediate any disputes.

The keeping of account books and receipts, the signing of standard contracts, and the reading of circulars all draw their power from repetitive discursive practices. Such rhetorical labor seemed a promising way to improve the economic agency of women who earned their livings as domestic workers and to mediate the relationships of well-to-do women and the women they employed in their homes.

The Domestic Reform League

The WEIU and its Protective Committee's advocacy of circulars, contracts, account books, and other repetitive forms of written documentation reflects a deep investment in the stabilizing power of texts and their seeming transparency as a fair means of recording economic exchanges. The use of reference letters in the field of domestic service, though, served as a serious challenge to the reliability of documents, a challenge that the WEIU would address in 1897 through its Domestic Reform League.

Reference letters were subjective, idiosyncratic, and, at times, unreliable texts. The author of a reference letter could exercise considerable creative license, and the reader of such a credential had to call upon all her critical faculties in plumbing its subtext, and even evaluating its authenticity. Kellor has documented the considerable chicanery involved in the circulation of written reference letters by the notoriously corrupt intelligence offices that operated as for-profit placement bureaus for domestic workers. According to Kellor, intelligence offices would claim that they could not be held responsible for the veracity of the references of the domestic workers they were attempting to place, alleging that "employees write their own references, that some people make a living by writing them, and that employers are not to be relied upon" to provide honest assessments of their former employees (59). Pettingill openly admits that she presented herself to an intelligence office with false references when she sought her first household job. As a college-educated woman, she had no references attesting to her skill as a domestic worker, so she fudged a letter and suffered no negative consequences as a result of her dishonesty. With a bit of ironic pride, Pettingill acknowledged, "I wrote my own reference—they say it is a good one" (x).

Those who employed domestic workers could be equally duplicitous. The proprietors of intelligence offices faulted employers for providing glowing reference letters to unsatisfactory household workers merely to rid themselves of a troublesome employee. Women who employed domestic workers were also known to refuse recommendations to valuable employees so as to avoid losing their services. Employers might also provide less than candid references out of sympathy for a domestic worker, not wanting to feel responsible for damaging a young woman's prospects for gainful employment.

While the intelligence offices pointed fingers at domestic workers and their employers, Kellor found that the small entrepreneurs who ran these placement firms often engaged in fraudulent practices as well. They would encourage potential household employees to bring any kind of reference, would allow them to use old references by changing dates and otherwise altering the text, and would sometimes steal strong reference letters from applicants in their waiting rooms (60–61).

In 1885, the WEIU established a Domestic Service Bureau as a subdivision within its Employment Department and differentiated its operation from the troublesome for-profit intelligence offices with the promise that the bureau would only place domestic workers with credible references (Osborn 31). Two years later, the Domestic Service Bureau was overwhelmed with requests from well-to-do women seeking dependable household employees. In her report from the Employment Committee in 1887, A. W. Chamberlin explained to the WEIU membership that the bureau's difficulties resulted from "our great care not to recommend those to fill places of trust, concerning whom we have no actual knowledge, either personally or through reliable reference" (31). After nearly a decade in operation, the Domestic Service Bureau was "still confront[ing] the old difficulties in the domestic problem": the demand for household workers was greater than the supply and "the impossibility under the present system of getting reliable reference." Even-handed in its analysis, the bureau went on to note that "we often find the employer as much or more to blame as the employed, and as both must be protected we at times have to decline to fill orders" (Burnham 40).

In response to the slipperiness of references and the shortage of women interested in domestic employment, the union authorized its Domestic Service Bureau in 1897 to organize employers and employees into a Domestic Reform League (DRL) that would serve as a more professional employment bureau as well as undertake investigations into the conditions of domestic service (Donham 113). By joining the league and paying a minimal registration fee, well-to-do women hoped to secure a "higher class of girls" for their household workers. For domestic workers, membership in the league held out the promise of entering into more equitable relationships with employers.

To accomplish its work, the DRL's placement bureau maintained its own copious files on "the useful domestic history of the members of the league" (Hersey 2). A mistress in need of a maid could check with the DRL to find out the work histories and wages of applicants for the position; domestic workers seeking positions could consult the DRL to determine if a potential employer had a high turnover rate among her household employees. Essentially, the DRL's card catalog transmuted the vexingly subjective and unmanageable reference letters into something like an accounting ledger with seemingly more objective and formulaic entries that could document how long a household worker had been employed and by whom, at what wages, and why she was dismissed or chose to depart. No longer would an employer need carefully to sift through the sentences and paragraphs of individual and idiosyncratic reference letters in an attempt to discern potential household workers' skills and limitations. Instead, the DRL's cards presented each woman's work history in an immediately recognizable format, and because each card repeated the same kinds of information in the same way, an employer could quickly make comparisons across several applicants. And in exchange for having their work lives thus reduced to series of reiterative card entries, women who worked as servants had access to similar information about their employers.

Through its card catalog, the DRL brought unruly reference letters into line with the same vision of textuality reflected in the Committee on Protection's circular, standardized contract, and account books and receipts. The seemingly neutral rhetoric of the cards would encode and repeat "facts" and could thereby stabilize relationships between domestic workers and the women who employed them. The leaders of the DRL thus felt that the work of the placement bureau was "informed by a genuinely democratic spirit, and appeals for a better understanding between employer and employee, and for more direct business methods. . . . It asks nothing from paternalism; it ignores the haunting tradition of feudal days; and it says squarely to employer and employee alike: this is a business contract, requiring a clear understanding as to wages, duties and conditions" ("Report of the Employment Committee . . . 1904" 42). The "most modern sort" of office "machinery," as Heloise E. Hersey dubbed the card catalog in her history of the DRL, schooled household workers in textual practices that afforded some measure of protection from unscrupulous employers (2). A household worker could be assured that the factual outline of her work history would be transmitted to a potential employer with minimal misrepresentation, and she could make her own inquiry at the DRL about any well-to-do woman who sought to secure her services. How often and why did a domestic employee leave their employer's household? What wages did the employer pay previous employees? Allowing the DRL to create a card catalog entry on one's work history required minimal effort from domestic workers, and the DRL held out the promise that women earning their livings as domestic workers could enter into more equitable relationships with their employers through such a system of documentation. Indeed, domestic workers seemed to view the DRL as an institution that could amplify their voices when they had disagreements with their employers. Domestic workers who joined the DRL and became dissatisfied with their employer would, as Donham explains, report cases of hardship or injustice with the question: "What does the League say to that?" (113–114).

The most powerful evidence in the archives, though, that household workers found the reiterative rhetorical activity of registering and updating their work histories in the DRL's card catalog to be an efficacious means of managing their work lives lies in the initiative's enrollment numbers. Within just four months of commencing operations, the DRL had enrolled 470 employers and 554 employees (Donham 113), and the DRL's files grew so robust that it eventually had to employ "six or seven clerks" to maintain its system of "card-cataloguing" (Hersey 2). After six years in operation, the DRL reported that it served 4,721 employers and 13,430 employees (Dennie 48).

The number of domestic workers who embraced the opportunity to have their work histories standardized and documented in the DLR's card catalog indicates that this form of repetitive rhetorical labor was widely viewed as worthwhile by low-wage women workers. A domestic worker would have to invest minimal discursive effort in having her employment history recorded in a standardized way by the DLR. Household workers were also likely to find the DLR's systematization and documentation an appealing form of repetitive rhetorical labor because it placed them on more equal footing with the well-to-do women who employed them. The card catalog of employment records replaced the slippery, unreliable reference letters that were written about domestic workers by well-to-do women for an audience of other well-to-do women. Moreover, well-to-do women had to agree to have their histories as employers similarly documented and available for domestic workers to peruse.

While household workers were attracted to the DRL and the particular forms of repetitive rhetorical labor that it promoted, they spurned the WEIU's most ambitious and expensive effort to address the troubled relationship between domestic workers and their employers—its School of Housekeeping.

School of Housekeeping

If standardized employment histories recorded in the DLR's card catalog relieved well-to-do women of the trouble of writing and interpreting idiosyncratic reference letters, a diploma or certificate from a training program for domestic workers might provide even more credible evidence of a domestic worker's qualifications, or so leaders of the WEIU thought. By professionalizing domestic work, a formal training school for domestic workers might also elevate the status of household labor and attract more women workers, or so leaders of the WEIU hoped. Appropriating five thousand dollars from its own funds and securing donations in excess of two thousand dollars, the WEIU thus opened a School of Housekeeping in two buildings on Saint Botolph Street in October 1897 (Donham 123).

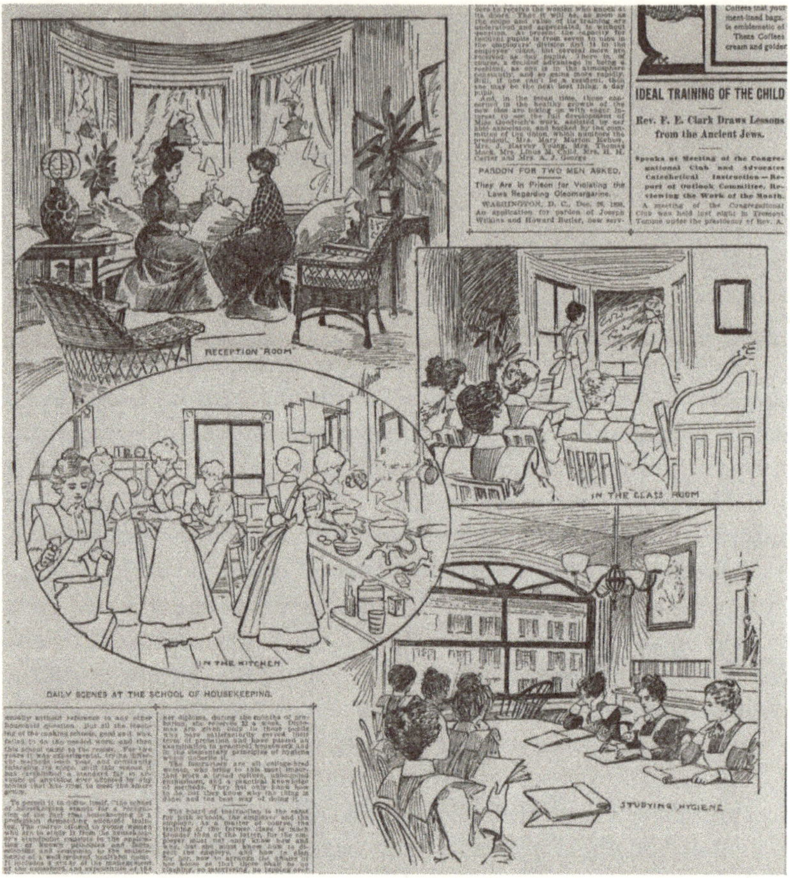

2.1. "Daily Scenes at the School of Housekeeping," *Boston Herald*, December 27, 1899. Image courtesy of Wisconsin Historical Society.

A reporter from the *Courier-Gazette* of Rockland, Maine, described the School of Housekeeping as "brightly and attractively furnished," and the nine young women who enrolled in the original three-month course for domestic workers received free room and board in "sunny dormitories with white iron beds, and blue screens" ("Comments of the Press" np). The students were not charged tuition, but they were required to purchase a blue-and-white uniform that would "paint the ideals of simplicity and cleanliness" ("Comments of the Press" np). The course of study for domestic workers included instruction on preparing and serving meals, cleaning parlors and bed chambers, and doing laundry.

The WEIU was not alone at the turn of the twentieth century in believing that such a school for domestic workers had the potential to address the tensions between them and their employers through particular kinds of rhetorical artifacts. Writing in the *Century Illustrated Magazine* in 1896, Carrie Niles Whitcomb argued that certificates earned by graduates of training schools for domestic workers would be "proof of skill, competence, and integrity; they should state exactly what a servant is fitted to do, and they should be so conscientiously given that a housekeeper might rest assured that she knew exactly the capabilities of the servant" (796). From the perspective of employers, training schools where domestic workers could earn diplomas seemed a most promising way to provide them with suitable domestic employees. Lucy Maynard Salmon recognized the appeal of such diplomas or credentials for employers. Salmon noted, "The plan . . . believed to contain the greatest possibilities for improvement in domestic service, is that of establishing training-schools for servants, such schools to have a regular course of study and to grant a diploma on the satisfactory completion of the work. . . . The diploma . . . would be a testimonial of capability and moral character more reliable than the personal recommendation of previous unknown employers. It would render possible a better gradation of wages, a more perfect organization of domestic work, and more satisfactory business relations between employer and employee" (180). In founding its School of Housekeeping, the WEIU believed it could contribute to the project of creating "more satisfactory business relations" between domestic workers and the women who employed them, and certificates and diplomas would be a critical component of the school. Even before they enrolled at the School of Housekeeping, potential students were educated on the value of certificates and diplomas. A recruitment brochure for the School of Housekeeping explained: "Upon satisfactory completion of her course, the pupil is given a certificate. She is then placed with an employer to serve a probation of three months before receiving her diploma." With a diploma in hand, a graduate was ensured of placement through the Domestic Reform League, and the grade of the diploma would determine the wage that the domestic worker could expect to receive. A parlor or chamber maid earning a Grade A diploma could expect a weekly wage of $4, while a pupil who earned a Grade D diploma could expect only $3.25 per week ("Course for House-Workers, 1900–1901").

Like the Committee on Protection's preprinted contracts and circulars and the DLR's card catalog of employment histories, such diplomas derive much of their rhetorical power from repetition. Institutions issue diplomas that vary only in terms of names, dates, and, in the case of the School of Housekeeping, a ranking (e.g., Grade A). Through their standardized language, diplomas attest to the uniformity of graduates' educational experiences and attainments in lieu of a more idiosyncratic, individualized assessment of their abilities, and potential employers could quickly decode the meaning of the diploma because its recurring form and message make it easily recognizable. The diploma or certificate bestowed on graduates of such a school would presumably serve as far more reliable documentation of a domestic worker's skills and competencies than any personal recommendation letter or other nonstandard text, thus assuring employers about the capabilities of the women they hired to work in their homes. For domestic workers, a diploma might seem to promise increased leverage in negotiating higher wages or more satisfactory workplace conditions.

But the WEIU's School of Housekeeping failed to attract suitable students, despite the positive press it received. School policy required that entering students be at least sixteen years old, but the instructors still found their pupils immature. In its first report to the WEIU, the organizers of the School of Housekeeping thought it prudent to remind the members and potential employers that "even with the careful instruction given and an exact statement of the preparation the pupils have received, it is essential that great care should be taken to place the graduates of the school at first with intelligent women, who will understand that training does not mean experience, and does not imply judgment. It should be understood that there is ample chance for mistakes, disappointment, and unjust criticisms regarding the work. These are possibilities which it is well to face and be prepared to meet" (Young, "Report of the Committee . . . 1898," 58). In 1899, the School of Housekeeping reported to the WEIU membership that "of the employees who have been in the school the past year, several proved physically unable to complete their course of training (Young, "Report of the Committee . . . 1899," 49).

Salmon's visits to a number of training schools for household workers point to the fact that a lack of suitable students was a widespread trend. She reported that many students in such training schools did not attend voluntarily but were instead placed there "by friends, guardians, pastors, or city missionaries" (182). Salmon also noted that "in one training-school with accommodations for twenty, where neither labor nor expense had been spared to make it a success, there were when visited but five persons in attendance, and these five were the most unpromising material that could be brought together to train for such service, one being a partial cripple, another very deaf, a third too young to take the responsibility of a general servant, a fourth was deficient in mental capacity, and the fifth was a Swedish girl who attended to learn English" (181–82).

By 1901, the School of Housekeeping was being referred to as the WEIU's "Expansion Policy," its "Philippine Problem." In the WEIU's annual report, the organizers of the school noted: "Like the nation, we are sure of only one thing—that we are not doing what we set out to do" (Goodrich 51). Attracting suitable students to the program for servants continued to prove difficult, and the course for household workers was discontinued.

In its failed attempts to train and credential domestic workers through its School of Housekeeping, the WEIU was in good company. After studying a number of largely unsuccessful schools, Salmon cited a variety of reasons for their failure: that there was no practical demand for such schools since the tight labor market made it possible for women to earn high wages without formal instruction in household work, that the school's instructional strategies were out of step with broader trends in education, and that such schools were "an anomaly in a democratic country" and introduced a "caste system utterly at variance with democratic ideas" (185–86). Most significantly, though, for Salmon, schools for household workers did not recognize that "educational forces do not push from the bottom, they pull from the top" (262). She argued that "the stream cannot rise higher than its source, and the training-school for employees cannot succeed so long as employers are content with unscientific methods in their own share of the household duties (183). Salmon thus advocated the establishment of a professional school open only to college graduates that would investigate all aspects of household work.[5] Like Ellen Swallow Richards, Alice Norton, Mary Converse, Margaret Dodd, and other domestic scientists studied by Jessica Enoch, Salmon was deeply invested in bringing the power of scientific inquiry into the home. As Enoch argues, elite women were able "to create a new professional ethos for themselves" by redefining the home as a site of "complex problems that could only be solved by rigorous intellectual engagement and scientific experimentation" (*Domestic Occupations* 76). For Salmon, the diffusion of such methodically acquired knowledge would lead to more efficient means of accomplishing household work, thereby also improving the lives of domestic workers.

Frances Kellor offered a different assessment of why such schools for domestic workers failed. She notes that "none of these schemes was based upon what the employee wished to study or enjoy, but upon what employers wanted or thought best. Some attractive features of training must be devised to reach employees" (132). As one of the domestic workers interviewed by Kellor explained, "Those schools are not for us; no one ever finds out what we want to learn; they start out with a theory and everything must fit that, and we won't fit—that's all" (130). Rather than a site for "head workers and hand workers" to engage in dialogue and constructive collaboration, the School of Housekeeping privileged the needs and desires of elite women and neglected the perspectives of low-wage women and what they might want from the experience of attending such an educational institution.

One of the things that domestic workers evidently wanted from such schools was a sense of community and common cause that was so lacking in their working lives and that the WEIU had espoused as a goal for all women—head and hand workers—when it was founded in 1877. They wanted more than just a diploma. The first class of students at the WEIU's School of Housekeeping were notorious for folding away the screens that divided their large dormitory into smaller apartments. After noting with perplexity this preference for common space, a writer for the *Boston Herald* could only conclude, "The girls like companionship" ("Housekeepers' School"). The school's organizers also noted in their 1899 report to the WEIU membership that "the past winter's pupils formed an association among themselves; had monthly meetings; adopted a badge and showed a desire for social intercourse and healthful amusement" (Young, "Report of the Committee . . . 1899" 49). Such actions speak to domestic workers' deeply felt desires to establish social connections and common cause among themselves. But finding only minor opportunities to develop such a sense of solidarity, working women rejected the School of Housekeeping as an institution that could improve their economic lives. Having not provided domestic workers with more sophisticated rhetorical opportunities to represent themselves and their labor or a space for dialogue, the leaders of the WEIU heard only the sound of low-wage white women's feet walking away from the organization's most substantial financial investment in empowering women who earned their living as household employees and mediating their relationship with their well-to-do employers.

John Schilb's work on "rhetorical refusals" serves as a productive reminder that even in rejecting much of what the WEIU's School of Housekeeping offered, domestic workers were engaged in their own powerful rhetorical performance. Schilb analyzes a number of significant moments in which rhetors refused to adhere to their audiences' expectations. For Schilb, such moments of defiance "involve more than just spitting in an interlocutor's eye" and are not just "mere expressions of 'tude." Instead, rhetorical refusals are "actively aimed at persuading their audience of something" (10). By rejecting the terms of engagement, a rhetor can make an audience aware of how its own assumptions and expectations make further dialogue untenable. Repudiating the terms of a rhetorical situation can be a strategy for disrupting existing hierarchies and redefining the terms of any possible exchanges in the future. Schilb goes on to speculate that "rhetorical refusals are most likely to be performed by people at polar extremes: that is, those who already enjoy high prestige (thus having little to risk) and those who feel quite abused by dominant powers" (20). Women earning their livings as household workers in Boston certainly felt exploited and ill-treated by economically elite women. By refusing to enroll in the School of Housekeeping, they forced the WEIU to reconsider its assumptions and approaches to mediating the troubled relationship between household workers and their employers.

In the case of domestic workers and the WEIU, newspaper reports that the women who attended the School of Housekeeping formed an association and rejected the isolation or privacy imposed upon them by folding screens suggest that the household workers who initially enrolled at the school were interested in developing a sense of community and common cause. Kellor's interviews reveal as well that the students would have been more interested in training schools based not on the desires of employers but "conducted for them alone, the courses based on their needs" (131). Finding their desires thwarted, the students at the School of Housekeeping refused the role of passive recipients in a one-way exchange and redefined the rhetorical situation by absenting themselves from the scene. While not advocating that rhetorical refusals should be common, Schilb notes that such moments of rebellion point to possibilities for "greater rhetorical adventurousness in the discourses of civic life" (23). The WEIU might have been more adventurous in its engagement with Boston's domestic workers by listening to them about the kinds of educational opportunities they might be interested in and by building creatively on household workers' desires for a sense of solidarity and connection with each other.

REPEATED EFFORTS TO STANDARDIZE HOUSEHOLD WORK

The Committee on Protection's promotion of preprinted contracts and publication of informative pamphlets, the Domestic Reform League's files of employment records, and the School of Housekeeping's diplomas all relied on the power of standardization and repetition to manage the vexed relationships between economically elite women in Boston and the women they employed as domestic workers. Recognizing the problematic nature of an affectively oriented parlor rhetoric and familial discourses (N. Johnson), the WEIU embraced systems of documentation that were developing in nineteenth-century business enterprises as they grew in geographic size and reach in the late nineteenth century (Yates).

Though the voices of women who earned their living through household work in the nineteenth century are difficult to discern in the archives, organizational records can on occasion be sifted through to determine how domestic workers chose to participate in the repetitive rhetorical labor encouraged by the WEIU. Notably, the record-keeping system of the DRL, which provided a standard structure for encoding employment histories for both employers and employees, attracted the greatest number of domestic workers. Registering with the DRL and allowing one's employment history to be systematically encoded within a system of standardized record-keeping required minimal rhetorical labor from low-wage women while offering some measure of control over representations of their lives and labors. Citing work by Edward Stevens and Dorothy E. Smith, Deborah Brandt has traced how economic and political processes were increasingly encoded in print over the course of the late nineteenth and twentieth centuries. In the emergent "documentary America," the ability to manage written accounting procedures can determine a person's ability to participate in civic life and to safeguard her economic interests (*Literacy in American Lives* 47–50). As a system of iterative documentation, the DRL instantiates the rise of a documentary culture in the United States in the late nineteenth century, extending the reach of such a textual system into the home and the work lives of low-wage women and their employers. The School of Housekeeping, though, with its promise of certification and a diploma, never attracted significant numbers of women workers. It demanded a substantial investment of their time, and household workers had little input into the curriculum, which was determined by elite leaders of the WEIU. By refusing to participate in the rhetorical labor of the School of Housekeeping, domestic workers made clear to the WEIU and elite women that the school was not a viable way forward for increasing the economic leverage of domestic workers, providing them with meaningful opportunities for connection and common cause, or for improving the relationships between them and their employers. At best, the WEIU's efforts over several decades spanning the turn of the twentieth century can be characterized as a series of partial successes intermingled with substantial failures.

Nevertheless, the repetitious rhetorical labor promoted by the WEIU prefigures ongoing efforts of activist domestic workers who were able to organize themselves in the twentieth and twenty-first centuries, efforts that were spurred in part by the shifting population of women who earned their living through household labor. Historians Vanessa H. May and Premilla Nadasen have both documented changes in the nature of domestic work over the course of the twentieth century—most significantly, the demographics of women who earned their livings through household labor shifted. According to Nadasen, an increasing number of jobs in industry and the service sector attracted working-class white women, who left household employment to become factory workers, department store clerks, office staff, and telephone operators. Restrictive immigration policies in the 1920s further limited the pool of women newly arrived from Europe who would have filled domestic jobs in Boston and other northeastern cities. Nadasen notes, "These trends resulted in a shortage of white and European-immigrant domestic workers, and women of color became the vast majority of domestic workers in all regions of the country. . . . In 1900 black women constituted 28 percent of domestic workers; by 1950 they were 60 percent" (11).

While the immigrant and other impoverished white women who worked as domestic employees in the Northeast during the late nineteenth century were often unmarried and lived in their employers' homes, Black women who came to dominate the ranks of household workers in the twentieth century frequently had their own families. They thus tended to "live out" and departed from their employers' households in the late afternoon or early evening to return to their own homes (May 8). Segregation meant that Black domestic workers' homes were typically located in Black neighborhoods where churches and community organizations served as sites for networking and building common cause. Moreover, in traveling to and from work each day, Black domestic workers often connected with each other while taking public transportation to reach their white employers' neighborhoods. May has argued that these circumstances helped give "birth to domestics who directly confronted employers' control over the occupation" (8–9). Forming a traditional labor union that could engage in collective bargaining and negotiate a contract on their behalf was not feasible since domestic workers were employed by countless individual households. But domestic workers formed advocacy groups, protested discriminatory regulations regarding household work, and lobbied government officials for equitable labor protections. Even as these twentieth-century household workers came to this work with a keen awareness of racial injustice and the need for collective action, they often advocated for the same sorts of rhetorical labor the WEIU had imperfectly promoted decades earlier.

Founded by Dorothy Bolden and other Black women who earned their livings through household work in Atlanta, Georgia, in 1968, the National Domestic Workers Union of America (NDWUA) offered programs so that workers could access technical training in areas such as price comparison shopping, driver education, child and elder care, and first aid (Nadasen 42, 98). As at the School of Housekeeping, certificates were issued upon the successful completion of training. But the NDWUA's programs were run by household workers, not the women who employed them. A proposal for the NDWUA's training program spells out, "The best teachers in any training program would be the domestics themselves" (qtd. in Nadasen 98). Similar training programs were promoted by the Household Workers Organization (HWO), a local organization of domestic workers founded in Detroit in 1969 by Mary McClendon, who had begun her career in household work as a young girl in Alabama before migrating to the North in 1955 (Nadasen 98). According to Nadasen, McClendon believed "'household labor' was a catch-all label that masked domestic workers' many roles" (100). She thus developed training in specialized areas such as Kitchen Manager, Child Supervisor, Geriatric Aide, and Party Supervisor. Like the School of Housekeeping's diplomas, such specialized job titles and certificates of completion have the potential to elevate the work of household labor while also creating equivalencies among employees and a repeatable shorthand way of communicating about individuals' skills and talents.

The first national organization of domestic workers was the Household Technicians of America (HTA), formed in 1971. Domestic worker Geneva Reid from Warren, Ohio, served as the first chair of HTA, and the organization came to represent an estimated twenty-five thousand household workers organized in more than three dozen local groups in cities such as San Francisco, Tulsa, Detroit, Cleveland, and Atlanta (Nadasen 79). According to Nadasen, local organizations of household workers issued model contracts and codes of standards, including delimiting chores that domestic workers would not do, such as washing windows, climbing ladders, and scrubbing floors on their hands and knees (96). The Washington, DC, chapter of HTA, for example, circulated a "Code of Standards" that included the suggestion that "a written agreement between employer and employee should clearly define the duties of the position, including specific tasks, how often they must be performed and the desired standards" (qtd. in Nadasen 96). Echoing the WEIU's Committee on Protection in its advocacy of pamphlets and model written contracts, the HTA sought to level the playing field between employers and household workers. Just as the WEIU had advocated a century earlier, the HTA and other organizations led by domestic workers promoted written contracts and codes of standards for household work in order to spell out the expectations and responsibilities for the signatories. Moreover, such standardized documents repeat the same information to every reader, thus stabilizing relationships and making it possible for third parties to intervene and adjudicate disputes.

This sort of rhetorical labor that derives its power from repetition continues to reverberate in discussions of household labor in the twenty-first century, even as the population of domestic workers has once again shifted. An increasingly significant portion of the number of women who strive to earn a living through household labor in the United States today are migrants in a globalized economy, and the American Community Survey estimates that a significant number of these women are undocumented (Burnham and Theodore 11–12). Founded in 2007, the National Domestic Workers Alliance (NDWA), led by Ai-jen Poo, advocates for "respect, recognition, labor rights and protections" for these vulnerable workers (www.domesticworkers.org). The NDWA has promoted a National Domestic Workers Bill of Rights, which includes "a standard written agreement to ensure that workers and employers understand the rights domestic workers have under the law, and that full terms, duties, and conditions of their employment are clear and explicit." The NDWA also advocates for "new domestic worker training programs, including new grants for sector-wide training programs, as well as the first national study of long-term career development and training standards for the care workforce with a focus on how to ensure that improved skills and training lead to better wages and career opportunities" (www.domesticworkers.org.).

Informational pamphlets and codes of conduct, model contracts, employment histories encoded in card catalogs, and diplomas. Such seemingly mundane documents stand as a complex legacy. Women engaged in domestic work have often viewed such rhetorical labor as a way to gain control over their lives and economic situations while well-to-do women have viewed such documents as a way to gain control over the women they employed. By considering how such repetitious rhetorical labor has been used to standardize and stabilize working relationships between women of different economic standing, rhetorical scholars can better understand how diversely circumstanced women have exercised power through language and how power has been exercised over them. Despite their marginality in our histories of feminist rhetoric, such documents migrated quickly in the nineteenth century from industrial enterprises into the home, promising to improve the lives of low-wage women workers by making their labor visible in codified, standardized, and repeatable ways. While standard contracts, receipts, systematized employment records, and diplomas afforded domestic workers new discursive tools for managing their relationships with the women who employed them, such documents did little to create a sense of common cause or collectivity among domestic workers in Boston at the turn of the twentieth century. The handful of students who attended the WEIU's School of Housekeeping seemed interested in fostering a greater sense of community among domestic workers, but since the perspectives and desires of employers shaped the school's pedagogical agenda, most domestic workers refused to engage with the WEIU's most substantive investment in solving the "servant problem." The persistent appearance of standardized documents in the agendas of grassroots organizations led by household workers themselves in the twentieth and twenty-first centuries serves as a reminder of the power of such forms of repetition as well as the persistent tensions threaded through the relationships of women in different economic circumstances.

CHAPTER 3

REVISITING *IMITATIO*, REINFORCING NEIGHBORLY NETWORKS OF SOLIDARITY

Appalachian Farm Women and the Moonlight Schools, 1911–1920

On September 5, 1911, more than a thousand residents of Rowan County, in the eastern mountains of Kentucky, left their fields and farmhouses as the sun began to set. Navigating treacherous footpaths and makeshift roads, rural families traveled to their local, segregated schoolhouses to participate in the moonlight schools launched by the county school superintendent, Cora Wilson Stewart.[1] Often queried about the institution's romantic name, Stewart would explain that moonlight schools were not sites where "children studied, and played, and scampered on the green like fairies in the moonlight . . . where lovers strolled arm in arm, quot[ing] poetry . . . or where moonshiners . . . were instructed in the most scientific methods of extracting the juice from the corn" ("Address before the Kansas State Teachers Association"). Instead, the moonlight schools provided adult learners with opportunities to acquire and improve basic literacy skills. The beginning of the eight-week session was scheduled to coincide with the full moon because "bad roads with innumerable gullies, high hills and unbridged streams were obstacles to overcome" for residents traveling from remote farms (Stewart, *Moonlight Schools* 14). Once rural families arrived at the schools, volunteer teachers would lead the two-hour classes that included singing hymns and patriotic songs, using grooved tablets that allowed students to practice writing their names, and discussing short articles in local newspapers. After several weeks of study, many students were reading longer texts and composing letters to family members and public officials.

Within a decade, every Kentucky county had an "illiteracy agent" and 130,000 Kentuckians had learned to read and write at moonlight

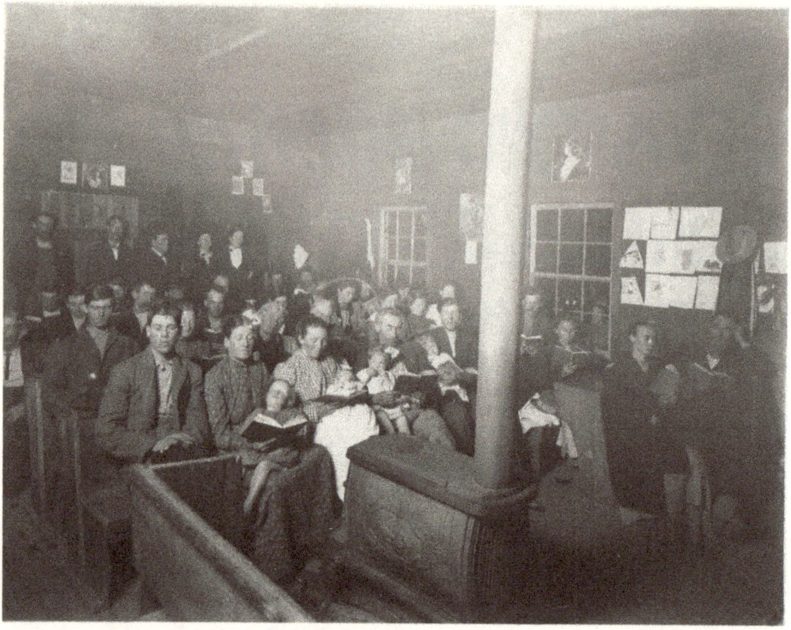

3.1. Moonlight School, 1911. Image Courtesy of Special Collections Research Center, University of Kentucky Libraries.

schools (Kentucky Illiteracy Commission 7, 9). County enrollment figures in the moonlight schools were celebrated locally and across the state. In Magoffin County, the county school superintendent touted that 1,400 people had been taught to read and write between 1916 and 1920 (Kentucky Illiteracy Commission 31). In Clark County, 203 Black students attended a moonlight school in 1915 (Baldwin 49), and R. D. Grant and Mrs. LaVinia Littleton, teachers from Mason County, reported: "Our moonlight school for colored persons has been a grand success" (Kentucky Illiteracy Commission 54).[2] Stewart authored a series of three textbooks, the *Country Life Readers*, for use in rural literacy classes across the country, and she carried her "crusade" against illiteracy to prisons, Native American communities, and, as Deborah Brandt has documented, to army induction centers during World War I ("Drafting U.S. Literacy").[3] In 1925, the *Pictorial Review* awarded its annual prize to Stewart, recognizing her as the woman who had made the greatest contribution to American life in the past year.

The moonlight schools and Stewart's *Country Life Readers* have merited the attention of scholars interested in pedagogies designed for adult learners (Canipe and Decker); in the history of literacy "crises" and the cultural work that representations of illiteracy accomplish (NeCamp;

Bevilacqua); and in the rhetorical construction of popular mythologies about Appalachia (Bryson). While Stewart's efforts to end illiteracy and her pedagogical materials serve as a rich site for pursuing a variety of significant research questions, I turn to the moonlight schools as an opportunity to investigate the working lives and repetitious rhetorical labors of rural women.

Rural women of all races have too rarely been included in rhetoricians' discussions of women and work. In editing *Who Says? Working-Class Rhetoric, Class-Consciousness, and Community* (2007), William DeGenaro included only one essay devoted to rural labor—Emily Plec's analysis of interviews that Daniel Rothenberg conducted with migrant farm workers in the late twentieth century. *Women at Work: Rhetorics of Gender and Labor* (2019), a collection of essays edited by David Gold and Jessica Enoch, offers insights into the rhetorical labors of women who earned their livings as seamstresses, photographers, metallurgists, musicians, entrepreneurs, and athletes, but no women whose livelihoods were tied to farming are included in the collection.

This long-standing omission can perhaps be explained by the fact that women who lived and worked on small farms in the early twentieth century were not typically considered wage earners, and the boundaries were blurry between a woman's domestic labor in a farmhouse and the work she undertook in fields, barns, chicken coops, and other spaces. Bringing in hay or other crops, milking cows, gathering eggs, butchering hogs, making cheese, stitching quilts, or nursing ill or injured family members did not result in a regular paycheck, but such labor was crucial as women sustained themselves and their families on small farms. Despite the fact that farm women and their labor posed a definitional challenge to widespread conceptions of women's work, nearly 16 percent of women workers in 1910 listed their occupation as agriculture on the US Census ("Comparative Occupation Statistics" 101), and some 53 percent of the US population were living on farms at that time (Bowers 13).

Women living and laboring on farms were a significant portion of the workforce just after the turn of the twentieth century, but they did not attract the attention of labor organizers or unions. Instead, they were often the target of educational activists and reformers, like Cora Wilson Stewart, who were invested in Progressive Era notions of social reform and uplift. From the moonlight schools, to Appalachian settlement programs modeled on Jane Addams's Hull House, to the US Department of Agriculture's widespread extension and home demonstration programs, educational reformers promoted entrepreneurial activities among farm women and espoused the importance of formally organized civic activities in rural communities. They also positioned the white, middle-class housewife as a model of gendered behavior for all women.[4] In doing so, reformers in Appalachia created "zones of neediness" in which rural women workers lacked economic agency and required intervention so that they could be productively aligned with the national economy (Stump 1020–121). This mapping of power and positionality prefigures the rhetorics of development and neoliberalism often invoked at the turn of the twentieth-first century in regard to rural women workers in the Global South (Mohanty 29–30; Escobar 8–9; Dingo, *Networking Arguments* 114–18). From small farms in Appalachia to small plots of land that sustain families in Brazil, South Korea, Zimbabwe, and other countries, women living in rural communities have been and continue to be seen as workers in need of intervention and organization by a variety of stakeholders.

Such efforts, though, often fail to recognize the existing systems of solidarity and collective action that sustain many rural communities. In the case of the moonlight schools, Stewart's pedagogical agenda overlooked how Appalachian farm women had for generations carefully cultivated and maintained networks of kith and kin that served as social safety nets in difficult times and allowed them to pool the benefits of economic windfalls in good times. Trading surplus vegetables from a kitchen garden with neighbors, inviting family and friends to help prepare dinner for the hands who helped butcher livestock, participating in quilting bees and communal corn-huskings, sharing transportation resources with other residents living in their vicinity, opening one's home to relatives in need of safe harbor from a family member struggling with addiction or engaged in dangerous criminal activity—all were common practices among rural women in the early twentieth century (Walker; Neth; Holt; Greer, "Women's Words"). Such alliances and collaborative strategies have long helped farm women cope with poverty, inadequate educational opportunities, and a legal system unresponsive to their needs. These flexible, everyday systems of solidarity are rarely remarked upon as a form of low-wage workers' activism, and investigations of such ordinary survival tactics may appear on the surface to be nostalgic or naive. But just as much as women employed in the Lowell textile factories in the 1830s and 1840s and as domestic workers employed in the private homes of Boston in the late nineteenth century, Appalachian farm women were investing their physical energies and their rhetorical labor in negotiating their "differential access to and control over the means of provisioning and survival" (Acker 68). Arising in response to local circumstances and deeply rooted in rural traditions, the neighborly networks of women living on small farms in Appalachia were a significant element of their working lives and an important expression of their solidarity.

By overlooking such a significant portion of women workers and how they engaged in cooperative activities in the early twentieth century, rhetoricians risk developing a stunted sense of the diverse forms of rhetorical labor that allow women to claim a greater sense of economic agency as well as strengths and limitations of efforts to create common cause and organization. Similarly, drawing sharp distinctions between traditional forms of workers' activism and other forms of solidarity by which people with few economic resources have nurtured their families and communities unnecessarily limits the range of possibilities that might be available for reconstructing the economic and social landscape in the twenty-first century. I thus contend that the tenacity of rural women's support structures and the repetitious rhetorical labor that sustains them merit the attention of rhetorical scholars as well as researchers, teachers, and activists interested both in rejuvenating traditional labor unions and in imagining new kinds of advocacy groups for people with limited economic resources in the United States and around the globe.

In this chapter, I first describe the educational opportunities farm women encountered when they attended the moonlight schools, a pedagogical program grounded in repetition, or *imitatio.* By asking students to parrot statements from their teachers, to copy sentences from their textbooks, and to use textual templates for their own discursive productions, Stewart sought to impress upon students that white, heteronormative farm families exemplified traditional agrarian values and labor practices that made them central to the life of the nation. But the moonlight school pedagogies and *Country Life Readers* also encouraged farm families to embrace more capitalistic forms of economic activity and more structured forms of community engagement. However, rural women did not necessarily embrace new economic and civic behaviors, no matter how often the benefits of such behaviors were repeated and reinforced.

The second half of this chapter turns to letters written by women, mostly white, who attended the moonlight schools, letters that are loosely threaded throughout Stewart's collected papers. These missives allow me to argue that farm women in Appalachia opted to use their expanding literacy skills not to adopt the new organizational behaviors and economic identity Stewart continually advocated but instead to engage in their own forms of repetitive rhetorical labor as they sought to reinforce their traditional neighborly networks.

In focusing my attention on texts produced by students in response to a particular pedagogical program, I am in a sense following in the methodological footsteps of numerous historians in rhetoric and writing studies who have probed the degrees of success (and failure) that diverse educational institutions have achieved in carrying out their ideological and cultural agendas (Simmons; Fitzgerald; Rothermel; Hays; Welsch; Ritter). In her afterword to *Local Histories: Reading the Archives of Composition*, Jean Ferguson Carr cites Gabriel Compayré, a nineteenth-century French educational historian and pedagogical theorist. Compayré urged educators to study "not the great writers on education and their doctrines, not the great teachers and their methods, but the pupils themselves" (239). Patricia Sullivan has more recently echoed Compayré in urging historians in rhetoric and writing studies "to feature those voices of past students whenever and wherever they appear" (367).

My interest in the writing produced by women who attended the moonlight schools, though, extends beyond their identities as students. Instead, my focus is on rural women's labor outside the classroom and their forms of unorganized activism to improve the lives of their families and their communities. In their articulation and exploration of feminist rhetorical practices, Jacqueline Jones Royster and Gesa E. Kirsch remind scholars of "the twofold challenge of being aware, not only of what enters our field of vision—what we see and recognize—but attuned also to our blind spots in order to consider with critical intensity what may be more in shadow, muted, and not immediately obvious" (76). In the case of women who attended the moonlight schools, their lives as workers beyond the classroom are "not immediately obvious" in the letters Stewart preserved. Jennie L. Vaughn has urged feminist scholars seeking to recognize the shadowy and less apparent elements of the lives of their research subjects to draw upon "living archives" as well as traditional archives housed in institutional repositories. For Vaughn, living archives include "people, relationships, conversations, and sources that the researcher cultivates alongside their work in traditional, institutional locations" (126). In reading the letters written by women who attended the moonlight schools to see them as workers, rather than as students, I thus draw upon my own rural roots and lived experiences in Appalachia as well as my abiding connections with family who still live in the region. I have also immersed myself in the rich body of research produced by other scholars who study rural women and communities from a range of disciplinary perspectives, including LuAnn Jones, Mary Neth, Anita Puckett, Katherine Kelleher Sohn, Sara Webb-Sunderhaus, and Melissa Walker. Bringing this living archive into conversation with the letters written by rural women and contained within Stewart's collected papers allows me to recognize how their epistolary efforts function as a form of repetitive rhetorical labor that enabled rural women to reinforce existing forms of solidarity in their communities.

By reinforcing their existing community networks and traditions through repetitive rhetorical labor, the rural women who attended the moonlight schools engaged in a project that differed from how the Lowell mill girls deployed and redeployed commonplaces through their regularly appearing periodical as they sought to craft a new public identity for themselves as white women in an industrial setting in the mid-nineteenth century (chapter 1). Rather than trying to craft a new public identity for themselves as women workers, the women who attended the moonlight schools used their expanding literacy skills to buttress the rural identities that they already inhabited. The repetitive rhetorical labor of the farm women who attended the moonlight schools also stands in contrast to the standardization of language and documents that domestic workers in Boston encountered as means of managing their economic lives (chapter 2). Rather than using forms and systems of workplace documentation that could objectively be (re)read by multiple individuals, the documents composed by moonlight school students were deeply personal. These rural women celebrated their own sense of accomplishment as they expanded their abilities to read texts central to their lives, such as the Bible; described their joy in being able to maintain connections with distant friends and family; and expressed gratitude to their teachers. Instead of embracing a depersonalized notion of textuality as the path to economic agency, the women who attended the moonlight schools fully marshaled the affective, interpersonal dimensions of their repetitive rhetorical labor.

Throughout this book, I am seeking to document the varied ways in which women workers with limited financial resources sought to gain greater economic agency and how they responded to a range of opportunities to find common cause with other women working in similar circumstances. Featuring the women who attended the moonlight schools as one of my historical case studies allows me to call attention to the ways in which low-wage working women have not always sought to create new possibilities for themselves and their communities or embraced innovations but have instead relied on well-established traditions and sought to reinforce long-standing communal practices of solidarity. Such seemingly unorganized women workers have much to teach us about possibilities for collective action and about the repetitious rhetorical labor of low-wage women workers seeking to improve their working lives today. I begin with an overview of the moonlight school curriculum and Stewart's *Country Life Readers* and how they reiterated messages of reform in terms of rural women workers.

IMITATIO AT WORK IN THE CLASSROOM: SCHOOLING RURAL WOMEN ON NEW ECONOMIC IDENTITIES

Rural women who attended the moonlight schools encountered pedagogies based on imitatio, a long-standing form of rhetorical education grounded in various forms of repetition—paraphrase, translation, the study of exemplar texts, and other forms of reiteration. As Cora Wilson Stewart explained, the essential elements of the first sessions at the moonlight schools were "simple words, much repetition and a content that related to the activity of the reader" (*Moonlight Schools* 21). At the nightly class meetings, rural women would have recited in unison with their classmates scripted answers to their teachers' questions. For the drills, teachers were instructed to ask scripted questions in a "quick, snappy fashion," and the students would repeat the answers in unison (*Moonlight School Course of Study* 13). For example, in drills on food and nutrition, the teacher would ask students to "name the two large classes of foods," and students were to respond "Body builders" and "Energy producers." Or a teacher might ask, "Should [children] have tea or coffee?" and the students were to respond, "No—they do not make bone or muscle" (28, 31)

Repetition was also a key pedagogical strategy throughout the *Country Life Readers*. In the first of the *Country Life Readers*, rural women found lessons that included a short list of related vocabulary words, a series of six to eight sentences to read and recite, and a final sentence, printed in script, that they were instructed to copy ten times. The lessons in the second of the *Country Life Readers* follow the same format, but the students encountered more polysyllabic words, a wider range of intricately structured sentences to copy, longer reading selections (100–150 words), and more complex sample documents to use as models for their own writing. According to Stewart, repetition was necessary "until the right habit was formed" (*Moonlight Schools* 27). The final reader in the series contains no vocabulary lists or sentences to be copied ten times. Instead, rural students were offered a collection of inspirational readings drawn from popular authors like Gene Stratton-Porter, Henry Wadsworth Longfellow, Washington Irving, and Louisa May Alcott. While students would not necessarily repeat or imitate the works of these well-known writers, the reading selections represented an inventional storehouse of ideas and attitudes to be adopted by the students.

The roots of this pedagogical practice of imitatio can be traced to ancient rhetoricians, including Isocrates, Plato, Aristotle, Dionysius of Halicarnassus, Longinus, Cicero, and Quintilian (McKeon; Corbett; D. Sullivan; Hawhee). Through the centuries, imitatio has signified a range of discursive activities in the Western world—memorizing and repeating word-for-word the writing of respected authorities, mimicking the intonation and bodily gestures of effective public speakers, adopting the prose style of revered texts, or translating and paraphrasing the key ideas in an argument. By imitating discursive models, students expand their vocabularies and are exposed to new linguistic forms and structures; engagement with exemplary texts also provides students with culturally sanctioned resources for invention and potential road maps for their own discursive productions. Imitatio remained an essential component of education through the nineteenth century in the United States. According to Dale L. Sullivan, John Witherspoon and John Quincy Adams both recognized the value of imitation for students. (5). Though contemporary classrooms may look quite different than the pedagogical spaces familiar to Witherspoon and Adams, review, repetition, and modeling continue to be critical components of literacy education today. The International Literacy Association notes that as people are learning to read, repetition allows them to bridge from their current knowledge base to new discursive practices (3). And as sites of twenty-first-century literacy education, coding boot camps, where people develop critical literacy skills in computer languages, also typically involve "close order drill," or continual repetition until an action is "instinctive" (Waguespack, Babb, and Yates 54).

But imitatio has also been viewed as a tool for indoctrination. Drawing upon the work of Homi K. Bhabha, Robert E. Terrill notes that imitation can be "a powerful instrument for sustaining the supremacy of a dominant culture" as the discursive forms of those in power are replicated and their hegemony reinforced ("Rhetorical Imitation and Civic Diversity" 169). Writing of rhetorical education and imitatio or mimêsis in the nineteenth century, Kirt H. Wilson observes that "imitation was embroiled in a struggle for power, social status, and identity" (90). As Wilson argues, "the repetitive copying of forms taught students the skills of literacy, and the imitation of exemplars instructed the young white mind in the virtues of republicanism and the responsibilities of citizenship." For Black people who were free in the antebellum period, imitating "the dominant culture" allowed them to "obtain a measure of independence and to establish grounds for their inclusion in the body politic" (89). After the Civil War, the abilities of Black people to claim a modicum of power by successfully imitating the norms of European Americans prompted mimêsis as a rhetorical performance to be recast as a "primitive instinct," according to Wilson (89), while in classroom, imitative pedagogies came to be seen as most appropriate for the least cognitively sophisticated students.

Stewart, too, was deeply invested in the hegemonic power of imitatio and its pedagogical potential to mediate "power, social status, and identity." She believed that copying model sentences from the *Country Life Readers* and using the letters and longer passages in the textbooks as models would have a "fine psychological effect" on the farm families who attended moonlight schools (*Moonlight Schools* 72). The psychological effect Stewart hoped to have on farm women was twofold—she sought both to reinforce the value of a white, heteronormative agrarian lifestyle and to reform their labor and community life.

Reinforcing Rural Values and Valuing White Women's Work

As farm women moved through *Country Life Readers*, they repeatedly encountered lessons that lauded rural life. The first textbook celebrates the beauties of the countryside and reminds rural women that natural features of the landscape, such as wild flowers, are "half the joy of country life" (68). The second *Country Life Reader* opens with Norman Gale's brief poem "Life in the Country," which characterizes rural life as "the best of all!," a statement that students would have been instructed to copy ten times (9).

In the third of the *Country Life Readers*, students encountered longer texts that venerate the mundane tasks accomplished every day by rural women: Silas Dinsmore's "The Churning Song," Louisa May Alcott's "A Song from the Suds," and an anonymous poem on the making of jams and jellies. The third textbook also features Paul Hamilton Hayne's poem "The Farmer's Wife," which exalts the rural woman's "sun-burnt hands and buxom arms" and reveres her for being "Blithe as a bee, with busy care," for ensuring that the "home chords of toil are all in tune," and for draining the use of "each richly bounteous hour" (204). The poem concludes with an admonition to "Ye dames in proud, palatial halls—/ Of lavish wiles and jeweled dress." Such wealthy women are reminded that "Your sister 'mid the country dew / Is three times nearer Heaven than you" (206). Hayne's poem contributes to Stewart's unremitting message about the nobility of an agrarian lifestyle and the place of white farm women in the cultural life of the nation. Stewart also chose to include Mary N. Prescott's poem "Work" in the third reader. In each of the poem's four stanzas a feminized force of nature or creature is questioned about her labors: the "sweet . . . fair wind" sweeps cobwebs from the sky, the "soft rain" waters the crops and fills wells, a red-breasted bird nurtures her offspring, and a honeybee pollinates flowers. More significantly, the wind and rain, birds and bees also seem to respond to unstated questions about the value of their work. For example, after explaining that "I'm urging the corn to fill out its cells; / I'm helping the lily to fashion its bells; / I'm swelling the torrent and brimming the wells," the rain turns the table on her interrogator and poses a question whose answer is self-evident: "Is that worth pursuing?" (178). Similarly, the honeybee reminds the questioner that as she fills her "basket with precious pelf," she "toil[s] for my neighbor as well as myself" (178). Making such a poem part of her educational program for farm families allowed Stewart to call attention to the importance of the chores farm women completed every day, often without recognition or remuneration. In sum, all three *Country Life Readers* emphasize "those things which relate to the usefulness and dignity of the farmer and the farmer's wife, and the importance of their work in the world" (Stewart, *CLR3* 1).

To be sure, the vision of rural life and women's work that Stewart celebrated was grounded in nativism, white supremacy, and heteronormativity. Stewart castigated immigrants who sought "to advance the welfare of the country from which they came rather than the welfare of the nation which has received them into its bosom," and she characterized the "millions of pure Anglo-Saxon Americans" living in Appalachia as "a reservoir of strength and patriotism" (*Moonlight Schools* 5). Samantha NeCamp has argued that throughout Stewart's career as an educational activist, she was "particularly incensed by the fact that educational programs for the foreign-born were liberally funded by many state and local governments while she struggled to locate minimal funding for illiteracy programs targeting the native-born" (28). For Stewart, the native-born white residents of Appalachia were more worthy beneficiaries of educational and philanthropic outreach, and they were more likely to repay the efforts of reformers by embracing capitalistic economic behaviors and stalwart patriotism.

Stewart's characterization of the residents of Appalachia as "pure Anglo-Saxon Americans" also occludes the presence of Black farm families in the region. In a 1916 article in the *Journal of Negro History*, Carter G. Woodson called attention to the erasure of Black residents in Appalachia. Woodson's efforts to challenge the whiteness of the region have subsequently been taken up by anthropologists (Anglin; Hartigan); historians (Inscoe; Griffin), sociologists and linguists (Brown; B. Smith; Mallinson and Childs), and rhetoricians (Taylor). Recent scholarship has also participated in the queering of Appalachia, challenging the notion that all farm families are comprised of a heterosexual couple and their offspring (Glasby, Gradin, and Ryerson). Black farm families did attend segregated moonlight schools, but they and other nonwhite, nonheteronormative families who engaged with Stewart's curriculum would have encountered lessons that celebrated, rather than complicated, the image of the white, yeoman farmer, ensconced on his own small plot of land with a wife and children.

All the authors whose literary works are included as exemplars or inventional models in Stewart's textbooks are white, and only two images across the three *Country Life Readers* clearly feature Black people. Among the twenty-two visual representations of people that illustrate lessons in *Country Life Readers: First Book*, there is a single image of Black families working in a cotton field. This image accompanies a lesson on cotton as a staple crop in the South that is imperiled by the boll weevil (42–43). In the *Country Life Readers: Third Book*, there is a similar singular, identifiable image of Black people, again working in a cotton field; a white man sits astride a horse in the middle of the field and appears to menace the Black workers as they tend the plants (71). This disturbing image appears above an unattributed poem that celebrates the various uses of cotton. The *Country Life Readers* thus reinforce the racist linkage between the cultivation of cotton and Black people—while enslaved or under systems of exploitive tenant farming. In the pages of Stewart's textbooks, white farm families were positioned as the normative residents of rural America and were worthy of respect and celebration. But even the white, native-born farm families that Stewart prioritized were viewed as subjects in need of reformation.

Reforming White Rural Women and Their Communities

For all of the ways the moonlight schools and the *Country Life Readers* venerated the traditions of a white, heteronormative agrarian lifestyle, Stewart's pedagogy was intended to bring dramatic changes to rural communities, and she was part of a broader rural reform movement in the first decades of the twentieth century. New technologies, scientific advances in agriculture and domestic science, and modern business practices had all begun to disrupt rural traditions (Bowers 8). So dramatic was the impact on rural communities that in 1908 President Theodore Roosevelt established the Commission on Country Life (CCL) to investigate the challenges faced by farm families and recommend possible solutions.[5]

The CCL advocated a number of solutions to improve rural life, but central to all of them was organization (Bowers 62–63). CCL member Walter Hines Page believed that organization was "the greatest invention in modern times and the greatest engine of all progress" (qtd. in Bowers 38), and the CCL's final report declared that rural citizens had failed "to adjust to the fundamental change from an agriculturally based economy with its concept of individualism to an industrially centered one with its principle of organization of interests" (Bowers 62). The CCL thus encouraged white farm families to form cooperatives in order to gain access to more profitable business opportunities and to participate as both producers and consumers in marketplaces organized by capitalist principles. Moreover, by joining formalized civic organizations, farm families could improve the social and cultural life of rural communities, according to the CCL. The instructional materials that farm women encountered at the moonlight schools and in Stewart's *Country Life Readers* were intended to facilitate these kinds of adjustments to their working lives and their communities.

While the *Country Life Readers* repeatedly celebrated the rural lives and labors of white women in Appalachia, farm women were also encouraged to assume new economic identities and to participate in the marketplace as producers and entrepreneurs. For example, the second of the *Country Life Readers* alerted women that the poultry industry generates about six hundred million dollars a year in the United States (40). The lesson goes on to urge women to invest in a good breed of hens and provide them with a good house and clean nests in order to "get your part of that six hundred million dollars" (41). The lesson then concludes with the commissive statement "I will raise more poultry" for students to copy ten times. In a later lesson, farm women encountered a basic recipe for making cottage cheese accompanied by the observation that "city people gladly pay a good price for it." The lesson concludes with this sentence for copying: "A woman that can make good cottage cheese can increase the value of the cow $40 or $50 a year" (*CLR2* 77).

Not only were women urged to become entrepreneurs and producers, but they were also instructed to become consumers of mass-produced commodities and to adopt the behavioral norms of middle-class white women. The first of the *Country Life Readers* features a drawing of a commercially manufactured toothbrush, and the lesson proceeds with a series of sentences that link dental hygiene to the appropriate expenditure of economic resources:

> See my new toothbrush!
> It did not cost much, but it will save me money.
> It will save me from pain.
> If I use it after every meal, my teeth will not decay.
> If my teeth do not decay, they will not ache.
> If I take care of them, I shall not have to buy new ones.
> I will brush my teeth and save them. (45)

Beyond encouraging women to purchase mass-produced consumer goods to meet rising standards of personal hygiene, the moonlight schools also celebrated particular norms of middle-class housekeeping that would require women to use cash to purchase materials and devices. Products such as house paint in tasteful colors; crocks, pails, and sieves for dairy work; egg timers; cooking thermometers; and rubber rings for canning were all lauded in the *Country Life Readers*. By becoming purchasers of such goods, rural women could hope to achieve a level of "cleanliness" that would reflect positively on the "moral condition of the entire household" (*CLR3*, 217).

In addition to embracing middle-class norms of consumption and becoming more robust purchasers of mass-produced goods, farm women were also encouraged to use their developing literacy skills to access other sources of knowledge and domestic science expertise to improve their work lives and their communities. For example, in a lesson from the *Country Life Readers: Second Book* titled "When Foods Are Scarce," the following dialogue unfolds between two women:

> "I have a little book that gives directions for making twenty-seven kinds of corn bread. I like to vary the kinds of bread I make. How glad everybody is when they see a different kind of bread on the table! . . . You can also make cakes, dumplings, and puddings of corn meal."
>
> "Is it possible? I should like to see the little book that tells how to cook all these things." (82)

In later lessons, a physician belittles a woman for not preparing nutritious food for her sick husband. She then hurries to a neighbor's house to learn how to make a restorative beef tea. Rather than drawing upon her own expertise, the neighbor responds, "Let me get my cookbook. I cook most things by recipe, and then I know that I am making them right" (90–91). In the pages of the *Country Life Readers*, women are repeatedly depicted as passive recipients of expert knowledge that is not rooted in local community practices. They must refer to cookbooks to know they are preparing meals "right." Along with encouraging women to consult the expertise of cookbook authors, lessons in the *Country Life Readers* offer brief descriptions of the latest "cold-pack" method of canning and encourage women to use modern methods as they make cheese for their families. More detailed information about these new procedures would be available through farm journals and other publications.

The model letters in Stewart's textbooks even guided women living in Appalachia through the process of acquiring print materials and accessing expertise and consumer goods from afar. In one lesson, a student corresponds with the editor of *Progressive Farmer* about obtaining a subscription; another lesson features a student requesting a catalogue of "household conveniences" from a mail order merchandiser. In speeches she gave around the nation, Stewart further emphasized the importance of relying upon the knowledge circulated through printed texts and of the value of consumer goods. In an often repeated address titled "Mountain Jewels," Stewart urged farm women to eschew neighborhood visits and gossiping in favor of reading nationally circulating magazines like *Ladies' Home Journal* and *Twentieth Century Home* (Baldwin 24–25). In

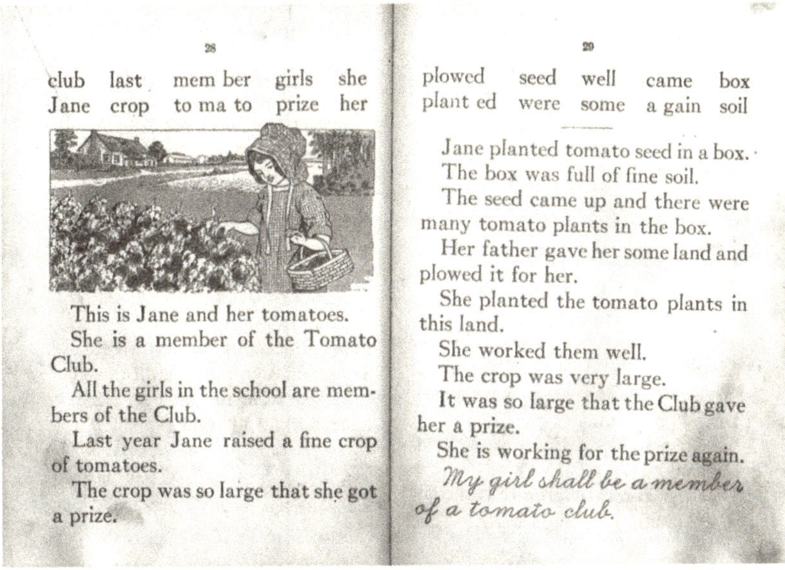

28

club last mem ber girls she
Jane crop to ma to prize her

This is Jane and her tomatoes.
She is a member of the Tomato Club.
All the girls in the school are members of the Club.
Last year Jane raised a fine crop of tomatoes.
The crop was so large that she got a prize.

29

plowed seed well came box
plant ed were some a gain soil

Jane planted tomato seed in a box.
The box was full of fine soil.
The seed came up and there were many tomato plants in the box.
Her father gave her some land and plowed it for her.
She planted the tomato plants in this land.
She worked them well.
The crop was very large.
It was so large that the Club gave her a prize.
She is working for the prize again.
My girl shall be a member of a tomato club.

3.2. Jane and the Tomato Club. From Cora Wilson Stewart's *Country Life Readers: First Book*, B. F. Richmond, 1915.

such periodicals, women living in Appalachia would have encountered advice to guide them toward the norms and behaviors of middle-class white housekeepers, including how to prepare meals on a budget, decorate their homes, and rear their children. Such magazines also brought women living in rural communities into contact with advertisements for commercially branded food products, cleaning supplies, and personal hygiene items.

While the moonlight schools offered rural women the opportunity to reshape their own labor and their families' lives through new economic activities and literacy practices, the *Country Life Readers* also encouraged them to undertake the work of organizing a more structured community life of clubs and formal institutions. For example, the first of the *Country Life Readers* features a young girl who is a member of her school's Tomato Club and wins a prize for raising a particularly fine crop. The lesson concludes with this commissive sentence for her parents to copy: "My girl shall be a member of a tomato club" (29). Similarly, a lesson in *Country Life Readers: Second Book* urges students to support a Sunday school because "the Sunday school is a 'get together' affair, and the country needs more of such things" (131).

The model letters in the *Country Life Readers* echo the importance of formally organized institutions. In the first book, "Sallie Spell" writes this letter to her sister: "Our moonlight school is still in session. There are many men and women in the school. . . . We are going to form a health league and a good roads club. The league will work for better health and longer life. The club will aid in making roads better" (54–55). By positing the formation of Sunday schools, health leagues, cooperatives, libraries, and good roads clubs, the *Country Life Readers* repeatedly underscore the link between the new literacy skills moonlight school students were developing and the new forms of organized activity in which they should engage.

While not the labor unions that have enabled industrial workers to participate in collective bargaining with their employers, the structured civic endeavors promoted by the moonlight schools and throughout Stewart's *Country Life Readers* seem to hold out the possibility that formally organized rural residents with few economic resources might work together to improve their own communities and even engage with state legislators and other officials to secure needed services and resources. Such civic engagement might have been what CCL member Walter Hines Page hoped for as he urged rural citizens to embrace the "principle of organization of interests" (Bowers 62).

But informal networks of support and solidarity had already existed for generations among women living in Appalachia, and they repurposed the new literacy skills they developed at the moonlight schools to engage in their own repetitive rhetorical labor to buttress these resilient networks. Contemporary scholars of imitatio would not be surprised that farm women repurposed the lessons Stewart offered them.

IMITATIO REPURPOSED

From the vantage point of the twenty-first century, the repetitive pedagogy that rural women encountered at the moonlight schools might seem to engage them in "withered and withering classroom exercises" (Terrill, "Mimesis" 308). A number of scholars have, though, revisited imitatio, noting its potential as a pedagogical practice that creates a space in which students bring their own needs and desires into conversation with the perspectives of others. Robert E. Terrill observes that "a student schooled through imitation attends to both her own discourse and the discourse of another, simultaneously." Terrill goes on to note that students shaped through imitatio are "inherently bifurcated, influenced by their individual motives as well as their understanding of cultural norms and traditions" ("Mimesis" 300). Frederick Douglass's famous description of his engagement with the *Columbian Orator*, a text rife with messages about republican virtue, patriotism, and white supremacy, serves as an illustration of this bifurcation. Douglass describes reading passages from the volume "over and over again with unabated interest" (44). Douglass then elucidates the complexity of his iterative encounters with ideas advanced by the exemplar texts. He writes that his repeated reading "gave tongue to interesting thoughts of my own soul" and "enabled me to utter my thoughts" (44). But the *Columbian Orator* also induced a complexly layered range of emotions in Douglass—a palpable hatred for those who profited from the slave trade, a heightened sense of self-awareness and outrage over his own enslavement, and a stubborn sense of hope (44). Douglass's narrative underscores that imitatio does not necessarily result in mere mechanical reproduction and indoctrination.

Robert Brooke has similarly documented a range of student responses that extends well beyond mechanical reproduction and indoctrination in a college-level, first-year writing class structured around principles of imitation. For Brooke and for the teacher whose class he observed, an imitative writing pedagogy involves more than the rote reproduction of words, phrases, or larger discursive units. Instead, imitation involves a complex negotiation between the psychosocial identities students bring to the classroom and the models they encounter there (24–26). In the class Brooke observed, Margaret Laurence's *A Bird in the House* was presented to the students as a model for "using writing to explore the complexity of their own lives and to communicate this complexity to other readers" (30). Among the eight students that Brooke followed closely, he documented a range of responses—some students accepted the writerly identity modeled by Laurence; other students "transform[ed] . . . their understanding of . . . [the] course so they could keep what excited them and avoid what was threatening" (32); and still other students ultimately rejected the writerly identity in the exemplar text that they were asked to consider as a model (35). In sum, imitatio opened up a range of choices and possibilities in the classroom.

Like the students studied by Brooke who rejected the writerly model they were asked to imitate and like Douglass, the farm women who attended the moonlight schools in Appalachia did not embrace the identities and behaviors that were held up as models for them. Instead, they marshaled the new literacy skills they acquired through Stewart's repetitive pedagogy to reinforce the long-standing neighborly networks that had sustained their families and their communities for generations. Such networks have been an important means of economic agency for rural women through the years. The diverse forms of labor that rural women undertake in their farmhouses as well as in fields, barns, chicken coops, and other spaces are recognized as valuable forms of life-sustaining work within such neighborly networks. Moreover, such networks are structured through tenaciously affective connections, rather than strictly rational calculations about the immediate costs and benefits of any particular forms of economic activity. These resilient, neighborly networks have been well documented by a range of scholars and researchers.

A LIVING ARCHIVE: UNDERSTANDING NEIGHBORLINESS IN APPALACHIA AS A FORM OF ECONOMIC AGENCY

In the early decades of the twentieth century, rural women of all races rarely held title to land or other economic assets. Through reciprocal exchange networks, though, they could gain access to vital resources. Pooling labor to butcher livestock, sharing tools and expertise, bartering one's surplus eggs for some of a neighbor's bumper crop of pole beans, opening one's home to relatives in need of shelter, or going "visiting" to care for an elderly or ill neighbor—all were forms of neighborly activity in which farm women typically participated. Rural historians and sociologists, like Melissa Walker, Mary Neth, and Marilyn Irvin Holt, have established the sustaining power of these informal social networks for rural women. A significant though often unrecognized form of solidarity, such "neighborliness" allowed women in rural communities to create a sense of mutuality among themselves and established an informal system of social welfare that could see farm families through hard times.

James Watt Raine, a rhetoric professor at Berea College from 1906 to 1939, notes that such "neighborliness" was a fundamental trait among Appalachian families. Writing in 1924, he noted: "A sister-in-law with a shiftless husband and half a dozen children descends without invitation and almost without warning upon a family whose house has two rooms and a lean-to shed for cooking. The family 'have mighty leetle to do with.' It is a hard struggle to provide for their own little brood . . . but they welcome her without comment. . . . as week follows week. . . . [And] they never hint that the visit is unduly prolonged" (74). Seventy years later, Loyal Jones, also a professor at Berea College and a key player in the establishment of the college's Center for Appalachian Studies, included neighborliness among the core values he felt were central to the lives of Appalachian residents, along with religion, independence, patriotism, humor, humility, familial connection, love of place, cooperation, and appreciation of beauty.[6] Research by scholars in rhetoric and composition has similarly brought to light the support networks of kith and kin that remain a powerful force in the lives of women in the region. When Katherine Kelleher Sohn asked the "whistlin' and crowin' women" in her study to define Appalachia, they focused on "close family ties [and] neighborliness" as key characteristics that keep them rooted in the region (425).

Arising out of long-standing mutual interests and personal relationships, such neighborly practices of sharing resources and pooling labor should not be dismissed as little more than the quaint norms of a bygone era or a romantic ideal. Instead, they can stand as a critique of capitalism, the commodification of goods and services, and the modern labor market. After doing an interview with Nellie Stancil Langley, who farmed in rural North Carolina in the first half of the twentieth century, oral historian Lu Ann Jones notes that "like many members of her generation of farmers, Langley laments the demise of an ethic of sharing and trust that she believes once characterized her rural community. The labor demands of the traditional tobacco culture had encouraged mutual aid, and families routinely swapped work during harvest time. But her jeremiads do not invoke a naïve nostalgia for 'the good old days.' Rather, implicit in her comments is a thoughtful critique of capital-intensive agriculture and rural modernization and changes that have come in their wake" (21). More recently, linguist Anita Puckett has documented how the particular speech patterns of the current residents in an eastern Kentucky community, Ash Creek, assign value to economic items, situate labor within the context of "helpin out," and create social webs of kith and kin with whom they exchange goods and services within networks of "belongin" (24–25). For Puckett, the "helpin out" communicative practices of Ash Creek residents "function to reproduce a local organization of labor that contradicts or is partially syncretic with wage-labor and capitalistic commodification of labor expectations" (25). Such resistance to narrow understandings of production and consumption can also be seen in how students from Appalachia negotiate the literacy work they are asked to undertake on college campuses. In her research on first-year writing students at an open-admissions public university in Appalachia, Sara Webb-Sunderhaus found that the students' "performance of an Appalachian identity that is neighborly and 'helps out' others played a significant role in their development of another metaphor of literacy: literacy as communion. In this metaphor, literacy is a communal resource, one to be shared among friends and neighbors" (221). Webb-Sunderhaus demonstrates how such an understanding of literacy as a valuable resource to be shared within a network of affective relationships countered the university's construction of literacy as consumption—a possessable object an individual acquires and then uses for their personal advancement (210).

My intensive reading of these scholarly sources—from James Watt Raine to Sara Webb-Sunderhaus—affects my appreciation of how networks of kith and kin function as a form of workers' solidarity in Appalachian communities. Spending extended periods of time on my grandparents' mountaintop farm near Pickens, West Virginia, and listening to oft told family stories has also schooled me in the value of neighborliness within rural communities. And in the memoir my grandma penned late in her life as a way to stay busy even when her body was too worn out to engage in physical labor, I can trace repeated examples of how she participated in the flow of economic resources through neighborly networks. Having cultivated this "living archive," I am better attuned to "consider with critical intensity what may be more in shadow, muted, and not immediately obvious" in the letters of moonlight schools students that are preserved in Stewart's institutional archive (Royster and Kirsch 76).

The Cora Wilson Stewart papers are housed in some seventy boxes at the University of Kentucky's Special Collections Research Center. Trying to trace the voices of women who attended the moonlight schools across Stewart's extensive archive is a complex task. A patient search yields the occasional letter among Stewart's many files of correspondence as well as in files that deal with the publication of the *Country Life Readers*, Stewart's own book-length account of the moonlight schools, and reports of the Kentucky Illiteracy Commission (KIC). Indeed, many of the original letters found in the archive seem to have been saved because they were reproduced in Stewart's *Moonlight Schools* or in KIC reports. Handwritten in large, often awkward script, the letter writers identify themselves as residents of some thirty-six different communities in twenty-six different Kentucky counties; the earliest letters date from 1913 and the latest from 1920.[7] There are also a handful of letters from students attending moonlight schools in Alabama, Georgia, and North Carolina, and from members of the Niitsitapi nation living on the Blackfeet Indian Reservation in Browning, Montana. The archived letters are typically quite brief, averaging about seventy-five words in length, and they are filled with idiosyncratic spellings and syntax.

Not a random or representative sample, the archived letters were saved by Stewart to promote her methods of educating rural citizens. As William Merrill Decker has noted in his history of epistolary practices, such collections of letters can blur "the boundaries between addresser and addressee" as the letter recipient's acts of selection, preservation, and arrangement shape the narrative that emerges from the authorial activity of the letter writer. Decker goes on to observe that collections of letters appealingly "create the illusion of individuals telling their own stories" while much of any single letter's story "may be invisible, buried, or lost" (8–9). The letters preserved in the archives and published more widely by Stewart certainly offer an affirmation of her education agenda as the individual letter writers testify to their positive experiences as students in the moonlight schools.

Though neighborly networks among Appalachian women are not addressed in the *Country Life Readers* or in the pedagogical materials associated with the moonlight schools, the importance of such networks can be traced in letters written by women who attended the moonlight schools. Their epistolary efforts stand as forms of repetitive rhetorical labor that rural women used to reinforce their neighborly networks. With a neighborly frame of mind, I turn now to the voices of women who attended moonlight schools as they engaged in repetitive rhetorical labor to reinforce their neighborly networks.

"I JUST FEEL SO GRAND AND BIGGETY": RURAL WOMEN REINFORCE THEIR EXISTING NEIGHBORLY NETWORKS

Given that the available letters are archived in Stewart's collection and that she used many of them to promote the pedagogical efficacy of the moonlight schools, one would anticipate reading positive accounts of reformed working habits among rural women and tales of (re)organized Appalachian communities. But none of the women's letters that I encountered in the archive mention the acquisition of new consumer goods, financial gain, specific home renovations, or the formation of tomato clubs and health leagues.[8] Like the contemporary college writers studied by Robert Brooke, the letter writers seemed to have rejected the identity of the middle-class white housewife that was presented to them as a model or exemplar they might imitate. Though the moonlight schools' pedagogy of imitatio and the *Country Life Readers* advocated for new economic identities for rural women and structured forms of interacting with family and neighbors, farm women's letters reveal their own motives were not necessarily aligned with the lessons they were asked to repeat.

Most poignantly, the letters reveal again and again that acquiring the ability to read and write profoundly impacted the self-worth and identity of many moonlight school students. "You k[n]ow life is a failure without learning," wrote Mrs. A. A. Eudy. "If I could only have had this oppartunity when I was young it would have been a blessing to me, . . . I am glad to say I can reaid just a little now" (CWS Papers, Box 2, folder 8). Such a growing sense of self-worth is also evident in the three-page letter that Ann Armstrong, a white widow living with two of her sons on a farm in Marshall County, sent to Stewart on October 24, 1918 (1920 US Census). She refers to herself and fellow moonlight school students as "scholars" and concludes with: "I thank the Lord for permitting me to live long enough to learn to read and write" (Kentucky Illiteracy Commission 85). Mrs. Cansalevady Jones attended a moonlight school in Whitley City, Kentucky, at the age of fifty-two. In her letter to Stewart, she listed her accomplishments: "I have read the first reader. I have the second reader and will soon have it read. . . . I can read the Bible . . . and have had some number work" (114–15). A Fulton County student perhaps says it best: "I just feel so grand and biggety sitting down reading and writing by myself" (48). The pride that echoes through the statements of Mrs. Eudy, Ann Armstrong, Cansalevady Jones, and the student from Fulton County serves as a salient reminder that the ability to read and write can profoundly affect a woman worker's sense of her identity and agency. As David Gold argues in his book-length study of postsecondary institutions serving disenfranchised students in Texas at the turn of the twentieth century, "What may ultimately serve to liberate and empower students may simply be the ability to write with confidence to contemporary rhetorical norms" (8). Farm women referring to themselves as scholars and describing their affective state as "grand" underscores the significant ways in which learning to read and write can afford students a stronger sense of self-efficacy.

While farm women seemed to have developed a sense of personal empowerment from their increased facility with the written word, the norms of the white middle-class housekeeper that the *Country Life Readers* held up as an aspirational identity are never mentioned in their letters. "Influenced by their individual motives" as much as by the new norms that Stewart was promoting, the students celebrated their acquisition of literacy skills and their ability to undertake print-based rhetorical labor (Terrill, "Mimesis" 300). The women's letters speak to how their abilities as readers and writers resulted in a new, more empowered sense of personal identity based on their academic accomplishments, rather than their abilities to conform to the new economic identities Stewart promoted. They embraced the sense of agency that came from expanding their repertories as readers and writers of the printed word but did not seem to adopt the values of entrepreneurship or embrace ideas about women's responsibilities to achieve particular forms of middle-class decorum.

More, though, than documenting their own educational achievements and the sense of agency they derived from such attainments, rural women described engaging in the repetitive rhetorical labor of (re)circulating news of family milestones and local events via letters. They thus fortified their existing networks of support and neighborly relationships. The mother of twelve children, Patience M. Lunsford was a white woman living with her husband Elijah (or Elisha) on a farm near Burning Spring, Kentucky (1910 US Census). She addressed Stewart as "Dear Friend" and shared how she has "rat lots of leters since last year" and that writing to her many children "keeps [her] bisy" (Stewart, *Moonlight*

Schools, between 190 and 191). Similarly, Amanda McKinney of Carrollton, Kentucky, informed Stewart in 1914 that she enjoyed attending a moonlight school and that she had "written [her] first letter to [her] mother" (CWS Papers, box 2, folder 8). That McKinney designates her letter to her mother as a "first" suggests that a second, third, and many more letters will follow. Through ongoing epistolary circuits, vital information could be shared, requests for assistance could be issued, and expressions of gratitude could be offered. The repetitive rhetorical labor of ongoing written correspondence allowed women to maintain connections and affiliative relations, helping ensure that supportive networks remained strong. Indeed, teacher Alma Porter reported that among her moonlight school students, "the most fascinating work was letter writing" (Kentucky Illiteracy Commission 53).

Several letter writers even enacted collaborative forms of rhetorical labor. In the archives, one finds letters coauthored by adult siblings as they reached out to their parents, extended family members, and friends. Stewart herself received a number of such letters in which parents, siblings, and other family members would add postscripts to each other's letters, compose their own short cover notes, and engage in other acts of collaborative authorship. Even the process of attending a moonlight school could require collective effort. A white woman, forty-four-year-old Martha J. Kinder lived on a farm three miles from the nearest schoolhouse with her husband, Barney, and their six children, ages five to twenty (1910 US Census). In her August 27, 1913, letter to Stewart, Kinder noted that the teacher, Miss Lottie, "sends a copy for me every evening by them children. I copy them and send them back next morning" (Stewart, *Moonlight Schools*, between 44 and 45). For women living on small farms, accessing the educational opportunities available at the moonlight schools and the processes of letter writing were deeply intertwined with the networks of kith and kin that served as invaluable social and economic safety nets.

Indeed, the letters written by women enrolled in the moonlight schools can be read as evidence of their desires to integrate their teachers and Stewart herself into their neighborly networks. Expressions of praise and gratitude are the most repeated features in letters written by moonlight school students. Kittie Wimms was a thirty-nine-year-old Black woman who lived with her husband, Tom, on a tenant farm in Allensville, Kentucky (1910 US Census). She wrote to Stewart: "I thank you for getting up this school" (Kentucky Illiteracy Commission 113). Mrs. Jones from Whitley City, Kentucky, praised her "nice teachers" (114), and Ann Armstrong wrote "I certainly do think my teacher deserves all the praise which may be offered her and much more" (83–84).

Eula Thompson, a student in a North Carolina Moonlight School, described her teacher as "sweet" and applauded the way she "explains thing [*sic*] so we understand and make us enjoy night school" (CWS Papers, box 2, folder 8). Hailing from Partridge, Kentucky, Mary Jenkins was the wife of a white farmer and had three children ranging in age from eight to seventeen (1910 Federal Census). She was appreciative of the opportunities the moonlight schools afforded her—she thanked Stewart in both the opening and closing lines of her letter, ending her letter with "I thank you again and again" (Kentucky Illiteracy Commission 87). Such frequently repeated expressions of gratitude are essential in maintaining goodwill and a sense of mutuality in the rural women's systems of aid and informal exchange that did not mechanically balance debits and credits. These brief but affectively powerful testimonies to assistance received strengthened valuable social connections. While the women who earned their living as domestic workers in Boston needed to rely on depersonalized language and standardized documents to gain a greater measure of control over their economic lives, repetition was used by farm women to reinforce the affective relationships and connections that were vitally important to their economic survival.

The establishment and maintenance of strong communal ties, however, required personal interactions in addition to repeated accolades and expressions of appreciation. Among rural families, the social practice of "visiting" was a favorite pastime and the basis of economic exchanges among farm families (Walker 54; Neth 44). Not surprisingly then, many women enrolled in the moonlight schools sought to extend their hospitality to Stewart. "[I] hope you come pay us a visit soon," wrote Eula Thompson at the end of her letter to Stewart (CWS Papers, Box 2, Folder 8). Patience Lunsford hoped Stewart would be able to attend the local fair, and R. D. Grant and Lavinia Littleton, teachers at a segregated moonlight school for Black residents in Mason County, also wrote to Stewart, reporting on plans for a celebration and exhibition as their classes concluded. They noted that the students and teachers would have "a grand banquet" to end the moonlight school session, and they invited Stewart to attend (Kentucky Illiteracy Commission 54). Recognizing that Stewart might not be able to travel to McCreary County, Sarah Jane Coffey, a white woman who lived with her parents and four younger siblings on a farm (1920 US Census), indicated that she would be satisfied with a textual visit from Stewart. "I would be glad to get a letter from you," she wrote in her November 11, 1919, epistle (Kentucky Illiteracy Commission 93). Such visiting—textual or otherwise—functioned to expand one's network of supportive connections and to strengthen existing relationships with kith and kin.

Moonlight school students also offered gifts to their teachers and to Stewart herself. N. S. Shaw, the superintendent of schools in Allen County, reported that students in Oak Forest presented their teacher, Mr. R. O. Cliburn, with "a handsome suit of clothes" (Kentucky Illiteracy Commission 14). Stewart herself was the recipient of textual gifts in the form of students' poetry. One student mailed the following verses to Stewart along with Easter greetings: "It is good to be alive today / With Easter skies above / With friendly flowers to nod and sway / and kindly folks to love" (CWS Papers, box 2, folder 8). Another student enclosed the following verses in a letter to Stewart:

> Night school will shine to night
> Won't that be fine.
> When the sun goes down
> And the moon comes up
> Night school will shine. (CWS Papers, box 2, folder 8)

Like the presents of homemade food and fancywork that rural women used to maintain their ties with family and friends, these textual gifts cemented the bonds between Stewart and moonlight school students. Such homemade tokens of affection operate outside the imperatives of the market economy. Rather than circulating as commodities to be bought and sold for a profit, the transfer of a textual gift from one person to another cements the bonds of friendship. For rural women, gift giving, textual and otherwise, was an integral part of their systems of mutual support.

The art of writing friendly letters to relatives and friends would also, of course, have been familiar to middle- and upper-class women living in small towns and large cities. As Nan Johnson has documented, middle-class women were encouraged to view letter writing "in familial terms and bounded by the walls of the home" while men might engage in business correspondence and use letters to affect the disposition of public events and opinions (81). Within the middle and upper classes, femininized epistolary efforts established women's mastery of the rules of etiquette and cemented their moral authority in matters of the heart. But for women struggling with poverty on subsistence farms in Appalachia, the repetitive rhetorical labor of ongoing epistolary exchanges with family and friends could play an essential role in sustaining neighborly networks that helped them negotiate a troubled economic landscape.

In sum, letters written by women who attended the moonlight schools extended the work of care and community that had long been central to their economic lives. Their repetitive rhetorical labor of corresponding with family and friends stands as a reminder of the tenacity of existing social relationships and support networks among people with few economic resources. By affording Appalachian farm women the opportunity to expand their repertoire of reading and writing skills, the moonlight schools placed an additional tool for sustaining informal systems of solidarity and mutual assistance in their hands.

REVISITING WOMEN'S WORK, REENVISIONING WORKERS' SOLIDARITY

Keenly attuned to the needs and goals of their own communities and knowing full well the value of their work to their families and neighbors, the women who attended the moonlight schools call feminist rhetoricians and scholars interested in labor activism to consider alternative forms of solidarity. The neighborliness evidenced by women attending the moonlight schools productively disrupts the easy acceptance of widely circulating ideas about how capitalism, entrepreneurship, and relationships (re)defined by the labor market might transform impoverished communities both in the United States and around the world. More particularly, the repetitive rhetorical labor associated with such neighborliness—expressions of self-esteem, agency, and accomplishment; letters that strengthen support networks of kith and kin; textual gifts and other goods circulated through non-cash-based systems of exchange—adds nuance to understandings of the range of discursive activities that we associate with workers' efforts to gain leverage over their economic lives.

The emotionally rich letters of farm women contrast sharply with the impersonal, standardized documents that domestic workers used to mediate their relationships with their employers. And while the mill girls toiled mightily with the pen and used the power of the periodical to craft a new public identity for themselves as workers, moonlight school students invested their energy in sustaining long-standing, resilient forms of solidarity in their communities. With persistent ingenuity and creativity through the decades and across diverse workplaces and spaces, women with few financial resources have undertaken considerable rhetorical labor to improve their economic lives, rhetorical labor whose power lies in the ordinariness of repetition and reinforcement rather than in noteworthy speeches or dramatic acts of persuasion.

The neighborly and caregiving legacies of Mrs. A. A. Eudy, Ann Armstrong, Amanda McKinney, Patience Lunsford, Mrs. Jones, Eula Thompson, Kittie Wimms, Sarah Jane Coffey, and other Appalachian women in the early decades of the twentieth century have been carried forward in the work of more recent labor activists in the region. Historian Jessica Wilkerson has studied women who led movements for social justice and workers' rights in Appalachia in the 1960s and 1970s. She has documented that "women leaders who took up the fight for justice ushered in a web of activism that pulsed outward from a core ethic of care. The act of care-giving animated their understanding of politics and activism and infused their movements" (197).

Wilkerson cites as an example the Appalachian Women's Right Organization (AWRO), whose rural and working-class leaders disputed the Kentucky Commission on Women, which had focused its work on the concerns of white, middle-class women and removing barriers that limited their access to high-paying jobs (175). According to Wilkerson, "on a wintery evening in March 1975," women from eastern Kentucky affiliated with the AWRO "navigated difficult road conditions in the dark" and "made their way to the courthouse" in Hazard County to meet with commission members (180). The AWRO members challenged the "commission's vision of women's advancement by individual uplift" and "urged the commission *not* to create a false binary between work and welfare" (181, emphasis in original). The women affiliated with the AWRO had critical insights to share with the commission about their often unrecognized and unwaged work: feeding their families; providing childcare for young grandchildren, nieces, nephews, and others; nursing ill and disabled spouses and loved ones; affording safe harbor to family members endangered by domestic violence and substance abuse; reliably transporting family and friends to schools, medical clinics and regional hospitals, and social service offices. As Wilkerson concludes, when rural women like those aligned with the AWRO "politicized their caregiving labor and challenged the extraction of their work, they made their labor visible and generated critiques of capitalistic logic" (14). With a more holistic and nuanced view of women's labor, the AWRO in the second half of the twentieth century and the women who attended the moonlight schools decades earlier serve as salient reminders that solidarity among women workers continues to take many forms.

CHAPTER 4

PIECEWORK

Rhetorical Accrual at the Donnelly Garment Company, 1933–1937

On January 30, 1988, Gertrude Dora, age seventy-three, was invited by members of the Junior League of Kansas City to participate in an oral history interview and share her experiences as a worker in the garment industry. Recognizing that extant local histories gave scant attention to the region's economic development, the Kansas City Museum enlisted Junior League volunteers to document the work lives of local residents across a number of vital industries, including meat packing, railroads, real estate, and the garment industry. Dora had been employed at the Donnelly Garment Company (DGC) for forty-six years, starting in 1932. In the early twentieth century, the DGC was the largest dress label in the United States, having been founded by Nell Donnelly Reed in 1916. At the DGC, Dora worked as a machine operator, trained other women as operators, and eventually served in a quality control position. Even as she wrestled with fading memories in trying to respond to the interviewer's questions, her interview transcript is filled with a warm sense of nostalgia as she reflects on the meaning of her working life. What emerges most clearly from Dora's oral history is that she considered the DGC "a great big family" (6), and she goes on to note: "I don't think there was another—I didn't hear of another factory anyplace—I said the world, I really believe that, but not in America, that they took care of their employees the way Nelly Don did" (13).

Dora was not alone in recollecting a deep sense of affiliation with the DGC and affection for Reed, who was a compelling figure as a female entrepreneur in the early twentieth century. Three other longtime DGC employees who were interviewed by the Junior League in the late 1980s—Nevora Davis, Helen Little, and Helen Shelfo—echoed Dora's sentiments that Reed created a unique workplace in the early decades of the twentieth century. They spoke about the clean, safe working conditions in the factory; the above-average wages they earned; Reed's efforts to manage the production schedule and avoid seasonal layoffs during the darkest months of the Great Depression; employee benefits that included paid vacations, health insurance, and pensions; the crisp white uniforms provided by the company so that women did not risk damaging their own clothing on the factory floor; and the company's lavish Christmas parties. Archived at the Kansas City Museum, these four oral histories present remarkably consistent, retrospective accounts of what it was like to work at the DGC and how employees felt about their jobs.

A more sizeable body of texts written by the DGC's workforce, which consisted largely of white women, can be found in the archives of James A. Reed, Nell Donnelly Reed's second husband and attorney. Over several months in 1937, more than seven hundred of the company's employees composed short letters—145 words on average—about their work lives.[1] Though the letter writers do not seem to follow a shared template, they repeatedly and explicitly express their satisfaction with their jobs. More obliquely, the missives speak to the workers' resistance to a unionization campaign led by the International Ladies' Garment Workers' Union (ILGWU), which had begun in 1933. The ILGWU was ultimately able to bring its campaign to a successful conclusion in 1971, fifteen years after Nell Donnelly Reed had sold the company.

The ILGWU's decades-long drive to unionize DGC employees merits sustained scholarly attention and has much to teach us about labor organizing and persistence. My goal in this chapter, though, is to understand how the majority of the DGC's women workers chose to frame their work lives and economic agency in ways that ran counter to the unionization campaign in the late 1930s and how they used repetition to do so. I argue that the letters composed by the DGC's women workers to spurn the ILGWU's organizing overtures represent a particular kind of repetitive discursive action that I refer to as rhetorical accrual. Highlighting the cumulative force of voices that reiterate common ideas and shared perspectives, rhetorical accrual derives its power from similarity and commonality, rather than the originality of any singularly powerful message or rhetorical performance. In their individual letters, the white women who stitched, pressed, and packed Nelly Don dresses repeated shared experiences, ideas, and attitudes. Recognizing that there is strength in numbers, these low-wage women workers asserted their economic agency and their right to participate in decisions about their futures as employees through their accrued rhetorical labor. Moreover, the process of rhetorical accrual allowed the letters of the DGC's women workers to create a powerful impression of consensus within their workplace community. This impression gains even more credence some fifty years later, when the oral histories of DGC workers recorded in the 1980s accumulate alongside the letters from the 1930s. For low-wage women workers, rhetorical accrual places minimal demands upon the individual writer/speaker while delivering a highly impactful argument and creating a deeply felt sense of common cause among participants.

Both the power and perils of participating in the process of rhetorical accrual comes more clearly into focus, though, when we turn to the experiences of two groups of DGC employees who worked on the margins of the cohesive community that emerges from the letters—Black employees at the DGC, who were limited to working as janitors and maids, and the handful of white women workers who were sympathetic to the ILGWU's overtures. These Black workers chose to contribute their own, collaboratively written missive to the collection of letters that were amassed in 1937, echoing the same themes that emerge in the letters written by the white workers at the factory. Recognizing the power they might access by participating in the letter-writing campaign, the maids and janitors composed a letter that subtly insisted upon a recognition of their presence at the DGC and that seized a measure of control over processes of racialized identity formation at the factory. The experiences of the small number of white women workers at the DGC who held views counter to the mass of letter writers and were interested in affiliating with the ILGWU presents a stark contrast to the image of a like-minded community of workers created by the letters and oral histories. The verbal and physical harassment these workers endured underscores the dangerous potential of rhetorical accrual to silence dissenting voices.

This chapter begins with a brief historical overview of the DGC and its battle with the ILGWU. I then theorize the concept of rhetorical accrual and explore the methodological challenges of investigating the DGC workers' letters as an expansive body of repetitious discursive performances, challenges that tools from the digital humanities can help address. The theoretical and methodological work I undertake early in this chapter then frames my two-part analysis of the letters written by white women workers at the DGC. I demonstrate first that the repetitious process of rhetorical accrual allowed the DGC's white women workers to advance an argument based on evidence and ethos; I then examine how the process of rhetorical accrual provided an important occasion for building a sense of community among the majority of DGC employees. In the final sections of the chapter, I turn to the Black maids and janitors who opted into the letter-writing enterprise and to the handful of pro-ILGWU women who opted out of this repetitive rhetorical performance. Attending to their experiences serves as an occasion for bringing into focus both the powers and limits of repetitive rhetorical performances and for attending to the complexities of building meaningful coalitions in the workplace.

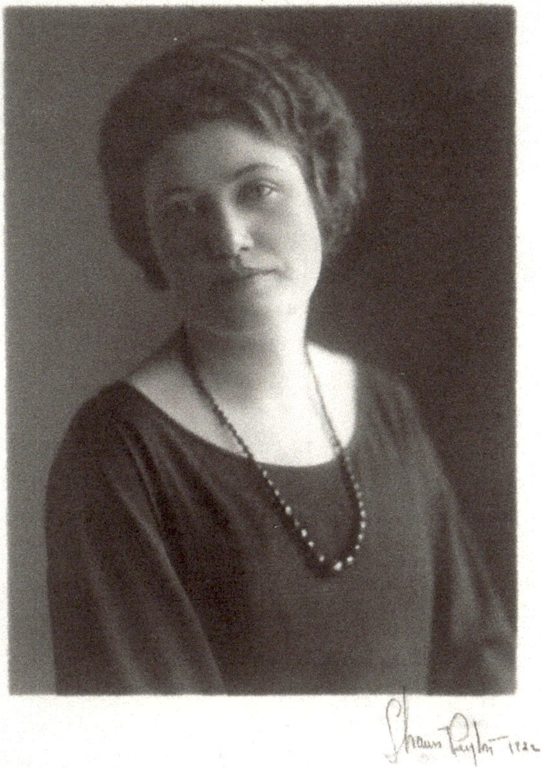

4.1. Nell Donnelly Reed, 1922. Image Courtesy of State Historical Society of Missouri, Kansas City Research Center.

(RE)FASHIONING THE GARMENT INDUSTRY: NELL DONNELLY REED, THE DGC, AND THE ILGWU

Dissatisfied with the poor quality and unattractive nature of housedresses in the early years of the twentieth century, Ellen "Nell" Quinlan Donnelly, a young housewife in Kansas City, began designing stylish yet affordable frocks for herself and other women in her social circle.[2] Encouraged by her friends, she marched into the George B. Peck Dry Goods Store in 1916 with a pink gingham sample dress that she dubbed a "Nelly Don." She convinced the store's buyer to order eighteen dozen, and when the dresses sold out in less than a day, the DGC was born. Caroline Bird notes that "the company prospered during the 1920s, sometimes grossing as much as $3.5 million a year" (194). Even after the stock market crash in 1929, the DGC maintained its sales and actually expanded its product line, a business success all the more remarkable given that more than one in three dress manufacturers on Seventh Avenue in New York City were forced into bankruptcy between 1929 and 1933 (Bird 194).

The DGC's success was due to the unique fashion sense of its founder and her innovative business practices. Using high-quality fabrics, Nell Donnelly designed attractive, comfortable dresses for everyday wear. Rather than trying to promote the latest fashion fads, Nell Donnelly cultivated repeat customers who had "to live in and with the clothes they bought" (Bird 195). To ensure women of all sizes and shapes would be satisfied with a Nelly Don purchase, a mock-up of every new design was created in each size and tried on an actual woman in the appropriate age demographic before the dress went into mass production (Bird 194; O'Malley 7).

Along with a keen eye for practical fashion, Nell Donnelly brought considerable business acumen to running her company. To lower costs and increase her control over production, she bypassed brokers and negotiated directly with fabric mills on issues of color, pattern, and price (O'Malley 30), and she brought some of the principles of scientific management to bear upon the garment industry. According to Terence Michael O'Malley, Donnelly turned to the aviation and automobile industries for lessons in efficiency, and she pioneered the use of section production principles in the dressmaking business (2–7).

Most importantly, though, Nell Donnelly was committed to creating a hospitable workplace for her largely white workforce. The DGC factory was spacious, well-lit, and clean, and the machines necessary for sewing and pressing garments were maintained in top condition to ensure workers' safety. Nell Donnelly paid wages above the industry average, covered 50 percent of the cost of employees' health insurance, funded a pension plan, provided two weeks of paid vacation each year for each employee, and hosted lavish DGC holiday parties (Swisher 21; O'Malley 65).

Despite the DGC's working conditions and personnel policies, the ILGWU targeted the company for unionization in the 1930s.[3] The DGC first came to the attention of the ILGWU in 1933–1934 when the National Recovery Administration (NRA) established the Codes of Fair Competition (CFC).[4] Because it primarily produced cotton housedresses, the DGC successfully argued that it should fall under the Cotton Code, rather than the Code for the Dress Manufacturing Industry, which governed firms that produced silk and wool garments and were required to pay higher wages (Swisher 20). Within the year, the ILGWU sought to unionize the DGC. In the ensuing months, the union invited DGC employees to several mass meetings but had little success in generating interest among the rank-and-file workers. Instead, the DGC employees opted to form their own Donnelly Garment Workers Union

(DGWU), which the ILGWU viewed as a sham union controlled by Nell Donnelly Reed. While frontline ILGWU organizers picketed the DGC's factory in Kansas City, lawyers for both the ILGWU and the company began a series of courtroom battles that would span nearly four decades.

In this chapter, I focus on the late 1930s, when the DGC's battle with the ILGWU was at a fever pitch and when some seven hundred letters written by DGC workers began to accrue. To be clear, I strive here to avoid simplistic narratives that would create easy villains or idealized heroes at the DGC. The archival records will not allow me to lionize the letter writers as a group of independently minded, white working-class feminists in the Midwest who preferred a local, cross-class alliance with the progressive woman who employed them, instead of aligning themselves with the ILGWU and the cadre of men who led the union from their power base on the East Coast. Nor am I able to cast the letter writers as naive women who were manipulated by a duplicitous employer into resisting the egalitarian, empowering overtures of the ILGWU. Instead, the letters suggest that the DGC was home to a complex group of women workers who were navigating a challenging economic and social landscape. By threading the voices of the DGC workers into feminist histories of rhetoric, I hope to foster more nuanced understandings of the diverse ways women have sought to claim economic agency in the past while also holding out future possibilities for fostering more resilient, inclusive, and flexible collectivities among women workers that are responsive to local exigencies.

RHETORICAL ACCRUAL: THE POWER OF MANY VOICES

When rhetors repeat shared feelings, understandings, and viewpoints, they can amplify the power of their individual voices. Repetition can create a substantial body of evidence and the powerful impression of consensus as dozens, hundreds, or even thousands of similarly aligned rhetorical performances accrue, becoming far more credible and urgent than any singular message.

Such a strategy of rhetorical accrual can be particularly attractive for ordinary speakers/writers who do not wish to call attention to themselves as individuals or to step into the spotlight of leadership. Rather than mark themselves as exemplary or unusual, rhetors who participate in processes of rhetorical accrual position themselves as one of many with common interests and shared concerns. By undertaking similar discursive performances, individuals suture themselves into a network of relationships, with each reiteration strengthening the affiliative bonds of the community. The letter writers at the DGC stand in a long line of women rhetors who have recognized the power of such rhetorical accrual and the value of echoing each other's voices.

Early examples of rhetorical accrual can be found in petition campaigns organized by unenfranchised women as a means of political participation. With multiple names affixed to it, a petition stands as a collective rhetorical performance, with each signatory repeating a shared commitment to the contents of the petition. Every individual signature makes the petition a more forceful representation of a shared viewpoint. For example, in 1774, women in Edenton, North Carolina, formed an organization in support of the American colonies' resistance to British rule. The organization published a petition signed by fifty-one women who pledged to boycott goods imported from England (Zaeske 16). In 1848, the Seneca Falls Declaration was signed by one hundred people, two-thirds of whom were women (Wellman 15). During the 1915 Panama-Pacific International Exposition in San Francisco, half a million people signed a petition for women's voting rights at a booth staffed by members of the Congressional Union for Woman Suffrage. The petition, 18,333 feet long, was then packed into a car dubbed the "Suffrage Flier" and driven across the United States, a journey that took three months, to be delivered to congressional leaders and President Woodrow Wilson (Cassidy 114–16). Whether a petition garners a few dozen signatures or thousands of individuals sign on, the accrual of voices expressing the same sentiment allows their shared argument to take on greater rhetorical heft.

A more contemporary example of rhetorical accrual can be found in the Me Too movement, which Tarana Burke started in 2006 in Alabama to support and empower girls and women of color who had been sexually harassed or assaulted. By making a space for sharing common experiences, Burke drew upon the power of repetition to demonstrate how many women experience sexual violence over the course of their lives. #MeToo exploded nationally and internationally in 2017 in the wake of highly public allegations of sexual assault against movie mogul Harvey Weinstein. According to Ashwini Tambe, #MeToo was retweeted half a million times within the first twenty-four hours after its launch in mid-October 2017 (197). The sheer number of sexual assault survivors who became visible as their stories accrued around the hashtag transformed public conversations about power, sex, and gender, particularly in the entertainment industry and the workplace.

Communications studies scholar Emily Winderman characterizes #MeToo as an example of "volume aggregation." For Winderman, volume aggregation occurs when "angry bodies that are physically or symbolically co-oriented together provide a visceral power in numbers"

(338). Tapping into the affordances of digital media with its potential for viral circulation, #MeToo brought together sexual assault survivors whose collective voice became louder and more powerful as they repeated all-too-common experiences and emotions. Volume aggregation serves as a useful framework for understanding the power of digital media and the immediacy of viral circulation available to rhetors in the twenty-first century.

The term "rhetorical accrual," as I use it in this chapter, differs in a subtle but significant way from Winderman's concept of volume aggregation. While volume aggregation is a process whereby a number of diverse voices come together seeking immediate impact, accrual underscores the importance of the passage of time for repetitive rhetorical performances. Rather than accumulating in blinding speed as tweets and retweets, the letters written by the DGC women accrued over several months in 1937. Each letter adds its own evidentiary weight to the argument as the workers repeat that they were satisfied with their jobs, helping to cement a shared identity among many of the workers. Though each letter stands on its own as a persuasive document, each letter's power is magnified by its position within a larger body of letters and other rhetorical performances by DGC employees. Fifty years after the ILGWU's initial attempts to unionize the company in the 1930s, Gertrude Dora and the other DGC employees who were interviewed by members of the Junior League about their long-ago work lives are still able to add to the rhetorical power of the letters by repeating many of the sentiments they expressed. Similarly, framing #MeToo as a process of rhetorical accrual, rather than more immediate volume aggregation, opens up questions about the relationship between Tarana Burke's important efforts in 2006, the virality of the #MeToo hashtag in 2017 that occurred primarily when it was taken up within the entertainment industry, and the continued use of the hashtag beyond social media. While volume aggregation focuses on the short-term, precipitate power of many angry voices speaking at once, the concept of rhetorical accrual affords feminist historians the opportunity to trace repetitive rhetorical performances as they unfold across months, years, decades, and even longer spans of time. The accrual of many individual discursive performances that repeat and reiterate shared concerns can, however, present new interpretive challenges for scholars and researchers in rhetoric.

RESEARCH METHODS: STITCHING TOGETHER COMPUTATIONAL TOOLS AND CLOSE READING

As a body of accrued rhetorical performances, the missives penned by the DGC workers initially seem confounding. The repetition of issues and ideas across all the DGC letters can too easily lull a reader into an overly quick, facile judgment about the meaning of letters and the women who wrote them. Why read seven hundred or more letters if the consistent outline of the argument they advance seems to emerge clearly after reading just one hundred of the letters, or even just ten of them? And with letters that repeat so many common ideas, those letters with more anomalous features can claim undue attention. In the case of the letters written by the DGC workers, a well-turned phrase praising Nell Donnelly or a particularly moving account of how a young woman uses her wages to provide for her aging parents can tempt a rhetorician to cull an individual letter from the archive for a more in-depth analysis that ultimately distorts the rhetorical work accomplished by the larger body of letters. Composed of many repetitive, individual discursive performances that accrued over several months, the collective body of letters does not easily yield to the traditional interpretive methods.

Digital tools for textual analysis can provide a way to begin probing the collective power of the letters written by the DGC employees and other accrued rhetorical performances. Rather than closely analyzing a single text, digital tools make it possible to read across hundreds, thousands, or even millions of texts, searching for particular words or discursive patterns. Digital humanities scholar Franco Moretti has dubbed these computational practices "distant reading," to distinguish them from the "close reading" of individual texts that has long been a foundational practice of rhetorical scholarship. Moretti argues that "the trouble with close reading . . . is that it necessarily depends on an extremely small canon. . . . you invest so much in individual texts *only* if you think that very few of them really matter" (48, emphasis in original). He suggests instead that scholars explore the value of other methods of encountering texts, including sampling, network analysis, and work with series, titles, concordances, and incipits (67). For feminist rhetoricians seeking to understand the power of repetition within a large body of texts that have accrued over time, Moretti's notion of distant reading and digital data-mining tools can be particularly efficacious.

Jessica Enoch and Jean Bessette have noted, however, that "very few feminist historiographers have taken up digital methodologies or engaged digital humanist conversations" (635). Citing Jacqueline Jones Royster and Gesa E. Kirsch's concept of strategic contemplation, they note that "the work of listening closely and carefully to our subjects" is a fundamental principle within feminist rhetorical historiography that may run counter to the practices of scholars in digital humanities who search across vast bodies of digitized texts for key terms or discursive patterns (642).[5] But feminist scholars do not necessarily need to choose between close, careful attention to the women whose words and visions we study and the computational tools of digital humanities. Indeed, Geoffrey Rockwell and Stéfan Sinclair, authors of *Hermeneutica: Computer-Assisted Interpretation in the Humanities*, explicitly position computational tools not as an "end game" that would replace a scholar's deeply attuned engagement with texts but as process of "playful exploration," a way to generate new hypotheses and prompt further conversation (148). Stitching together insights gained from the analytics tools of the digital humanities and from the processes of deliberative, thoughtful reading of textual artifacts can thus generate even more nuanced analyses of women's rhetorical performances.

In my work with the letters written by DGC workers, I strive to blend the use of digital tools with a sustained and sensitive reading of the letters. I center the DGC workers' voices by opening my analysis below with three of the letters in their entirety, and I ground my argument in extensive quotations from dozens of their letters. Digital tools and the distant reading they make possible supplement my efforts to listen carefully to the women's voices, allowing me to verify the repetitive themes as well as to identify silences and omissions across the entire body of letters.

"TO WHOM IT MAY CONCERN": RHETORICAL ACCRUAL AND THE EPISTOLARY LABOR OF WOMEN WORKERS AT THE DONNELLY GARMENT COMPANY

Sitting in the reading room of the Kansas City Research Center of the State Historical Society of Missouri and scrutinizing more than seven hundred letters written by workers in the garment industry in the 1930s is a complicated intellectual and affective experience.[6] I share transcriptions of three letters below to provide some sense of how these letters speak across the decades to contemporary readers. I have not altered the original spelling or syntax of any of the letter writers and only added clarifying corrections in brackets when a letter writer's meaning might be unclear.

> Being a widow with one boy, I am indeed thankful for the 12 yrs I have worked for the Donnelly Garment Company. The salary I received, I know is far above other women doing the same work in other factories. The security I felt in my job has enabled me to take on obligations for my future and also to give my son the best advantages possible both in school and music, and rear him in environments that I feel will make him an upright and useful citizen. I hope to spend many more years in their service so as to be able to finish his education.
>
> *Mrs. Nannie Barger*

I like to work at Nelly Don's because it is such a fine place to work on account of the fine surroundings, and fine associates. The wages are the best in the City for the kind of work. And everything is so clean. You have many more advantages than many of the other places. I hope I amy [may] have the pleasure of working for Nelly Don many more years.

An Ardent Employee
Bessie Taylor

July 15 – 1937

To Whom it May Concern:

I have been an employee of the Donnelly Garment Co. for five (5) years & can truthfully say that is the best place I ever worked.

I've worked in factories in Wichita, Denver, & Los Angeles. & have never worked in another that can in any way compare with the Donnelly factory. They (Donnelly's) have better working conditions, good pay & their employees are treated better than any other place I ever worked.

There were several things that impressed me especially when I first went to work at Donnelly's. One was the friendliness between the girls, floorladie's, & bosses. They all seemed to be old friends & really enjoyed talking & laughing together. I had always been used to floorladies and bosses being "big shot". I never had seen bosses and 'factory girl's on such friendly terms and at ease around each other like they were and still are at Donnellys.

Another thing is—when you have machine trouble & put in a call for a machinist, you don't have to wait & wait & wear yourself out trying to make it work. Your machinist is there within a few minutes and you are payed [paid] for the time you loose [lose] while he is fixing your machine.

Still another thing is the cleanliness of the toilets and washrooms. They have maids that clean the washrooms & toilets at least twice a day. We always have a good supply of sanitary towels and good soap. (Also individual drinking cups & ice water at all time to drink). Good clean mirrors to powder our noses when we like. Ever see all that in another factory? I never did.

I never worked in another factory where my employer was really a human being who believed in letting her employees make a good living wage & still have plenty of pleasure, too, like Nelly Don. I have received a five (5) bill for a Christmas present every year, also a paid vacation every summer since I've been working for the Donnelly Co. I have never received any thing like that from any other place I ever worked.

All during the depression I had steady work & made good money.

So as far as hard times were concerned I didn't really know there was a depression.

I can truthfully say that I am perfectly satisfied with my job, and feel it is a pleasure & an honor to be an employee of the Donnelly Garment Co. I am thankful for my good luck in having such a wonderful place to work.

Beulah Bond
2044 North Valley
Kansas City, Kans.

These letters vary in length, syntactic fluency, and level of detail. Barger emphasizes her responsibilities outside the workplace and the importance of job security so that she can take care of her family. Taylor offers little information about her personal life; instead, she underscores the cleanliness of the DGC factory, and as "an ardent employee," she is well aware that other garment factories in Kansas City offer women less appealing work environments. Bond's letter is the most detailed. She establishes her credibility as an industrial worker in cities across the West. She offers her assessment of the relationships between "factory girls" and "bosses" at the DGC as well as wages and benefits. Ultimately, she characterizes her employment at the DGC as both a "pleasure & an honor." Despite their differences, each of these letters is a powerful persuasive performance in its own right. The writers establish their credibility, make claims, offer evidence, and marshal the power of affect as they lovingly describe their workplace community and their familial ties outside the factory.

But as each woman's letter is folded into the larger collection of letters penned by coworkers, their rhetorical power is magnified. Shared experiences and perspectives are repeated over and over again across the letters. The unique voice of any single letter writer, such as Taylor, Barger, or Bond, echoes and reverberates with the voices of seven hundred or so other workers. As they accrue, the letters become a substantial body of evidence the workers have marshaled to represent their work lives and to explain their resistance to the ILGWU's organizing efforts. The credibility of the assembled evidence is further enhanced by the ways in which the women workers establish a collective ethos through the letters.

Rhetorical Accrual as Argument: Evidence

At the heart of the letter writers' accrued argument against the international union are the wages and working conditions at the DGC. Barger

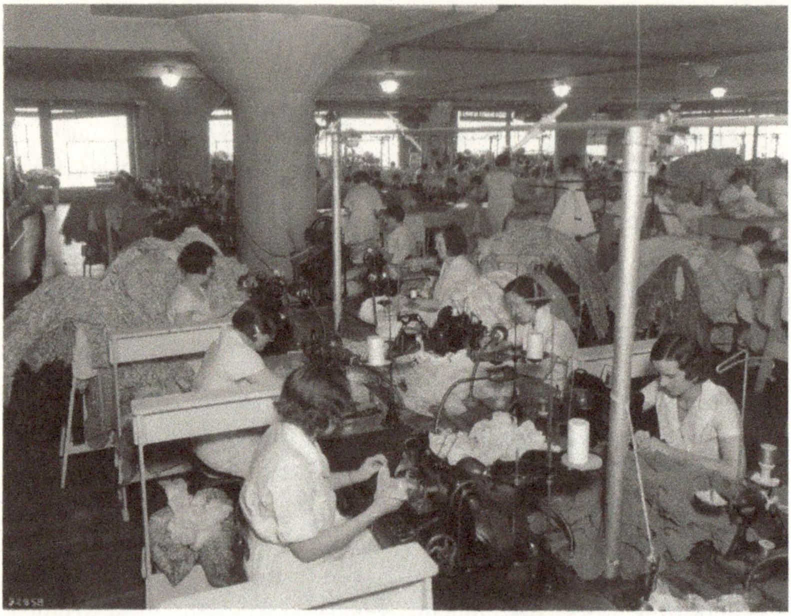

4.2. Factory Floor at the Donnelly Garment Co. Image Courtesy of State Historical Society of Missouri, Kansas City Research Center.

notes that her salary is far above what women working in other factories earn; Taylor writes that the wages "are the best in the city for the kind of work"; and Bond observes that she had "steady work & made good money" during the Depression. Taylor and Bond similarly comment on the working conditions inside the DGC factory, with Taylor describing her workplace as "so clean" and Bond indicating that she has "better working conditions . . . than any other place I ever worked," and she specifically calls out "the cleanliness of the toilets and washrooms." For Barger, Taylor, and Bond, satisfaction with their wages and working conditions are the foundation of their argument that the unionizing efforts of the ILGWU are not welcome at the DGC.

While this argument emerges after reading just a few letters, analytics tools from the digital humanities usefully substantiate the impression a reader forms as they move through the entire body of letters. Voyant Tools, developed by Stéfan Sinclair and Geoffrey Rockwell, is a user-friendly, freely available, online suite of analytics interfaces. I uploaded a zip file containing plain text versions of the letters, and Voyant Tools instantly provided me with a list of the most often repeated words across all the letters.

Not surprisingly, words that make up the company name ("Donnelly," "Garment" and "Company") are among the most frequently used words by the letter writers, along with words that situate the writers in time and place ("Kansas," "City," "Missouri," "MO," and "1937"). But "conditions" is the sixth most repeated word across the entire body of letters, appearing 514 times. Words related to compensation—"wages," "salary," and "pay"—become the fifth most addressed topic taken up by the letter writers when they are combined into a single category, appearing 707 times across the entire body of letters. Voyant Tools' context function then allows me to affirm that the writers are indeed repeatedly expressing their satisfaction with their wages and conditions. The context function shows me each occurrence of a key word, like "conditions," along with the surrounding text. This makes it possible to see how a key term is used in different contexts, or, in this case, by different letter writers.

The contexts surrounding all 514 occurrences of the word "conditions" involve positive statements in which the letter writers universally expressed their satisfaction with the cleanliness and safety of the factory floor and the amenities available to them at the DGC. Mrs. Minnie Allen wrote that "the company always kept the factory clean and sanitary provided nurses to care for our injuries and illness and have in every way possible made our working *conditions* pleasant and safe." Rose Gorman wrote: "As an employee of the Donnelly Garment Company for the past four years I have been satisfied with the working *conditions* and the management of the company." And Helen Reardon observed that "wages and working *conditions* are far above the average. I cannot see where a union would secure for us what we do not already have." This digitally enabled mining of the entire body of letters for the term "conditions" complements my experience of slowly reading each individual letter and affords me "a different way of encountering evidence," as Enoch and Bessette have suggested (645). Using Voyant Tools to access the letter writers' repeated expressions of satisfaction with the working conditions at the DGC makes visible and verifies the repetition of particular information that is the evidentiary foundation of their accrued argument.

Similarly, checking the contexts in which the words "wage," "pay," and "salary" appear allows me to document that the letter writers universally expressed satisfaction with their pay at the DGC. Lela Stevens wrote that "the hours and working conditions are swell, and *wages* so much above other places." Etta Mae Curry wrote that the DGC "has provided for me and my family a very good living with *wages* which are the best." Nola Leeds wrote: "I have been employed by the Donnelly Garment Co. nearly two years. On my *wages* I have been able to support my paralized [*sic*] husband and four boys, and keep them in school." And Lorene Dougan observed that "the hours are reasonable [and] the

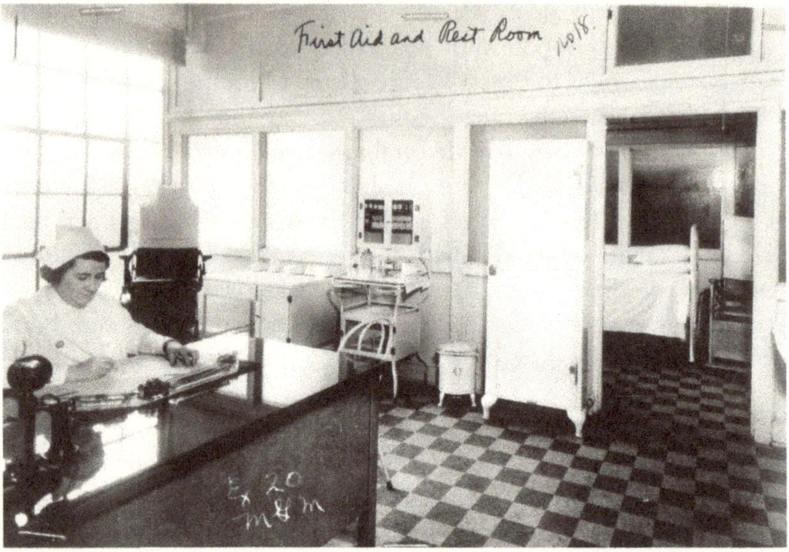

4.3. Infirmary at the Donnelly Garment Co. Image Courtesy of Kheel Center for Labor-Management Documentation and Archives, Cornell University Libraries.

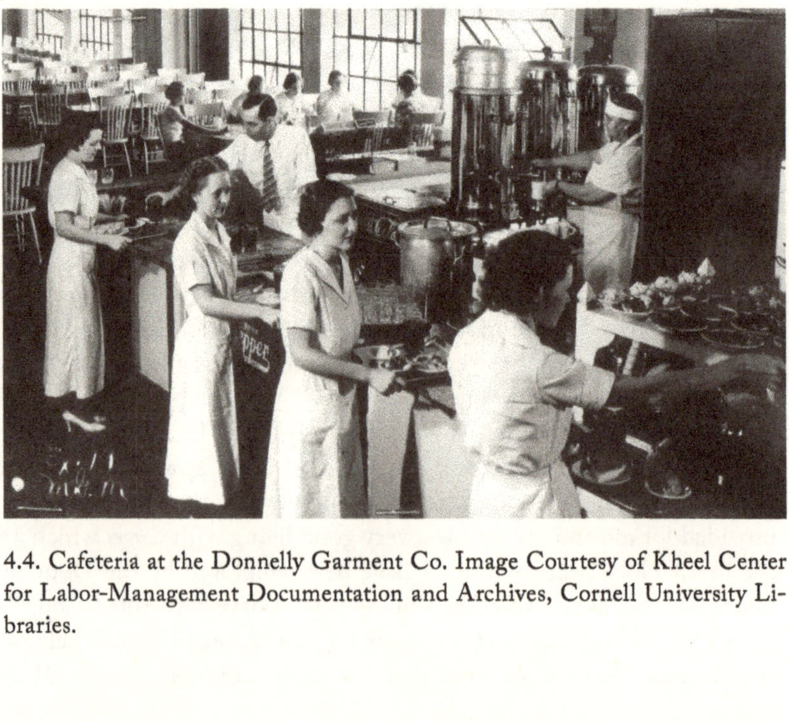

4.4. Cafeteria at the Donnelly Garment Co. Image Courtesy of Kheel Center for Labor-Management Documentation and Archives, Cornell University Libraries.

pay is the best of any in this line of work." Rather than applying simple labels, such as "good," to their wages/pay or working conditions, the letter writers have composed a range of nuanced, affirmative statements as they represented their work lives. As each of these statements evincing an individual worker's satisfaction with her compensation joins with the letters written by other DGC employees expressing similar assessments of the fitting nature of the DGC's wages, the letters become a hefty of body of evidence assembled by a like-minded community of women workers.

The oral histories recorded with DGC employees in the 1980s echo the argument that began accruing in the 1930s. Gertrude Dora recalled in her oral history interview that the washrooms were kept "just spotless as you would in your home" (5), and she offered extensive descriptions of the DGC's fully staffed infirmary and company cafeteria where "a wonderful chef" prepared meals. She summed up: "I know no other factory in Kansas City, probably in the United States, was never like that. . . . We had so many people come in there and marvel at the condition of our place and the cleanliness" (6). Writing in October 1937, Gertrude Dora had similarly praised the DGC's employment practices, including paid vacations and holiday bonuses, and she concluded her letter by observing: "One would travel a long ways to find another employer like Mrs. Reed. She is one in a *million*." In her 1980s interview, Helen Little described the $18 a week she earned at the DGC as "good wages back then" (2), echoing her letter from 1937 in which she wrote with satisfaction of her wages and the steady employment that allowed her to provide her son with necessary "medical care and eye treatment." The archives do not contain any letter Helen Shelfo might have written in the 1930s, but in her oral history interview in 1988, she observed that DGC employees "were making more money" than any other garment workers in Kansas City (8), a perspective that is consistent with the evidence that amassed in the collective body of letters. By recalling their work experiences at the DGC, Dora, Little, and Shelfo contribute to and affirm the evidence that began accruing some fifty years earlier when they and hundreds of DGC workers put pen to paper.

Rhetorical Accrual as Argument: Ethos

The accrued persuasive power of the DGC letters hinges, though, not only on repeated statements about the satisfactory wages and working conditions as a body of evidence. The letter writers are also engaged in a process of collective ethos building, a process that involves the DGC employees citing their firsthand knowledge of working conditions in other garment factories across Kansas City and the nation and framing their satisfaction with their wages in terms of their abilities to provide for their families.

Kathleen J. Ryan, Nancy Myers, and Rebecca Jones have demonstrated that "marginalized rhetors have a keen sense of the burdens of ethos negotiation" (3), and they argue that many women rhetors adopt an ecological approach to ethos construction, an approach that acknowledges the importance of "communicating relationally and locationally" (11). Knowing their credibility and suasive power is neither assumed nor stable, low-wage women workers must continually negotiate and renegotiate their ethos within a dynamic web of relationships. As women workers resisting the organizational efforts of one of the largest and most powerful international unions, the DGC letter writers were keenly attuned to the necessity of establishing their credibility as economic decision makers capable of managing their work lives. In their accrued missives, they thus often detail their work histories to establish their knowledge of conditions across the garment industry, locating themselves and the DGC within a unique space in the industrial landscape. Edna Tattershall wrote: "I have been employed by the Donnelly Garment Co. almost one and ½ years and I want to say it is the best place I ever worked at three other Garment Co. and they don't compare with Donnelly's in wages, working conditions or any other way." Mae Harcum offered a more detailed account of her work history. Though her sentence structure is unconventional, she begins by listing each of her employers, her years of service, and her job titles as she works to establish her ethos: "I was an employee of Montgomery Ward & Co of Kansas City from 1917 to Dec. 1920 as index clerk. By the National Cloak and Suit Co. From Jan 1921 to 1923, Ret. goods and complaint adj. The southwestern Bell Telephone Company at the Benton exchange from 1924 to 1930 as local opr. I have a complete Beauty culture course with diploma. Have had my own shop. Work for Normandman Bro. in Los Angeles Calif. Higginsbothom Baily in Dallas, Texas. Lees Overall factory in K.C." Harcum then went on to describe her work life at the DGC:

> None of the above mentioned places were more satisfactory as to working conditions, such as hours, wages or convenience, none were more thoughtful as to electric fans, light equipment, individual drinking cups, paper towels, sanitary wash rooms, of maid service, hospital, nurse first aid, lunch room, rest room, fire preventions, ventilation, elevator service, adjustable chairs. No instructor or her assistants are ever to [*sic*] busy to cooperate with the operator, such as showing her an easy way to handle her work, bring her thread, snaps, buttons or whatever she might need to

> complete her operation. . . . I would not quit my work for any of the above mentioned firms employment.

Having worked at the DGC for seven years, Pearl Uto similarly asserted that her current working conditions and wages "have been far above any of the five (5) different factories I have worked in here in Kansas City and in Chicago. . . . It is the easiest and cleanest work I have ever done." Like Harcum, Uto, and other letter writers, Rosie Christian Velghe cited her substantive work history and knowledge of the labor market to enhance her credibility as a savvy worker navigating the industrial landscape: "I have always been satisfied of all working condiontion [conditions] at the plant. I have worked in several Garment factorys and I must say there has never been one to compare with the Donnelly Garment Co. For it has the cleanest Washrooms I have ever seen in any factory. Best Machines available . . . More light than other factorys and so many other nice things that working at the Nelly Don Factory is a pleasure and also a great help." Velghe concluded her letter: "Words can not express my feeling for the Donnelly Garment Co. For I think it is the grandest place to work on earth. And I mean it." By citing their firsthand knowledge of labor conditions across the garment industry as well as other spaces in which women often found employment outside the home, individual letter writers situated themselves within a broader network of women workers. They recognized that their credibility hinged upon their ability to make well-informed, discerning judgments about the unique space the DGC created for its employees. Circumventing assumptions about their naivete and potential charges that they were easily manipulated by their employer, the letter writers repeatedly establish their ethos as knowledgeable participants in the labor market.

In addition to building their collective ethos by asserting their ability to assess the employment opportunities available to them, the DGC letter writers commonly write about how their wages allow them to provide for their families. Rather than positioning themselves as individuals seeking the highest possible remuneration for their labor as an indication of their value in the marketplace, the letter writers repeatedly stress that the value of their labor is rooted in how it sustains their lives and relationships beyond the factory floor. In their letters, the DGC's women workers make visible those who benefit from their wages. For example, Violet Hawkins wrote: "I have been able to care for my Mother and myself having most of the necessities needed also have a little savings account since I have been with the Donnelly Garment nearly 8 years." Zella Hemme wrote: "I am a mother. There are 4 children in the family. My husband is a carpenter and has had quiet [quite] a time making enough money to give the family the nessary provision for home education and recreation. I went to work to help solve this problem and have really injoyed the privilage of working in the Donnelly plant." In her letter, Lillian Toeneboehn noted that she "can't begin to tell what my checks have meat [meant] to me & my family," and she goes on write that "being a farmer's daughter I can tell you it would have been tough going if it hadn't been for my check each week. to me each check seemed like a rescue boat to a sinking ship at sea. Well I guess I could write a book and still not be able to tell you what Donnelly's has meant to me. And I only hope you will be able to understand in these couple of pages how I feel about it, and how much happiness it has brought me." When reading through the DGC letters, one finds countless stories of how the wages women earned at the DGC afforded them opportunities to sustain and support their families. As these stories accrue, they contribute to a collectively built ethos of the DGC letter writers as a group of women workers whose judgments about their employment are an artful intertwining of expertise and materiality, of ethics and relationships.

While the collective argument of the DGC letters centers on women's expressed satisfaction with their wages and working conditions, it is important to ask what is not represented in the letters. To preserve a particular kind of feminine ethos, women have long navigated around difficult topics, sidestepping directly agonistic positions and conflict. In their letters, most of the DGC employees avoid a direct epistolary confrontation with the ILGWU. Only a handful of letter writers explicitly addressed the ILGWU. Voyant Tools reveals that the words "union" and "unions" appear in only 92 letters, and in 45 of those letters, the woman worker is expressing her satisfaction with the Donnelly Garment Workers Union. "I am proud to belong to the Donnely Garment workers union. My wages are much higher, at the Donnelly plant, than I ever made before," wrote Opal Cox. Rose Lee Greeley similarly noted, "I couldn't begin to write all the reason's I am satisfied with my job because they are too numerous to mention, and I am so happy to have the job I have and make the money I make, and can proudly say I work for the Nell Donnelly Garment Co. and belong to the Donnelly Garment Workers Union. We do not need another union." Only three letter writers mentioned David Dubinsky, the president and public face of the ILGWU, albeit in uncomplimentary ways. The vast majority of letter writers do not demonize the ILGWU, its leadership, or its members—indeed, they invest very little of their rhetorical labor in writing about the international union. Collectively, the letter writers build a positive case for the DGC and the work experience it afforded its employees. They do not represent themselves as bearing animosity or antipathy to unions in general—they just do not believe that affiliating with the ILGWU would better their current economic circumstances. As Gertrude Dora summed up in her oral history interview in 1988, "Of course, unions were needed in some places where they didn't treat their employees like human beings. But not in our place" (18).

By repeating the same topics and reiterating shared affective experiences, the DGC letter writers who chose to compose letters built a weighty body of evidence and collectively constructed a credible ethos. As an act of rhetorical accrual, their letters represent an important strategy whereby low-wage women workers produced arguments about their labor and attempted to claim agency over their economic lives. The oral histories collected some fifty years later reinforce the rhetorical labor accomplished by the letter writers in the 1930s.

Rhetorical Accrual as Community Building

While writing letters allowed the DGC workers to amass a cogent body of evidence and build a collective ethos, participating in the process of rhetorical accrual also functions to strengthen their communal bonds. Seemingly individuated ideas, attitudes, and emotions accumulate and accrue into a shared repository of letters that externalizes the workers' common patterns of experience, thus helping to cement their group identity. As Winderman observes, "Bodies that are physically or symbolically co-oriented together provide a visceral power in numbers, potentially nurturing collectivization" (338). Through their epistolary labor, the DGC workers certainly co-orient themselves symbolically and cultivated a sense of common cause even deeper than what they might derive from their shared experiences on the factory floor. Indeed, the letter writers used the epistolary occasion to make this sense of affiliation and common cause visible to the wider public.

The letter writers often wrote explicitly about their relationships to each other and to their immediate supervisors. "An exceptionally lovely bunch of people to work among. Just stand outside at night and see them come out and anyone would know they are *not* coming out of a sweat shop," observed Rose Campbell (emphasis in original). For Mildred E. Brooks, the DGC employees were "the nicest group of girls I have ever worked with," and Mollie Cannon expressed in her letter that "it is a place I myself would feel honored if my daughter worked there, ever one [everyone] is congenial every body happy." The DGC letter writers also included their supervisors, or "instructors" as they were titled at the DGC, as they described their satisfying workplace relationships. Winnie Underwood wrote, "Because the floor lady for whom I work was once a worker just like me, she's fair, knows her business, and I'd also class her in my list of friends." Irene Tillery similarly noted, "My instructors do not take the role of bosses, but act as helpers, and are always fair to everyone. I am not made to feel that I'm only a wheel in the machine, but to feel that the management is interested in me personally and socially as exemplified through the giving of parties, gifts, bettering working conditions where possible, and the provision of recreational facilities." As the letters repeat, with slight variations, the workers' sense of appreciation for coworkers and supervisors, they build a cogent argument that the DGC is an emotionally satisfying, egalitarian workplace.

The appreciation that DGC letter writers expressed for their supervisors even extended up through the organizational hierarchy to Nell Donnelly Reed herself. Throughout her career, Nell Donnelly Reed was careful to craft an image of herself as nothing more than an astute housewife and savvy seamstress (Greer, "Rhetorical Domesticity" 160–62). She characterized her business as "a sort of glorified housekeeping" (Callen 82), and in narrating the history of the DGC, Reed would emphasize that in the company's early years she cut, stitched, and pressed Nelly Don dresses alongside the women who worked for her.

Not surprisingly, many of the DGC employees use their missives as a rhetorical occasion for expressing their admiration and affection for their charismatic employer. "Mrs. Reeds ideas of fair play, kindness & generosity to all employees have been wholly responsible for the success the business has attained. Through my contact with Mrs. Reed I have not only gained in a material way, but have learned more about my duty to mankind," wrote Lula Nichols. Anna Sosenski observed that "Mrs. Reed treats her employees royal she never high hats us she comes to our dances and parties and is just one of us. At Xmas time she gives one *big* party for us and our families and no one is forgotten. I can not express with words the many nice things Mrs. Reed does for us and I am writing this of my own free will just because I would like for other people to know Mrs. Reed as I do" (emphasis in original). And Ethel Hinckley used her Christian faith as a framework for lauding her employer: "I am sure Mrs. Reed is laying up treasures in Heaven for how well we know the scripture 'Whatsoever you do unto the least of these you do it unto me.' The Golden Rule is practiced in every possible way, and as for me, the Donnelly Garment Company is just a 'Little bit of Heaven,' and I surely appreciate my job." The DGC workers who wrote admiringly of Nell Donnelly Reed heard their perspectives echoed by other letter writers. By expressing their admiration and affection for their employer, the DGC workers strengthened their communal bonds and presented themselves as a unified community.

Through the process of rhetorical accrual, the DGC workers built a powerful case to justify their reluctance to affiliate with the ILGWU. Indeed, the ILGWU recognized the power of these accrued letters and the threat they represented to the union's organizing efforts. Frank P. Walsh, an ILGWU lawyer, argued in court to prevent the letters from becoming part of the legal record. He characterized the letters "as incompetent, irrelevant, and immaterial, not tending to prove any issues in this case as they are now before the Court" (ILGWU, Appellants vs. Donnelly Garment Co., Appellees, 292). The judge initially allowed just a few of the letters deemed "typical" to be admitted as evidence; the rest of the letters were omitted.

Beyond ILGWU's efforts to limit the impact of the letters in court, the collective power of brief, repetitive rhetorical performances that accrue into a larger body of persuasive discourse comes more clearly into focus by turning attention to the DGC employees who were not part of the congenial workplace community that emerges from the letters. Black workers, who were limited to serving as maids and janitors at the factory, opted into the letter-writing enterprise, thus making their presence visible and asserting their right to participate in discussions about the company's future. A handful of workers who were sympathetic to the ILGWU's organizing efforts opted out of the epistolary endeavors that engaged the attention of their coworkers, and they endured verbal and physical harassment for their decision to pursue potential union affiliation.

HIDDEN SEAMS: WHITE SUPREMACY, BLACK WORKERS, AND THE AFFILIATIVE LURE OF RHETORICAL ACCRUAL

For all the explicit expressions of affiliation, affection, and admiration within the letters, white privilege and racist hierarchies shaped the DGC. The white women workers who used the epistolary genre to express their job satisfaction and celebrate Nell Donnelly Reed made no effort to recognize the labor of their Black coworkers, whose occupational opportunities were limited to custodial labor at the factory. The white letter writers repeatedly celebrated the cleanliness of the factory, but they did not acknowledge the janitors and maids who produced the sanitary conditions they valued so highly as part of their emotionally satisfying workplace community. The letter writers seemingly accepted without question that their racial identity entitled them to higher-prestige jobs and economic opportunities unavailable to Black workers.

Notably, though, the DGC's Black maids and janitors insisted upon their right to make their voices heard, to register their opinions about their employment, and to participate in the process of rhetorical accrual as workers' letters began to accumulate in 1937. Within the archive of letters is a single missive attributed to "The Colored Force," with the names of five maids (Nora Williams, Dorothy Roberts, Nancy Black, Dora Perry, and Birdie Baker) and seven janitors (Calvin Burton, John Hoope, Gilbert Kemp, Eugene Valin, Ernest Riley, George Blair, and Dean Tutt) appended to it.[7] The only document in the collection that represents itself as more than the perspective of a single worker, the letter is a complex rhetorical performance that moves between singular pronouns ("I can safely say . . .") and plural pronouns ("We have never worked for a company or an individual that has treated us any better at all times . . ."). The letter is also baffling with its assertion that it represents the perspective of "fourteen of us," but only twelve names appear beneath the closing.

Despite its somewhat puzzling nature and its unique position as the only collaboratively authored letter in the collection, the missive from "The Colored Force" repeats many of the same arguments advanced across the entire body of letters. The "I" who writes the letter establishes credibility by attesting to the longevity of their employment at the DGC: "I can truthfully say that I have been an employee of this company for fifteen years, and steadily so—the longest I have been employed in any one place." The letter goes on to assert that the DGC has "paid us a good salary, as well as giving us favorable working hours." By citing their satisfaction with the above-average wages at the DGC as the reason for resisting the ILGWU's organizing efforts, the women and men of the custodial staff repeat the same argument advanced by the white women who stitched together Nelly Don dresses: the DGC offered its employees reasonable wages and terms of employment. The janitors and maids thus add their voices to processes of rhetorical accrual and contribute their evidence to the argument.

This letter attributed to the DGC's Black workers also invests considerable rhetorical energy in expressing admiration for Nell Donnelly Reed. The letter concludes: "I feel it is my duty to offer praise where praise is due. Allow me to say here, Nelly Don has been a Godsend to all the lest fortunate. Not just in the factory, but with a big heart and broad mind her hospitality has gone out to the outside world to give both aid and assistance to many a worthy cause. Her life portrays, as well as recalls to mind the old familiar poem from which I quote these lines, 'Let me live in the house by the side of the road and be a friend to man.' In conclusion, long live Nelly Don and The Donnelly Garment Sales Company." By offering this encomium to Nell Donnelly Reed, the maids and janitors who signed the letter contribute to the accruing argument of the entire body of letters that the DGC is a satisfying workplace and that the organizing efforts of the ILGWU were unneeded and unwanted.

To be sure, the maids and janitors at the DGC may have keenly felt a need to continually praise and appease their employer and their white coworkers. In his study of Black communities in Kansas City in the late nineteenth and early twentieth centuries, Charles E. Coulter has documented the discrimination and disproportionate economic hardship faced by Black workers. Drawing upon statistics compiled by the Kansas City Urban League, Coulter notes that in 1930, 89 percent of Black women workers in the city were employed in domestic and personal service while just 3 percent of Black women workers were employed at manufacturing companies, like the DGC, where wages were higher and working hours more regular than in private homes (274). Moreover, Black workers during the Great Depression were often "bumped" to provide jobs for white workers. Historians Carter G. Woodson and Lorenzo Greene documented that in 1929 all the Black waitresses at a Kansas City lunch counter were summarily fired and replaced by white women (Coulter 275). The racist context in which Black women worked and the precarity of their economic well-being may well have induced them to participate in the processes of letter writing and rhetorical accrual, regardless of how they might actually have felt about the circumstances of their employment and their employer.

But as the only letter in the collection that identifies its authors by race, this letter must be read with particular care for the complex layers of meaning it bears. Through this letter, the Black workers employed at the DGC are making visible their presence and asserting their right to participate in debates about the company's future. By advancing arguments similar to those put forward by white workers (i.e., wages are higher at the DGC than other factories) and by participating in the processes of community building through their praise of Nell Donnelly Reed, this epistolary effort helps them to legitimize their status as DGC workers and begins to destabilize the racial hierarchies that made them invisible to their white coworkers. A parallel might be drawn between this letter from "The Colored Force" at the DGC and the decision of Black students in the 1950s who wore suits and ties or "Sunday Best" dresses as they integrated lunch counters and other spaces in the South. Carmen Kynard has noted that activists from later generations have sometimes viewed such sartorial strategies as acts of acquiescence to racist standards of dress and comportment and the politics of respectability,[8] but she goes on to argue that the Black student activists in the 1950s who opted for more formal attire were making "a conscious decision to craft a black community presence" based on strength and dignity. They were strategic in their willingness "to engage the fact that whites did not have the capacity to moderately respect African Americans in public otherwise"

(64). So, too, does the deliberate rhetorical labor of the DGC's maids and janitors stand as a challenge to the white supremacy they experienced in the workplace and an effort to seize a measure of control over processes of racialized identity formation at the factory.

Taking these dimensions of the Black workers' letter into account makes apparent the rhetorical savviness of referencing the "old familiar poem" quoted in the missive's final paragraph. Published in 1897, Sam Walter Foss's "The House by the Side of the Road" is characterized by the New England Historical Society (NEHS) as a poetic celebration of "the common man in his battles against pretentiousness and authority" ("Sam Walter Foss Writes"). According to the NEHS, Foss's verses were often recited on public occasions and at civic gatherings, and even stitched into samplers in the early decades of the twentieth century. In five stanzas, the poem's speaker eschews the roles of contemplative hermit, trailblazing pioneer, and detached cynic, all of whom separate themselves from fellow human beings. Instead, the speaker delights in sharing in the lives of others who are in equal measure good and bad, weak and strong, wise and foolish, qualities the speaker also recognizes in their own character. By referencing this poem in their letter, the Black workers asserted their right to access epideictic tropes and themes that carried persuasive currency in the wider culture. And with a deft rhetorical hand, they expanded Foss's notion of the "common man" to include both the woman who founded and led the DGC and themselves in a vision of shared humanity. In short, participating in the shared rhetorical labor of documenting their work lives afforded Black workers at the DGC an important opportunity to make themselves visible as workers with considerable rhetorical skills and to participate in arguments about the future of their workplace.

PINPOINTS: SUPPRESSING DISSENT AT THE DGC

While the Black workers at the DGC chose to participate in the process of rhetorical accrual, a small group of white employees chose not to participate and expressed interest in affiliating with the ILGWU.[9] The experiences of these women workers reveal how rhetorical accrual can be a dangerous tool for suppressing dissent. Because accrued rhetorical performances can strengthen a sense of group identity and community, individuals within the group who might wish to directly challenge or complicate the argument that is being amassed may find themselves silenced, or worse. One can imagine the discomfit an antebellum woman might have experienced if all the members of her extended family or her church community were signing petitions to abolish slavery and she chose not to add her signature to the collective document. Similarly, someone seeking to defend a friend or colleague accused of sexual harassment would likely not find a receptive audience if they shared their perspective on social media using #MeToo. Sylvia Hull and Fern Sigler were two DGC employees who held opinions and ideas counter to the attitudes repeated in the body of their coworkers' accruing rhetorical performances. In 1939, Hull and Sigler were called to testify about their experiences at the DGC as lawyers for the company and the ILGWU battled in court.

Originally from Flint, Michigan, Sylvia Hull was the wife of a metalworker at one of Kansas City's automotive assembly plants, where he was a member of Local 39 of the United Auto Workers.[10] In court, Hull explained that she had worked at the DGC since 1929 and that she was interested in the ILGWU's overtures because she believed that the union might bargain for higher wages at the DGC. She also expressed that she did not wish to be constrained in choosing to associate with any organization. Under questioning from the ILGWU's counsel, Hull explained that she signed her union membership card in March 1937. Meyer Perlstein, an ILGWU vice president and southwestern regional director, then almost immediately invited her to attend the union's annual convention in Atlantic City as a delegate, an invitation her husband accepted on her behalf (ILGWU, Appellants vs. Donnelly Garment Co., Appellees 1949–1951). On April 22, 1937, the *Kansas City Journal-Post* carried an article announcing Hull's appointment as an ILGWU delegate representing the DGC.

Hull's account of what happened when she arrived at work that morning is disturbing. She testified that a group of fellow employees assembled at her machine before the workday began. They raised questions about her right to represent them as a delegate at the union's convention, and they eventually demanded that she surrender a pin worn by many workers to signify their commitment to Nell Donnelly Reed and the DGC. Hull testified: "When I first refused to give the girls my Loyalty League pin they told me that if they caught me with the pin on they would tear my clothes off. They also threatened to throw me out the window and I was seated with my back to the window and it was only two or two and [a] half feet and someone came along and opened the window and they threatened to throw me out" (ILGWU, Appellants vs. Donnelly Garment Co., Appellees 1958–1959). Staff from the personnel office interceded, and Hull reported that she was advised by members of the DGC management to leave the premises. Hull was assured that when her coworkers' frustration was resolved, she would be called back to work. Instead of returning to work at the DGC, Hull opted to do a brief stint as a paid organizer for the ILGWU before she eventually took a job at the Quality Hill Dress Factory in Kansas City, where the workers were represented by the international union (ILGWU, Appellants vs. Donnelly Garment Co., Appellees 1959–92). Hull did not directly challenge the letter writers' evidence that the DGC was a clean and safe factory nor did she express dissatisfaction with the DGC's management. But in affiliating with the ILGWU, Hull marked herself as outside the workplace community that so forcefully emerges in the accrued letters. Remaining employed at the DGC became untenable for her.

Fern Sigler was unable to appear in court due to illness, but her sister, May Fike, was also a DGC employee. Fike was called to the stand to provide an eyewitness account of what unfolded at the DGC when it became known that Sigler had opted to join the ILGWU. According to Fike, Sigler reported to work on April 23, 1937, and twenty to twenty-five DGC employees crowded around her machine. They were "singing songs, throwing slurs . . . about girls that joined the union, that they were not decent, they were streetwalkers, and things like that" (ILGWU, Appellants vs. Donnelly Garment Co., Appellees 1999). The verbal taunts quickly turned into a physical assault. Fike testified that "the crowd behind her [Sigler] pushed her chair up under the machine and held her so tight against the table she couldn't move. She couldn't work. They held her that way, I should judge about 10 minutes or more" (ILGWU, Appellants vs. Donnelly Garment Co., Appellees 2000). According to Fike's testimony and other evidence presented in court, Sigler was eventually escorted to the human resources office, as Hull had been. She too was advised to remain at home until the situation was less volatile and offered assurances that she would be recalled to the factory. DGC records that were accepted as evidence in the courtroom proceedings indicate that Sigler opted, though, to take an impromptu vacation with her husband that did not align with the scheduled vacation period for the section in which she worked at the DGC. Her position at the factory was not held for her.

These deeply troubling descriptions of the harassment and physical violence that Hull and Fike put forward certainly complicate the image of the DGC workforce that emerges from their accrued letters from the 1930s and the oral histories recorded in the 1980s. Instead of savvy economic decision makers who make a positive case for the wages and working conditions at the DGC, the women workers described by Hull and Fike are intolerant of alternative viewpoints. Rather than "an exceptionally lovely bunch of people to work among" that Rose Campbell described in her letter, or the coworkers who all "got along very nicely" that Nevora Davis described in her oral history (17), members of the DGC workforce take on a more sinister appearance as they harass and assault individuals they perceived as a threat to their workplace community.

The intimidation and violence experienced by Hull and Sigler is reprehensible, but there are rhetorical insights to be gained by moving beyond simple condemnation. Looking closely at the testimony of Hull and Fike underscores how processes of rhetorical accrual can nurture dangerously powerful communal impulses. In threatening their pro-ILGWU coworkers, the DGC employees who approached Hull and Sigler were no longer interested in making a positive case for wages and working conditions at Nell Donnelly's factory, nor were they interested in marshaling evidence about their work lives that might be used in a deliberative process to determine whether the ILGWU's organizing efforts would improve the work lives of the DGC employees. Instead, the women who confronted Hull and Sigler sought to shore up the boundaries of their workplace community. Hull was asked to surrender the pin that identified her as a DGC worker, while the women who approached Sigler emphasized the difference between DGC workers and "girls that joined the union," characterizing them as "not decent" and labeling them as "streetwalkers." By demanding that Hull surrender the physical symbol of her identity as a DGC employee (i.e., her pin), and hurling aspersions at Sigler, the DGC workers cast their pro-union coworkers as outsiders or interlopers, denying their place within the ideologically unified group of women workers evidenced in the accrued letters and oral histories. As the events at the DGC reveal, the process of rhetorical accrual very much has the potential to harden the social identities and realities it helps to create for both participants and nonparticipants.

The DGC workers' accrued letters and oral histories paint a powerful, consistent portrait of the lived realities of the majority of the workers—above average wages, clean and safe working conditions, a congenial sense of community on the factory floor. The majority of DGC workers voiced a shared identity and constructed a nearly impervious vision of the material realities of the DGC as a workplace where the intervention of the ILGWU was unneeded and unwanted. In the amassed letters and oral histories, there is no acknowledgment of different viewpoints or alternative perspectives at the DGC factory. As the rhetorical performances accrue, they are mutually reinforcing and cement a singular vision of how the DGC should move forward. Workers who refused to accept this vision were subjected to verbal and physical violence. The accrual of repetitive rhetorical performances by DGC workers served as a forceful mechanism to silence dissent. In sum, the repetitive force of rhetorical accrual can be a powerful tool for low-wage women, but like the sharp scissors and powerful sewing machines that the seamstresses at the DGC wielded with such dexterity, rhetorical accrual is a mechanism that has the potential to inflict serious injuries.

FINAL STITCHES

As I put the final stitches in this chapter, I must confess that when I began this project I expected to construct a very different narrative about the rhetorical endeavors of the women workers at the Donnelly Garment Company. I first learned of Nell Donnelly Reed and her fashion empire from her great-great-nephew, Terence Michael O'Malley, and his documentary film, *Nelly Don: A Stitch in Time* (2006). While focusing on Nell Donnelly Reed's colorful life and many accomplishments, the film also depicts the great affection the workers had for their employer, the comfortable working conditions they enjoyed, and their heroic efforts to fend off the meddlesome ILGWU. I was skeptical. Surely these women workers of the 1930s would seize any rhetorical opportunity for sly subversion, resisting their exploitive employer and pursuing unionization and class-based solidarity on the down low. But I am not the first scholar to enter the archives and find that the voices I encountered there confound and confuse me.

The work of Charlotte Hogg and other scholars who have studied women whose lives and viewpoints do not fit comfortably within established feminist frameworks have provided me with critical guidance in working with the DGC archives. Too often, Hogg notes, feminist scholars have worked mightily to recuperate and reclaim women who seem to accommodate and reinforce patriarchal norms, finding subtle ways in which their work and their lives can be (re)aligned with contemporary feminist goals. As an alternative, Hogg points to the valuable work of scholars across a range of disciplines who have productively documented "the interplay" of ideologies as groups of women with different beliefs, values, and goals clash with each other as well as how women navigate between dichotomous labels—conservative/liberal, patriarchal/feminist, oppressive/empowering, individualist/collective, anti-union/pro-labor. As Hogg argues, historians must not "*over*correct" the problematic nature of the voices of women that speak to us from the archives (400, emphasis in original). Instead, feminist historians of rhetoric must strive to generate scholarship "that acknowledges and analyzes, rather than bypasses," the lives of women whose rhetorical labor may be both disconcerting and uplifting (400). Jessica Enoch and Elizabeth Ellis Miller have similarly encouraged feminist rhetoricians to engage in "archival listening" when encountering the voices from the past that befuddle, disappoint, or even anger us. Enoch and Ellis Miller urge feminist historians to narrate their historiographic experiences, explaining their motivations and the materials they encounter in the archives (72); to articulate moments when they both identify with and feel divided from their historical subjects (77–78); to deeply contextualize the rhetorical situations of their subjects and the cultural resources available to them (79); and to "take the long view," attending to varied responses to a body of rhetorical performances rather than singular moments of success or failure, praise or blame (82). Such an approach allows us to reckon both with the complex humanity of the historical subjects we study as well as our own complexly entangled, always shifting positionalities as feminist researchers.

It has taken me over a decade to learn to live with the ambivalence created by the accrued rhetorical performances of the DGC women workers and to offer here what I hope is a narrative that exemplifies archival listening and accounts for the interplay between diversely circumstanced workers at the DGC. I have striven to acknowledge and analyze, rather than bypass, the complexities of their lives and labor. In doing so, I have found myself continually returning to a letter penned by a seamstress named Virginia Dare. In fewer than 170 words, she described the four and a half years she had been a Donnelly employee. She spoke of working conditions that were better than she "hoped for or expected"; a salary that was "far above that paid by other garment factories"; and the "spirit of fellowship and co-operation" that prevailed among employees and managers. And then she queried: "Why do people refuse to believe us?" Why, indeed.

For low-wage white women workers laboring in garment factories, on farms, in private homes, textile mills, or countless other workspaces, the challenges of controlling public representations of their lives and labors has been considerable. But when rhetoricians pause to take seriously their rhetorical labor—often repetitive and sometimes complexly entangled with contradictory notions of economic autonomy, workplace community, white supremacy, and class solidarity—there is much that can usefully frame discussions about the ongoing work of creating meaningful coalitions capable of working toward economic justice for all.

AFTERWORD

WORKING WOMEN, WORKING WORDS

From the Past to the Present, at Home and Abroad

"That gal there . . . she's pretty do-less." The greatest insult my grandma could level against someone was to label them "do-less," lacking a desire to roll up their sleeves and get things done, unwilling to put their hands to a task and see it through, failing to see that shared labor sustains families and communities. Though my grandma worked in a railroad camp, at a steel mill, on a farm, and at the local one-room schoolhouse, she was never a union member or part of any organized labor movement. Like the vast majority of low-wage women workers in the United States, she had to rely on different kinds of networks and forms of collective action as she sought to provide for herself and her family and to enrich her community. She was deeply committed to her extended family, to her local church and the school her children attended, and to the network of families who lived on nearby farms. I opened this book by describing my grandma's working life in the mountains of West Virginia. I return to her words and her life here because I believe the legacies feminist rhetoricians inherit from unorganized women who worked decades and even centuries ago still have much to teach us today, whether they are our direct ancestors or they speak to us from archives, libraries, and other repositories.

Though she passed before I began working on this project, I think my grandma would have appreciated the white women whose lives and labors I have represented in the preceding chapters. Whether weaving cloth in Lowell, mopping floors in Boston, tending to their farms and families in Appalachia, or stitching garments in Kansas City, none of these women workers were do-less. Even as they engaged in difficult, often dangerous, poorly remunerated labor, these women wielded the power of the pen to represent themselves and the value of their work and to participate in collective endeavors they judged to be most efficacious and satisfying. Careful attention to their work and their words reveals how repetitive rhetorical labor serves as a potent, flexible discursive tool for women struggling in a range of workplaces and spaces. In seeking to gain greater leverage over "their access to and control over the means of provisioning and survival" for themselves and their families, low-wage women workers have navigated complex relationships with coworkers, employers, educators, philanthropists, union leaders, government officials, cultural tastemakers, and others (Acker 68). Though not part of organized labor, the white women workers whose lives animate the pages of this book stand as evidence of the persistence and ingenuity with which they have engaged in a wide range of collective practices to gain a greater measure of power over their economic circumstances. Their repetitive rhetorical labor has also at times reinforced pernicious hierarchies based on race and white supremacy. The complex lessons these low-wage white women workers have to offer remain relevant today.

In seeking to articulate the power of linking the past with the present and potential futures, I follow in the footsteps of cultural theorist Kate Eichhorn. In her study of feminism's archival turn over the past two decades, she argues that the neoliberalism of the late nineteenth and early twentieth centuries has enervated our sense of political agency. We are encouraged to pursue entrepreneurial solutions to our problems and to focus on exercising our individual rights in the marketplace. For Eichhorn, the archive has "the ability to restore to us . . . not history itself but rather the ability to understand the conditions of our everyday lives longitudinally and, more important, the conviction that we might, once again, be *agents* of change in time and history" (6, emphasis in original). Eichhorn thus urges feminist historians to "activate" the archive by making connections across time and place, by tapping into the power of surprising disjunctures and contingencies, and by calling ourselves to account for silences and absences in historical records (160). In their recent collection, *Feminist Connections: Rhetoric and Activism across Time, Space, and Place*, Katherine Fredlund, Kerri Hauman, and Jessica Ouellette make a similar case for a "rhetorical transversal methodology" that allows "researchers to uncover rhetorical practices that are used repeatedly by specific groups with specific goals (across time, space, social identity markers, technology, etc.)" (4). Fredlund, Hauman, and Ouellette note that in geometry a transverse line is one that cuts across two parallel lines, "creating a connection between two lines that would never encounter one another (4). Studying the connecting lines of shared rhetorical practice between feminist rhetors who are historically or geographically remote from each other allows for more complex theorizations of those recurring practices and affords opportunities to consider previously unrecognized relationships.

Twenty-first-century women workers from around the globe might thus be productively placed in conversation with the low-wage white women workers whose lives and labors I encountered in the archive. Contemporary low-wage women workers certainly face different, though no less daunting, challenges than their foremothers. Multinational corporations and the transnational flow of labor and capital has seemingly "puncture[d] the century-old belief in worker power," according to Frances Fox Piven and Richard A. Cloward. They note that "if workers once seemed to have economic power over employers because they could withdraw their labor, now they have to worry about the virtually boundless army of workers across the globe ready to replace them or to replace at lower cost the goods and services they once produced" (413). Writing for *Economic Justice News*, Elmira Nazombe points out that "women and their labor are the unspoken factor in the globalization equation." Nazombe notes that "women's labor attracts investors" who "demand a cheap and 'flexible' labor force. Poor nations and communities recruit women workers in order to compete for investors by keeping wages as low as possible and safety requirements at a minimum." And in wealthier nations, like the United States, where women workers might expect greater protections on the job, the global flow of workers and capital enables exploitation regardless of national borders.

The transnational garment industry serves as a useful example. According to Mark Mittelhauser, few other industries have been as impacted by globalization as the textile and garment industry. The years between 1973 and 1996 saw a 39 percent decline in the number of workers employed in the industry in the United States (24). As garment production moved to Southeast Asia and Central America, wages and working conditions deteriorated rapidly. Tia Lessin's 2001 documentary, *Behind the Labels: Garment Workers on U.S. Saipan*, focuses on the lives of women who work six or seven days a week for up to fifteen hours a day, while residing in company-provided barracks that are "overcrowded, rat- and cockroach-infested . . . with no hot water or air conditioning" (Hesford and Kulbaga 92–94). In 2012, fire tore through the Tazreen Fashion factory outside Dhaka, Bangladesh, and inadequate exit routes left workers trapped on the factory's upper floors. Over a hundred workers, most of them women, lost their lives (Bajaj). Just five months later, more than eleven hundred workers in the same city perished when the Rana Plaza building, which housed five garment factories, collapsed. In the United States, a 2019 article in the *New York Times* exposed the conditions in the Los Angeles factories that produce garments for Fashion Nova, a "fast fashion" brand that markets trendy, inexpensive garments that consumers wear only a few times before discarding. The company contracts with factories where the workforce is comprised largely of undocumented women who have migrated to the United States seeking economic opportunities. The workers "must contend with rats and cockroaches" in "ramshackle buildings that smell like bathrooms," and they earn far less than the minimum wage under a piecework system (Kitroeff). Beyond the garment industry, women from low-income regions of the globe who are recruited to work as domestic workers for the economically elite in wealthier nations and women who labor in fields and on farms of large agricultural producers in North and South America, Europe, and Africa are vulnerable to exploitation and human trafficking.

The rise of a "gig" economy further complicates the agency of women workers in the twenty-first century. Facilitated by a wide range of proprietary internet platforms and smartphone apps, people seeking services can connect with a worker who will give them a lift across town, deliver their lunch, organize their closets, walk their dog, or take on just about any other task. Such freelance labor arrangements hold out the promise of flexibility and autonomy to workers who can seemingly decide when, for whom, and for what pay they will work. For women workers, who shoulder a disproportionate share of caregiving responsibilities for children and other family members, the flexibility of the gig economy may seem particularly appealing. This flexibility is, however, often illusory as opportunities for gig work are shaped by consumer demand. For example, some of the most lucrative hours to work as a point-to-point driver can occur in the late night or early morning hours of the weekends when demand surges as numerous potential customers seek transportation home from entertainment districts and event venues. As Alex Veen and his coauthors have noted, "whilst from the outside the gig economy can appear hyper-flexible, economic and social realities structure the working lives of gig workers and often result in gig workers having to fit their lives around the work and not the other way around, as often purported by the platforms" (25). Moreover, the gig economy and its promise of flexibility does not afford low-wage women workers relief from the gender earnings gap. In a study of more than a million rideshare drivers, Cody Cook and his coauthors documented that women earned 7 percent less than men, with the difference attributable to men's greater experience in using the rideshare platform; the areas in which men and women chose to drive; and an average higher driving speed among men (2–3). Gig work also provides few safety protections or benefits such as health care, retirement savings plans, or tuition assistance. And to date, gig workers in the United States have not been able to avail themselves of union representation and collective bargaining since they are viewed as independent contractors.

For women workers who might pursue the benefits of organized labor and collective bargaining, anti-union legislation and attitudes in the United States have eroded the gains made by organized labor since the middle of the twentieth century. Twenty-eight states have passed "right-to-work" legislation to preclude making union membership a condition of employment in the private sector. In 2018, the US Supreme Court's decision in *Janus v. AFSCME* overturned "fair share" provisions in public sector union contracts that required individual employees who opt out of union membership to still help cover the cost of negotiating the collective bargaining agreements from which they benefit. Moreover, many businesses have implemented a range of measures to forestall employees' impulses to seek union representation, including participatory management philosophies, alternative conflict resolution mechanisms, and the threat of outsourcing. For example, when a group of workers mounted a unionization campaign at an Amazon distribution center in Alabama in 2020, an anti-union website, Do It Without Dues, was quickly launched (Hayasaki 33). Employees visiting the site were reminded of existing systems that afford them input on working conditions at the warehouse, including an Associate Safety Committee, an appeals process for workplace concerns, and "open door avenues" for sharing their opinions and ideas for improving warehouse procedures and processes (doitwithoutdues.com). Amazon's efforts were successful, and the majority of workers at the warehouse voted against unionization in the spring of 2021. Coupled with anti-union legislation and judicial rulings, such corporate efforts to undercut organized labor have led to a US workforce in which just 9.7 percent of women workers were represented by unions in 2019 (Bureau of Labor Statistics 2), just 3 percent higher than the estimated 6.6 percent of women wage earners who were members of trade unions in 1920 (Kessler-Harris, *Out to Work* 152).

Despite the headwinds faced by traditional labor unions and the challenges of globalization and the gig economy, low-wage women workers across a variety of occupations continue to strive to gain greater economic leverage over their lives. They undertake substantial rhetorical labor within the context of a wide range of coalitions, collectives, and associations, not unlike the Lowell mill girls, domestic workers in Boston, Appalachian farm women, and the DGC workers. In Honduras and other Central American countries, women with few economic resources are often employed in *maquiladoras*, or factories owned by foreign corporations that have offshored the manufacturing of clothing, shoes, electronics, and other products. Women working as seamstresses in maquiladoras found, according to Nicole Helmerich, Gale Raj-Reichert, and Sabrina Zajack, that male-dominated trade unions did not welcome their participation (151). The Colective de Mujeres Hondureñas (Collective of Honduran Women), or CODEMUH, has served as an alternative organization for women working in the maquiladoras. Founded in 1989, CODEMUH is a feminist grassroots organization that focuses on workplace issues, such as occupational health and wellness, as well as on issues like domestic violence and reproductive issues that shape women's lives within and beyond the factory gates. CODEMUH's campaign "Labour, Yes, but with Dignity" seeks to create a positive image of women workers "as essential agents in the economic and social development of the nation, achieved through the exercise of their civic and labour rights" (Tórrez 10). Through this campaign, women workers addressed an audience consisting of not just their local factory bosses and the multinational corporations who own or contract with the maquiladoras but also national, state, and local governmental bodies, national and international NGOs, and other women working in similar circumstances. In their rhetorical labor, they strike a careful balance to engage these diverse stakeholders to improve working conditions without causing corporations to disinvest and relocate their factories (7). Relying on the power of repetition, CODEMUH used more than nine hundred radio announcements, along with thousands of leaflets, posters, T-shirts, and tote bags, to gain control over public representations of their lives and labors. They circulated and reinforced positive messages about the dignity of women workers and insisted on their right to fair wages and safe working conditions (10–12).

In Brazil, Joyce Fernandes, who earned her living as a domestic worker for seven years, created a Facebook page, "Eu, Empregada Doméstica" (I, housemaid), as a space where domestic workers, most of whom are Black or *Preta* in Brazil, can share their experiences (Fernandes). Domestic workers, sometimes with the assistance of daughters and granddaughters, compose and circulate representations of their lives and their labor, repeating all too common experiences of degrading working conditions, wage theft, and verbal and physical abuse (Blankenship 151). This drumbeat of the difficulties and degradations endured by domestic workers has drawn international attention. When "Eu, Empregada Doméstica" was featured in a story by the British Broadcasting Corporation (BBC), it picked up more than one hundred thousand followers in twenty-four hours (144).

Household workers in Brazil can also turn to an app, Laudelina, that provides them with easy-to-understand explanations of labor laws, a salary and benefits calculator, and a way to connect with other household workers. The app is named for Laudelina de Campos Melo, who first worked to organize domestic workers in Brazil in 1936 (UNWomen). Spanning the globe, the International Domestic Workers Federation (IDWF) has affiliates in sixty-five countries and more than six hundred thousand domestic workers as members, including migrant workers. In some locations, domestic workers have affiliated with trade unions, while in other contexts domestic workers are linked through associations, networks, and worker cooperatives (International Domestic Workers Federation, "About Us"). The IDWF amplifies the voices of domestic workers as it lobbies on behalf of international campaigns to end gender-based violence. The IDWF's My Fair Home initiative calls upon the employers of domestic workers to pledge publicly to pay fair wages, provide reasonable working conditions, and ensure workers' access to health care. Notably, My Fair Home also urges that all the conditions of employment be documented in "a written agreement" (International Domestic Workers Federation, "My Fair Home"). The power of standardized, accessible language that delineates women workers' rights and responsibilities and employment agreements that repeat their meaning to any and all readers remain critical tools for low-wage women workers, particularly those who are employed in private homes or are otherwise isolated from fellow workers.

From South Korea to Zimbabwe to the United States, women working in agriculture and the global food chain are similarly engaged in efforts to increase their economic agency, improve the lives of their families, and enrich their communities. In rural South Korea, women make up more than half the farmworkers. In the final decades of the twentieth century, free trade agreements and neoliberal agricultural policies devastated their rural economy and "contributed to eroding the traditional knowledge of peasants, but particularly, rural women's knowledge and by extension, their place in society" ("Women Peasants Change the World"). The Korean Women Peasants' Association (KWPA) responded to these challenges by documenting and archiving the work of women farmers, particularly in their efforts to protect seed biodiversity, promote sustainable farming, and challenge gender injustice. Through ZIMSOFF, or the Zimbabwe Smallholder Organic Farmers Forum, women farmers engage in peer-to-peer learning about local seed saving, soil conservation practices, and sustainable water management policies, thereby increasing the food sovereignty of their communities. Rather than contract with foreign firms to produce lucrative commodities like tobacco or cotton that can be sold in distant markets, ZIMSOFF and its women farmers focus on local needs and networks of knowledge. United Farm Workers has been a powerful voice for agricultural workers in the United States since the 1960s, negotiating contracts with large employers and pursuing legislative action, particularly in California, to improve working conditions on farms and in agricultural processing centers. But other organizations have emerged to address more particularly the challenges faced by women farm workers. For example, Justice for Migrant Women seeks to ensure that migrant women are guaranteed "the ability to live and work with dignity," and it makes gender-based violence a particular focus of its efforts ("Our Mission"). The organization is "engaged in culture shift and narrative work that centers migrant women and their families and experiences," and it offers a Rural Women's Collective Fellowship to help migrant women develop their "strategic storytelling skills." By repeating specific details of their experiences within powerful narrative frameworks, women who earn their living as migrant agricultural workers increase awareness of the challenges they face and create new possibilities for mobilizing other women workers and a range of allies, including legislators and government officials, employers, consumers, faith-based advocacy groups, and members of the legal community.

In sum, low-wage women workers around the globe and through the decades have undertaken considerable rhetorical labor as they have persistently sought to improve their lives and their communities. Their names do not always appear on the membership rosters of labor unions, nor have they been represented in feminist histories of rhetoric. But they have taken part in a diverse range of often unrecognized cooperative endeavors, and the discursive work they have undertaken is manifold. They have engaged in strategic storytelling practices, participated in peer-to-peer educational programs, documented and archived their long-standing work practices, posted on social media, organized public relations initiatives, engaged in letter-writing campaigns, shored up existing networks of communal support, used systems of documentation to protect their rights as workers, and launched periodicals. In doing so, they have sought to control representations of themselves and their work. At times they have forged powerful coalitions and alliances; at times they have created distinctions between themselves and other groups of women. They have addressed diverse audiences that often include their employers but also reach far beyond their immediate workplace and address legislators and governmental officials, leaders of nonprofit organizations and social service organizations, the consumers who use the products they produce, members of their own communities, family and friends, their fellow workers, and the general public. Rather than tap into the force of dramatic speeches or large rallies, unorganized women workers have relied on the steady, persistent power of a range of repetitive, seemingly unremarkable, rhetorical performances. Though the "dull daily reinforcement" of ideas and identities rarely attracts headlines or precipitates immediate change, low-wage women workers have deftly deployed various forms of "trivial repetition" to represent themselves and their labor and to gain a greater measure over their economic lives (Burke 26).

The historical case studies that I have shared in this volume anchor the rhetorical labor of contemporary women workers within longstanding, though previously unacknowledged, traditions of women workers' activism. Doing so contributes to the transnational feminist project of troubling simplistic dichotomies between women workers in low-income countries and in high-income countries and allows for the identification of moments when women workers in a variety of locations and time periods have creatively resisted having their lives and labors subsumed within the narrow logic of the marketplace (Dingo, "Networking" 531, 533). While feminist rhetoricians, including Jessica Enoch, David Gold, Sarah Hallenbeck, and Michelle C. Smith, have demonstrated the need for greater attention to rhetorics of women's work, there has been a reluctance to study low-wage women workers who sought to empower themselves outside of traditional labor unions. "Working-class" women have been narrowly constructed as those who can be found marching on the picket line or speaking from the podium during a union rally. Seeking to expand the possibilities for meaning making and alliance building, Charlotte Hogg has challenged the tendency of feminist rhetoricians to focus our scholarly endeavors on women who can be accommodated within the ideological frameworks with which we are most comfortable. Hogg cites the work of historian Joan Wallach Scott, who cautions feminists against constructing "a fantasized narrative that imposes sequential order on otherwise chaotic and contingent occurrences" in order to construct a habitable political identity in the present moment (qtd. in Hogg 396). As Hogg sums up, we do ourselves and our historical subjects a disservice when we tidy up the "messiness of reality" (397) and overlook women and their rhetorical labors who do not fit within our established stories of how women gain economic agency in the world.

However, rhetoricians might well follow the lead of scholars and researchers in the field of labor studies who have in recent years recognized the need to reimagine worker empowerment and reinvigorate a labor movement that includes, but is not limited to, traditional unions. Often labeled as "alt-labor," organizations such as workers' centers that battle wage theft on behalf of immigrants, faith-based organizations, NGOs, local community coalitions, and creative collaborations between unions and other types of organizations have yielded significant gains for workers. Steven K. Ashby invites scholars and activists to consider how "alt-labor" movements and traditional unions can both "strengthen the workers' rights movement by seeing themselves as allies and collaborators, seeking to achieve the same broad goals through different means" (101). Tom Juravich similarly cautions against viewing alt-labor "as a simple alternative to the labor movement" (105), and he documents the importance of marshaling different messages and means to address different audiences and achieve different goals. A wide range of organizations and efforts are needed so that low-wage women workers have greater control over the strategies and tactics used to reconstruct public perceptions about them and so that they can engage in efforts to ensure their economic needs are met in ways they determine to be meaningful and empowering.

Ultimately, the stories and legacies of low-wage white women workers in the century spanned by this study help us better understand the current moment and make us better listeners as women share their working lives by saying the same things again, and again, and again. Whether they are (re)circulating cultural commonplaces, reiterating the terms of their employment in standardized documents, reinforcing long-standing communal relationships, or repeating accounts of their work experience that accrue into a hefty body of evidence, low-wage women workers have much to tell us about varied ways in which they pursue their material interests and about their identities as economic agents.

For too long histories of working-class women's rhetorics have helped to recirculate the entrenched iconography of organized labor, which draws a stark contrast between the silent, victimized worker who is hunched over a machine in a sweatshop and the vocal, empowered worker who marches defiantly on the picket line with an upraised fist. Feminist rhetoricians need opportunities to think beyond this dichotomy and to investigate alternative kinds of economic and social lives that make sense across a range of locations and circumstances. We need to be attuned to the myriad ways rhetoric is entwined with our economic identities—that it can be used to get a job and ensure fair payment of wages, to construct women's public identities as workers, to sustain alternative forms of solidarity, as well as to organize a mass protest against workplace conditions or wage cuts. When we make space for the voices of a wide range of women workers, we will truly be able to say that our feminist histories of rhetoric are rich in all the right kinds of ways.

I'm not naive enough to presume that in another hundred years low-wage women workers will no longer face significant economic and social challenges, but I take to heart Rebecca Solnit's observation that "the best way to resist a monolithic institution or corporation is not with a monolithic movement but with multiplicity itself" (114). The stories I've shared here of unorganized women workers can, I hope, contribute to the power of this multiplicity.

NOTES

INTRODUCTION: WORKING WOMEN, WORKING WORDS

1. The complexities of naming the women working in Lowell's mills signal how their entrance into the industrial labor force ruptured existing understandings of work and gender in the United States during the first half of the nineteenth century. In the 1830s and 1840s, the term "mill girl" spoke to the hope that a woman's status as an industrial worker might be temporary—a "mill girl" might well grow up and return to the domestic sphere where she would fulfill more traditional womanly roles. The term "factory operative" was also used, making a woman worker seem like yet another piece of industrial equipment. I use "factory operative" and "mill girl" interchangeably throughout this volume because women working at Lowell used both terms to refer to themselves, and both terms continue to be used in public memory work at the Lowell National Historical Park.

2. As Goldfield notes, assessing the historical relationship between labor unions and Black workers is no simple task. Racial solidarity would seem essential to the success of the labor movement and the organization of economically disadvantaged workers. But examples abound in the late nineteenth and early twentieth centuries of a wide range of labor unions and other workers' organizations espousing racial equality while at the same time bargaining for seniority rights, job classifications, and pay scales that advantaged white men, and organizing segregated locals that diminished the power of Black workers to press for their demands at the bargaining table. While there is no denying the white supremacy threaded through the labor movement, Goldfield makes a cogent argument for disaggregating the labor movement and investigating union practices in local and specific contexts in order to understand how local and national leadership, rank-and file workers, and structural elements within particular industries and companies did (or did not) promote interracial solidarity (3).

CHAPTER 1: WEAVING NEW IDENTITIES

1. Cultural tastemakers and pundits like Orestes Brownson amplified the negative stereotypes that circulated about women workers employed in the tex-

tile industry. Even as he called upon mill owners to improve working conditions, Brownson avowed that the young women workers in the mills "wear out their health, spirits, and morals, without becoming one whit better off than when they commenced labor. . . . What becomes of them then? Few of them ever marry, fewer still ever return to their native places with reputations unimpaired. 'She has worked in a factory,' is almost enough to damn to infamy the most worthy and virtuous girl" (11). Sarah Josepha Hale similarly gave voice to negative perceptions of women working in industry when she reminded readers of *Godey's Lady's Book* that they should not try to distinguish themselves with expensive apparel because "many of the factory girls wear gold watches" and otherwise imitate "the ornaments which grace the daughters of our most opulent citizens" (3). While their industrial labor produced countless yards of cloth, the factory girls who first entered the industrial workforce in the United States troubled the social fabric of the young nation.

2. See Josephson, *Golden Threads*, 185–203, for further information about the publication history of the *Lowell Offering*, including the possible editorial influence of William Schouler, who owned the conservative *Lowell Courier* and was viewed as an ally of the mill owners. Benita Eisler notes, though, that "the *Offering* was not born a house organ, nor did it ever actually become one," and she suggests that the mill owners benefited more from the "uncensored and independent" reputation of the periodical produced by its workers (36).

3. Judith Ranta's index of the *Offering* identifies many of the women working in the mills who published under pseudonyms. Where possible, I have included both the name and the pen name of authors who contributed to the *Offering*.

4. In her study of the LFLRA, Amy Wan documents how religiosity was also a key rhetorical strategy used by contributors to the *Voice of Industry*, further underscoring the significant and complex ways in which faith and activism were intertwined for women in the nineteenth century.

5. Sarah Robbins provides a nuanced analysis of how middle-class and well-to-do women responded to the "troublesome mass of native laborers and new immigrants" in the 1830s and 1840s by composing and circulating their own "domestic literacy narratives" in which they assumed the role of motherly managers who were responsible for supervising reading and writing activities in their homes and across the nation. See chapter 3 of *Managing Literacy, Mothering America*.

CHAPTER 2: SERVICE(ABLE) RHETORICS

1. Only in large southern cities, such as Atlanta and New Orleans, was "living out" a more common arrangement. In these cities, Black women and married women comprised the majority of women who performed household labor. By 1912, roughly two-thirds of domestic workers in these cities were "day workers," and this trend took hold across the United States as the Great Migra-

tion brought increasing numbers of Black women to northern cities (Katzman 297, table A-19).

2. Focusing more particularly on Boston, the city that is at the center of this chapter, Sarah Deutsch affirms that white women dominated the ranks of household workers in the final decades of the nineteenth century. Deutsch reports that "although over half of Boston's Black female workers were domestic servants, as late as 1908 they had never comprised even 5% of Boston's domestic servants." This is due in part to the fact that Black people were less than 3 percent of Boston's total population in the final decades of the nineteenth century (*Women and the City* 55). Research conducted by the Women's Educational and Industrial Union (WEIU) in 1907 also pointed to the fact that "the three races that predominate in Massachusetts among women wage-earners in Domestic Service are: Irish (almost 50%), Canadians, Native Whites" (*Bulletin of the Domestic Reform League*, np).

3. For further information on domestic workers and labor organizations, see chapter 7 of Van Raaphorst's *Union Maids Not Wanted.* Van Raaphorst documents the existence of a number of intriguing though short-lived efforts to organize domestic workers in the late nineteenth century, including the 1881 strike of Black laundresses in Atlanta and Mary Hartropp's efforts to create a Servant Girl's Association in Kansas City in 1897. Like Tera W. Hunter, Van Rappahorst concludes that "domestic unions resembled the proverbial ephemeral ship in the night" (209).

4. That domestic workers and the women who employed them might be party to legal contracts was a relatively novel idea in the late nineteenth century due in part to lingering associations between hired servants and chattel slaves as well as questions about whether married women were sui juris and had the right to make valid contracts. In 1883, Oliver E. Lyman needed more than twelve pages of meticulously executed argumentation in *Popular Science Monthly* to establish that "notwithstanding their humble social condition, and although they are too frequently regarded as a lower race of beings . . . [servants] have reached a stage of progress that entitles them to the protection of law" (806). He concludes that "being human beings . . . the law clothes [servants] with rights similar to those possessed by other persons, who are not compelled to undertake what we call menial work. Their property rights, for instance, are as sacred as those of princes. To a steal a dollar from a cook is as wrong as to break open the safe of a banker. Their rights of life and limb also are just as inviolable as those of their employers. To kill a waitress is murder as well as when a queen is put to death violently. To chew up the thumb of a chamber-maid is mayhem just as surely as if it were the thumb of the President" (814–15). Like the women of the WEIU, Lyman determined that domestic relations would be greatly improved if household workers and their employers signed written contracts.

5. The WEIU followed Salmon's advice and the School of Housekeeping

began offering a course of study for well-to-do women who wanted to improve how they managed their own homes and for college graduates who wanted to become professionals in the emerging field of home economics. The curriculum for this course of study included nutrition, home construction, drainage, heating and cooling systems, and public health and sanitation. As Laurie Crumpacker notes, though, the school was still very expensive to operate and consumed a substantive portion of the WEIU's budget. Simmons College interceded and purchased the School of Housekeeping to use as the foundation on which to build its own Department of Home Economics (216).

CHAPTER 3: REVISITING *IMITATIO*, REINFORCING NEIGHBORLY NETWORKS OF SOLIDARITY

1. The daughter of a country doctor and a schoolteacher, Stewart was born and raised in eastern Kentucky. At the age of fifteen, she began her career in Morehead, the seat of Rowan County, as a teacher in the public schools, and she attended classes at Morehead Normal School, earning her teaching certificate by the time she turned seventeen. When her brother was elected mayor of Morehead in 1900, he encouraged Cora to run for county school superintendent. For full details on Stewart's life and her career, see Nelms's *Cora Wilson Stewart: Crusader against Illiteracy.* See also Yvonne Honeycutt Baldwin's book-length study of Stewart and her work.

2. Precise knowledge about the number of moonlight schools open to Black families and the racial identities of students who attended the schools is difficult to ascertain based on extant records. Reports from "illiteracy agents," as Stewart termed them, and county school superintendents that are included in publications of the Kentucky Illiteracy Commission are inconsistent in terms of whether they break out the number of moonlight schools open to Black students or pool all schools and students into their reported enrollment numbers. Additionally, some superintendents and agents acknowledge that their reports are incomplete because not all the moonlight schools in their counties filed reports in time for them to be included in aggregate data.

3. See Erica Abrams Locklear for a discussion of how the moonlight schools were taken up by teachers and students in North Carolina.

4. Inspired by the work of Jane Addams and other urban reformers, missionaries and teachers founded settlement schools throughout Appalachia in the early decades of the twentieth century. As Nancy K. Forderhase has noted, the leaders of such settlement schools often believed that "lack of community spirit" lay at the root of many of problems faced by rural residents, and they organized various educational and entrepreneurial initiatives, focusing particularly on transforming the lives of women and children (256). In 1914, the Smith-Lever Act established the Cooperative Extension Service to bring the agricultural research conducted by land grant universities into rural communities so

that farm families might benefit from the latest scientific advancements. For both white and Black women, this often meant they found university-trained experts in home economics coming into their communities to offer demonstrations and lectures. Such extension agents also urged farm women to form clubs and engage in organized activities so that they could collectively learn how to improve their work lives (Brooks; Domosh, Hoffschwelle; Karmen).

5. Liberty Hyde Bailey, dean of the New York State College of Agriculture at Cornell University, was tapped to head the Country Life Commission (CCL), which circulated a twelve-question survey to more than half a million people and held public hearings in twenty-five states/territories. Rural residents who could not meet with commission members were encouraged to gather at their local schoolhouses in early December 1908 and then submit summaries of their discussions on improving country life to the CCL. According to historian Clayton Ellsworth, the CCL received about two hundred such summaries (163). The CCL participated in the same white supremacy that is reflected in the pages of Stewart's *Country Life Readers.* W. E. B. Du Bois, then on the faculty at Atlanta University, wrote to Bailey requesting that the CCL's work include a study of tenant farming and agricultural peonage in the South. Ellsworth reports that the request was turned aside with the explanation that the CCL was not charged to study race relations (163), and the CCL canceled a public hearing at Tuskegee Institute in order "to avoid raising race relations to a fever pitch" (Ellsworth 164). The CCL also sidelined the experiences of immigrant farm families. Upon reading a draft of the report that included several pages highlighting the successes of immigrants as farmers, CCL commissioner Charles S. Barrett vociferously objected. He wrote to Bailey, "I am surer of nothing on this earth, than that the overwhelming majority of the farmers in the south and west are unalterably opposed to foreign immigration" (qtd. in Ellsworth 163). Barrett carried the day, and the several pages dealing with immigrants and country life were excised from the CCL's work.

6. A complex text that relies on both verbal and visual forms of argumentation, Jones's work has been both praised and panned; see, for example, Snyder.

7. Using US census data and other public records to glean further information about the letter writers presents an additional set of research challenges. Among a population for whom print literacy was not a primary means of communication, census enumerators would have struggled to determine whether a woman's name should be recorded as "Amanda McKinney," "Amanda Mckinny," or "Mandy McKiney," and within any rural community, there are often networks of extended family with the same last name and generations of women with only slight variations in their first names, as daughters were named to honor grandmothers, aunts, and other relatives. When I refer to specific letter writers, I include as much information as I could glean from public records, primarily the US censuses of 1910 and 1920, including the racial identity recorded

in the census. Unlike many other states, Kentucky did not conduct state censuses in the years ending with five (1915, 1925, etc.).

8. Many of the reports of the county school superintendents that are included in the 1916–1920 report of the Kentucky Illiteracy Commission do mention that the moonlight schools engendered a greater sense of community spirit among rural residents, though there are few details about collective actions undertaken by community members. Instead, the reports tend to shift from a general summation of the work accomplished by the moonlight schools to requests that the state legislature provide funding so that the volunteer teachers could be compensated and so that each county could have an attendance officer for public schools. Baldwin also comments on the politicized nature of the reports from county school superintendents regarding the value of the KIC; she focuses on dramatic swings between the positive reports filed in 1919 and the less enthusiastic responses that George Colvin, a republican newly elected to the post of superintendent of public instruction, received when he distributed a questionnaire to county superintendents in 1920 asking about the value of Stewart's work to end illiteracy in the state (120–21).

CHAPTER 4: PIECEWORK

1. Sources disagree on the total number of workers at the DGC during the months the letters began to accrue. Marguerite Water Keyes, a bookkeeper at the DGC, provided payroll records and an affidavit establishing that 850 employees were working at the DGC for the week ending March 5, 1937 (ILGWU, Appellants vs. Donnelly Garment Co., Appellees 131). Kyle Anthony estimates that the company consistently employed approximately 900 women and 100 men in full- and part-time positions during the Depression (142–43). Terence Michael O'Malley, Donna Swisher, and Judy Ancel assert that the DGC employed 1,300 people in the 1930s (O'Malley 69; Swisher 27; Ancel n.p.).

2. My focus here is on women who worked for the DGC, but Ellen "Nell" Quinlan Donnelly also merits the attention of feminist rhetoricians. See Greer, "Profiting from Rhetorical Domesticity."

3. Historians Donna Swisher and Kyle Anthony provide the most comprehensive accounts of the ILGWU's battles with the DGC. Neither Swisher nor Anthony discusses the DGC employees' letters in depth.

4. A key component of Franklin D. Roosevelt's New Deal, the National Recovery Administration (NRA) brought together labor leaders, industry representatives, and governmental officials to set minimum wages, maximum weekly work hours, and minimum prices for finished products across broad sectors of the economy. The NRA's primary goal was to forestall a spiral of destructive competition—a race to the bottom—during the darkest days of the Great Depression.

5. Since Enoch and Bessette's work on feminist historiography and digital humanities was published in 2013, much of the exciting scholarship at the intersection of these two fields has been focused on the locatability and linking of archives. See Gutenson and Bachelor; De Hertogh; Graban, Ramsey-Tobienne, and Myers; Rivard; VanHaitsma; and Fancher, Kirsch, and Williams.

6. All the letters are contained in three unnumbered folders in Box 34 of the James A. Reed Collection (K0433) at the State Historical Society of Missouri. I include them as "DGC Employee Letters" in the works cited.

7. George Blair also worked as a chauffeur for Nell Donnelly Reed. In 1931, when Reed was kidnapped from her driveway and held for a $75,000 ransom, Blair was also abducted. The pair were held captive for thirty-four hours before they were rescued from a small cabin on the outskirts of Kansas City (O'Malley 52–53).

8. Evelyn Brooks Higginbotham first articulated the notion of a "politics of respectability" in her 1993 study of Black churchwomen at the turn of the twentieth century; more recently, Brittney C. Cooper has explored respectability in the work of Black women intellectuals and activists from the final decades of the nineteenth century through the early decades of the twenty-first century.

9. Determining how many DGC employees were interested in the ILGWU's overtures is difficult. DGC employees who were called by the ILGWU to testify on the union's behalf in court estimated that they only knew of between five and twelve fellow employees who wanted to affiliate with the union. ILGWU lawyer Frank P. Walsh introduced signed union cards from twenty-nine DGC employees, but company lawyers provided evidence indicating that some of the twenty-nine cards had been signed when the workers had been employed at other garment manufacturers.

10. In a 1941 letter to David Dubinsky, ILGWU vice president Meyer Perlstein noted the efficacy of approaching DGC employees who had husbands or "sweethearts" working in the heavily unionized automotive industry as the ILGWU continued its efforts to gain sufficient support for organizing the company.

WORKS CITED

Acker, Joan. *Class Questions, Feminist Answers*. Rowman and Littlefield, 2006.

Allen, Julia M. "'Dear Comrade': Marian Wharton of the People's College, Fort Scott, Kansas, 1914–1917." *Women's Studies Quarterly*, vol. 22, no. 1/2, 1994, pp. 119–33.

Ancel, Judy. "The Garment Workers: Talk for Kansas City Labor History Tour—October 17, 24, 1992." www.kclabor.org/garment_workers.htm.

Anderson, C. Arnold, and Mary Jean Bowman. "Education and Economic Modernization in Historical Perspective." *Schooling and Society: Studies in the History of Education*, edited by Lawrence Stone, Johns Hopkins UP, 1976, pp. 3–19.

Anglin, Mary K. "Erasures of the Past: Culture, Power, and Heterogeneity in Appalachia." *Journal of Appalachian Studies*, vol. 10, no. 1/2, 2004, pp. 73–84.

Annaline. "The Wanderer." *Lowell Offering*, ser. 3, no. 9, June 1843, pp. 193–98.

Anthony, Kyle. "The Bitterest Battle: The Effort to Unionize the Donnelly Garment Company." *Wide-Open Town: Kansas City in the Pendergast Era*, edited by Diane Mutti Burke, Jason Roe, and John Herron, UP of Kansas, 2018, pp. 139–56.

Ashby, Steven K. "'Traditional' Labor and 'Alt' Labor: Comparisons, Critiques, and Perspectives." *Labor Studies Journal*, vol. 43, no. 2, 2018, pp. 101–3.

Bagley, Sarah. [S. G. B.] "Pleasures of Factory Life." *Lowell Offering*, ser. 1, no. 4, Dec. 1840, pp. 25–26.

Bajaj, Vikas. "Fatal Fire in Bangladesh Highlights the Dangers Facing Garment Workers." *New York Times*, 26 Nov. 2012, p. A4N.

Baker, Josephine L. [J. L. B.] "A Second Peep at Factory Life." *Lowell Offering*, ser. 5, no. 5, May 1845, pp. 97–100.

Baker, Josephine L. [B.] "Woman's Proper Sphere." *Lowell Offering*, ser. 1, no. 1, Oct. 1840, pp. 3–4.

Baldwin, Yvonne Honeycutt. *Cora Wilson Stewart and Kentucky's Moonlight Schools: Fighting for Literacy in America*. UP of Kentucky, 2006.

Baxter, Pamela, and Susan Jack. "Qualitative Case Study Methodology: Study Design and Implementation for Novice Researchers." *Qualitative Report*, vol. 13, no. 4, 2008, pp. 544–59.

Beecher, Catharine. *Miss Beecher's Domestic Receipt-Book*. 3rd ed., Harper and Brothers, 1862.

Beetham, Margaret. "Open and Closed: The Periodical as a Publishing Genre." *Victorian Periodicals Review*, vol. 22, no. 3, 1989, pp. 96–100.

Bevilacqua, Kathryne. "'What a Farmer Reads Shows in His Farm': Performing Literacy with Adult Reading Primers." *PMLA*, vol. 133, no. 5, 2018, pp. 1118–34.

Bird, Caroline. *Enterprising Women*. Norton, 1976.

Blair, Cynthia M. *I've Got to Make My Livin': Black Women's Sex Work in Turn-of-the-Century Chicago*. U of Chicago P, 2010.

Blankenship, Lisa. "From US Progressive Era Speeches to Transnational Social Media Activism: Rhetorical Empathy in Jane Addams's Labor Rhetoric and Joyce Fernandes's #EuEmpregadaDoméstica (I, Housemaid)." *Feminist Connections: Rhetoric and Activism across Time, Space, and Place*, edited by Katherine Fredlund, Kerri Hauman, and Jessica Ouellette, U of Alabama P, 2020, pp. 143–60.

Boehnlein, James M. *The Sociocognitive Rhetoric of Meridel Le Sueur: Feminist Discourse and Reportage of the Thirties*. Edwin Mellen Press, 1994.

Boryczka, Jocelyn M. "The Virtues of Vice: The Lowell Mill Girl Debate and Contemporary Feminist Ethics." *Feminist Theory*, vol. 7, no. 1, 2006, pp. 49–67.

Bowers, William L. *The Country Life Movement in America, 1900–1920*. Kennikat Press, 1974.

Branch, Enobong Hannah. *Opportunity Denied: Limiting Black Women to Devalued Work*. Rutgers UP, 2011.

Brandt, Deborah. "Drafting US Literacy." *College English*, vol. 66, no. 5, 2004, pp. 485–502.

Brandt, Deborah. *Literacy in American Lives*. Cambridge UP, 2001.

Brooke, Robert. "Modeling a Writer's Identity: Reading and Imitation in the Writing Classroom." *College Composition and Communication*, vol. 39, no. 1, 1988, pp. 23–41.

Brooks, Cecelia. "'Touch the Bottom and Lift': Black Women Home Extension Agents in Oklahoma, 1912–1935." *Chronicles of Oklahoma*, vol. 86, no. 1, 2008, pp. 88–108.

Brown, Karida L. *Gone Home: Race and Roots through Appalachia*. U of North Carolina P, 2018.

Brownson, Orestes. "The Laboring Classes." *Boston Quarterly Review*, July 1840, pp. 358–95.

Bryson, Krista. "Conflicted Rhetorics of Appalachian Identity in the Moonlight Schools." *Rereading Appalachia: Literacy, Place, and Cultural Resistance*, edited by Sara Webb-Sunderhaus and Kim Donehower, UP of Kentucky, 2015, pp. 33–54.

Buehl, Jonathan, Tamar Chute, and Anne Fields. "Training in the Archives: Archival Research as Professional Development." *College Composition and Communication*, vol. 64, no. 2, 2012, pp. 274–305.

Bulletin of the Domestic Reform League. Apr. 1907, no. 4. Women's Educational and Industrial Union, Boston, MA, Papers, 1878–1919, 1927–1932, B8, Box 1, Folder 5, Schlesinger Library, Radcliffe Institute, Harvard University.

Bureau of Labor Statistics. "Union Members—2021." News release. 20 January 2022, pp. 1–12.

Burke, Kenneth. *A Rhetoric of Motives*. U of California P, 1969.

Burnham, Katherine D. "Report of the Employment Committee for the Year Ending May, 1896." *The Women's Education and Industrial Union, 264 Boylston St., Boston, Mass., for the Year Ending, May 1896*, pp. 39–41. Women's Educational and Industrial Union Papers, ACC#81-M237, vol. 2, Schlesinger Library, Radcliffe Institute, Harvard University.

Burnham, Linda, and Nik Theodore. *Home Economics: The Invisible and Unregulated World of Domestic Work*. National Domestic Workers Alliance, 2012.

Burton, Gideon O. "Silva Rhetoricae." www.rhetoric.byu.edu.

Cady, Kathryn A. "'Ann and Myself': Rhetoric, Sexualities, and Silence at Lowell." *Southern Communication Journal*, vol. 77, no. 1, 2012, pp. 24–44.

Callen, Charles Lane. "It's All Right to Be a Wife if You Don't Look like One!" *American Magazine*, vol. 104, Nov. 1927, 18+.

Canipe, James B., and Martha M. Decker. "Kentucky's Moonlight Schools: An Enduring Legacy of Adult Learning Principles and Practice." *Adult Learning*, vol. 15, no. 3–4, 2004, pp. 19–21.

Carr, Jean Ferguson. "Afterword." *Local Histories: Reading the Archives of Composition*, edited by Patricia Donahue and Gretchen Flesher Moon, U of Pittsburgh P, 2007, pp. 237–40.

Cassidy, Tina. *How Long Must We Wait? Alice Paul, Woodrow Wilson, and the Fight for the Right to Vote*. 37 Ink, 2019.

Chamberlin, A. W. "Report of Employment Committee." *Report of the Women's Educational and Industrial Union for the Year Ending, May 1, 1877*, pp. 30–32. Women's Educational and Industrial Union Papers, Acc#81-M237, Carton 1, volume 1. Schlesinger Library, Radcliffe Institute, Harvard University.

Chateauvert, Melinda. *Marching Together: Women of the Brotherhood of Sleeping Car Porters*. U of Illinois P, 1998.

Clisby, Harriet. Excerpt from *Reminiscences*. ms. Women's Educational and Industrial Union Papers, Acc#81-M237. Carton 1, Folder 7. Schlesinger Library, Radcliffe Institute, Harvard University.

"Comments of the Press." School of Housekeeping. Women's Educational Industrial Union, Women's Educational and Industrial Union, Boston, MA, Papers, 1878–1919, 1927–1932, B8, Box 1, Folder 9. Schlesinger Library, Radcliffe Institute, Harvard University.

Cook, Cody, Rebecca Diamond, Jonathan Hall, John A. List, and Paul Oyer. "The Gender Earnings Gap in the Gig Economy: Evidence from over a Million Rideshare Drivers." Working Paper 24732, NBER Working Paper Series, National Bureau of Economic Research, June 2018.

Cook, Sylvia Jenkins. *Clothed in Meaning: Literature, Labor, and Cotton in Nineteenth-Century America*. U of Michigan P, 2020.

Cook, Sylvia Jenkins. "'Oh Dear! How the Factory Girls Do Rig Up!': Lowell's Self-Fashioning Working Women." *New England Quarterly*, vol. 83, no. 2, 2010, pp. 219–49.

Cooper, Brittney C. *Beyond Respectability: The Intellectual Thought of Race Women*. U of Illinois P, 2017.

Corbett, Edward P. J. "The Theory and Practice of Imitation in Classical Rhetoric." *College Composition and Communication*, vol. 22, no. 3, 1971, pp. 243–50.

Coulter, Charles E. *"Take Up the Black Man's Burden": Kansas City's African American Communities, 1965–1939*. U of Missouri P, 2006.

"Course for House-Workers 1900–1901. The School of Housekeeping." Women's Educational and Industrial Union, Boston, MA, Papers, 1878–1919, 1927–1932, B8, Box 1, Folder 9, Schlesinger Library, Radcliffe Institute, Harvard University.

Crumpacker, Laurie. "Beyond Servants and Salesgirls: Working Women's Education in Boston, 1885–1915." *Women of the Commonwealth: Work, Family, and Social Change in Nineteenth-Century Massachusetts*, edited by Susan L. Porter, U of Massachusetts P, 1996, pp. 207–32.

Curtis, Harriot F. [C.] "A Pic-Nic Party." *Lowell Offering*, ser. 1, no. 4, Mar. 1841, pp. 63–64.

Curtis, Harriot F. [Grace.] "The Young Wife." *Lowell Offering*, ser. 3, no. 3, Dec. 1842, pp. 49–54.

Curtis, Harriot F. [Kate.] "The White Dress; or, Village Aristocracy." *Lowell Offering*, ser. 3, no. 8, May 1843, pp. 169–70.

Davis, Nevora. "Nevora Davis Oral History Interview Conducted by Rebecca Lightfoot, in Kansas City, Missouri, 1987–14–11." *Economic Development of Kansas City Oral History Project*. Kansas City Museum, Kansas City, MO.

De Hertogh, Lori Beth. "Vanishing Acts: Theorizing Digital Iterations in Feminist Archives." *Enculturation*, Issue 26, 2018. enculturation.net/vanishing-acts.

Decker, William Merrill. *Epistolary Practices: Letter Writing in America before Telecommunications*. U of North Carolina P, 1998.

DeGenaro, William, editor. *Who Says? Working-Class Rhetoric, Class Consciousness and Community*. U of Pittsburgh P, 2007.

Dennie, Ellen M. "Report of the Employment Committee." *Women's Educational and Industrial Union Report for the Year Ending April 1903.* Women's Educational and Industrial Union Papers, Acc# 81-M237, Carton 1. Schlesinger Library, Radcliffe Institute, Harvard University.

Deutsch, Sarah. "Learning to Talk More Like a Man: Boston Women's Class-Bridging Organizations, 1870–1940." *American Historical Review,* vol. 97, no. 2, 1992, pp. 379–404.

Deutsch, Sarah. *Women and the City: Gender, Space, and Power in Boston, 1870–1940.* Oxford UP, 2000.

DGC Employee Letters. Unnumbered Folders, Box 34, James Alexander Reed Papers (1861–1944) Papers, K0443, State Historical Society of Missouri.

Diaz, Abby Morton. "Address of the President." *Report of the Women's Educational and Industrial Union for the Year Ending May 1, 1887.* Women's Educational and Industrial Union Papers, Acc# 81-M237, Carton 1, Schlesinger Library, Radcliffe Institute, Harvard University.

Dillane, Fionnuala. "Forms of Affect, Relationality, and Periodical Encounters, or 'Pine-Apple for the Million.'" *Journal of European Periodical Studies,* vol. 1, no. 1, 2016, pp. 5–24.

Dingo, Rebecca. *Networking Arguments: Rhetoric, Transnational Feminism, and Public Policy Writing.* U of Pittsburgh P, 2012.

Dingo, Rebecca. "Networking the Macro and Micro: Toward Transnational Literacy Practices." *JAC,* vol. 33, no. 3/4, 2013, pp. 529–52.

Domosh, Mona. "Practicing Development at Home: Race, Gender, and the 'Development' of the American South." *Antipode,* vol. 47, no. 4, 2015, pp. 915–41.

Donham, S. Agnes. *History of the WEIU.* ts. (1955) Women's Educational and Industrial Union Papers, Acc#81-M237, Carton 1, Folder 11. Schlesinger Library, Radcliffe Institute, Harvard University.

Dora, Gertrude. "Gertrude Dora Oral History Interview Conducted by Rebecca Lightfoot, in Kansas City, Missouri, 1988-30-1." *Economic Development of Kansas City Oral History Project.* Kansas City Museum, Kansas City, MO.

Douglass, Frederick. *Narrative of the Life of Frederick Douglass.* 1845. Edited by Deborah E. McDowell, Oxford UP, 1999.

Dublin, Thomas. *Transforming Women's Work: New England Lives in the Industrial Revolution.* Cornell UP, 1994.

Dublin, Thomas. *Women at Work: The Transformation of Work and Community in Lowell, Massachusetts, 1826–1860.* Columbia UP, 1979.

Dublin, Thomas. "Women, Work, and Protest in the Early Lowell Mills: 'The Oppressing Hand of Avarice Would Enslave Us.'" *Labor History,* vol. 16, no. 1, 1975, pp. 99–116.

Dudden, Faye E. *Serving Women: Household Service in Nineteenth-Century America.* Wesleyan UP, 1983.

Eaton, Mrs. S. E. "Report of Industrial Department." *Report on the Women's Educational and Industrial Union for the Year Ending May 2, 1882*. Women's Educational and Industrial Union Papers, Acc#81-M237, Carton 1. Schlesinger Library, Radcliffe Institute, Harvard University.

"Editorial Corner." *Lowell Offering*, ser. 1, no. 1, Oct. 1840, p. 16.

Ehrenreich, Barbara. *Nickle and Dimed: On (Not) Getting By in America*. Metropolitan Books, 2001.

Eichhorn, Kate. *The Archival Turn in Feminism: Outrage in Order*. Temple UP, 2013.

Eisler, Benita, editor. *The Lowell Offering: Writings by New England Mill Women (1840–1845)*. W. W. Norton, 1998.

Ellen. "Divine Love." *Lowell Offering*, ser. 1, no. 1, Oct. 1840, p. 12.

Ellis, Grace A. "Our Household Servants." *Galaxy*, vol. 14, Sept. 1872, pp. 349–54.

Ellsworth, Clayton S. "Theodore Roosevelt's Country Life Commission." *Agricultural History*, vol. 34, no. 4, 1960, pp. 155–72.

Enoch, Jessica. "Changing Research Methods, Changing History: A Reflection on Language, Location, and Archive." *Composition Studies*, vol. 38, no. 2, 2010, pp. 47–73.

Enoch, Jessica. *Domestic Occupations: Spatial Rhetorics and Women's Work*. Southern Illinois UP, 2019.

Enoch, Jessica, and Jean Bessette. "Meaningful Engagements: Feminist Historiography and the Digital Humanities." *College Composition and Communication*, vol. 64, no. 4, 2013, pp. 634–60.

Enoch, Jessica, and Elizabeth Ellis Miller. "Historiographic Disappointment: Archival Listening and the Recovery of Politically Complex Figures." *Ethics and Representation in Feminist Rhetorical Inquiry*, edited by Amy E. Dayton and Jennie L. Vaughn, U of Pittsburgh P, 2021, pp. 70–88.

Escobar, Arturo. *Encountering Development: The Making and Unmaking of the Third World*. Princeton UP, 1995.

Ethelinda. "Prejudice against Labor." *Lowell Offering*, ser. 1, no. 5, July 1841, pp. 136–45.

Eveleen. "Forgiveness." *Lowell Offering*, ser. 1, no. 1, Apr. 1841, pp. 29–31.

F. "Disasters Overcome." *Lowell Offering*, ser. 2, no. 10, July 1842, pp. 289–97.

Fancher, Patricia, Gesa Kirsch, and Alison Williams. "Feminist Practices in Digital Humanities Research: Visualizing Women Physicians' Networks of Solidarity, Struggle, and Exclusion." *Peitho*, vol. 22, no. 2, 2020.

Farley, Harriet F. "Editorial, Report of the Committee of the Massachusetts Legislature upon the Hours of Labor." *Lowell Offering*, ser. 5, no. 4, Apr. 1845, p. 96.

Farley, Harriet F. "Editorial—The Aim of the *Offering*." *Lowell Offering*, ser. 5, no. 1, Jan. 1845, pp. 22–24.

Farley, Harriet F. "Editorial—The Suicide." *Lowell Offering*, ser. 4, no. 9, July 1844, pp. 212–15.

Fernandes, Joyce (Preta Rara). "Me, the Maid." Translated by Maria Isabel Menendez-Leon. TEDxSãoPaulo 12 Jan. 2017, www.youtube.com/watch?v=_d_n-z3s8Lo.

Fitzgerald, Kathryn. "The Platteville Papers: Inscribing Frontier Ideology and Culture in a Nineteenth-Century Writing Assignment." *College English*, vol. 64, no. 3, 2002, pp. 273–301.

Flyvbjerg, Bent. "Five Misunderstandings about Case-Study Research." *Norwegian Journal of Sociology*, vol. 12, 2004, 117–42.

Foner, Philip. S. *The Factory Girls*. U of Illinois P, 1977.

Foner, Philip S. *Women and the American Labor Movement: From Colonial Times to the Eve of World War I*. Free Press, 1979.

Forderhase, Nancy K. "Eve Returns to the Garden: Women Reformers in Appalachian Kentucky in the Early Twentieth Century." *Register of the Kentucky Historical Society*, vol. 85, no. 3, 1987, pp. 237–61.

Frank, Dana. "White Working-Class Women and the Race Question." *International Labor and Working-Class History*, vol. 54, 1998, pp. 80–102.

Fredlund, Katherine, Kerri Hauman, and Jessica Ouellette. "Introduction: Exposing Feminist Connections." *Feminist Connections: Rhetoric and Activism across Time, Space, and Place*, edited by Katherine Fredlund, Kerri Hauman, and Jessica Ouellette, U of Alabama P, 2020, pp. 1–16.

Gere, Anne Ruggles. *Intimate Practices: Literacy and Cultural Work in US Women's Clubs*, 1880–1920. U of Illinois P, 1997.

Glasby, Hillery, Sherrie Gradin, and Rachael Ryerson, editors. *Storytelling in Queer Appalachia: Imagining and Writing the Unspeakable Other*. West Virginia UP, 2020.

Glascott, Brenda. "Affection, Intimacy, and Labor Organizing: Queering Public Activism in the Long Nineteenth Century." *Nineteenth-Century American Activist Rhetorics*, edited by Patricia Bizzell and Lisa Zimmerelli, Modern Language Association of America, 2021, pp. 163–75.

Glenn, Cheryl. "Silence: A Rhetorical Art for Resisting Discipline(s)." *JAC* vol. 22, no. 2, 2002, pp. 261–91.

Goggin, Maureen Daly, and Peter N. Goggin. "Stumbling into Wisdom in Rhetoric, Writing, and Literacy Research: An Introduction." *Serendipity in Rhetoric, Writing, and Literacy Research*, edited by Maureen Daly Goggin and Peter N. Goggin, Utah State UP, 2018, pp. 3–14.

Gold, David. *Rhetoric at the Margins: Revising the History of Writing Instruction in American Colleges*, 1873–1947. Southern Illinois UP, 2008.

Gold, David, and Jessica Enoch, editors. *Women at Work: Rhetorics of Gender and Labor*. U of Pittsburgh P, 2019.

Goldfield, Michael. "Race and the CIO: The Possibilities for Racial Egalitarianism during the 1930s and 1940s." *International Labor and Working-Class History*, vol. 44, 1993, pp. 1–32.

Goldman, Anne E. *Take My Word: Autobiographical Innovations of Ethnic American Working Women*. U of California P, 1996.

Goodrich, Henrietta I. "Report of the School of Housekeeping for the Year Ending April, 1901." *Women's Educational and Industrial Union, 264 Boylston St., Boston, Mass., for the Year Ending April, 1901*, pp. 51–56. Women's Educational and Industrial Union Papers, Acc#81–237, Carton 1. Schlesinger Library, Radcliffe Institute, Harvard University.

Graban, Tarez Samra, Alexis Ramsey-Tobienne, and Whitney Myers. "In, Through, and About the Archive: What Digitization (Dis)Allows." *Rhetoric and the Digital Humanities*, edited by Jim Ridolfo and William Hart-Davidson, U of Chicago P, 2015, pp. 233–44.

Gray, LaGuana. *We Just Keep Running the Line: Black Southern Women and the Poultry Processing Industry*. Louisiana State UP, 2014.

Green, Venus. *Race on the Line: Gender, Labor, and Technology in the Bell System, 1880–1980*. Duke UP, 2001.

Greer, Jane. "Profiting from Rhetorical Domesticity: Fashion Magnate Nell Donnelly Reed's Discursive Seams, 1916–1956." *Women at Work: Rhetorics of Gender and Labor*, edited by David Gold and Jessica Enoch, U of Pittsburgh P, 2019, pp. 158–71.

Greer, Jane. "Women's Words, Women's Work: Rural Literacy and Labor." *Reclaiming the Rural: Essays on Literacy, Rhetoric, and Pedagogy*, edited by Kim Donehower, Charlotte Hogg, and Eileen E. Schell, Southern Illinois UP, 2012, pp. 90–106.

Gries, Laurie E. *Still Life with Rhetoric: A New Materialist Approach for Visual Rhetorics*. Utah State UP, 2015.

Griffin, Larry J. "Whiteness and Southern Identity in the Mountain and Lowland South." *Journal of Appalachian Studies*, vol. 10, nos. 1/2, 2004, pp. 7–37.

Guppy, Betsey. [Betsey] "Recollections of an Old Maid." *Lowell Offering*, Oct. 1840, pp. 5–7.

Gutenson, Leah DiNatale, and Michelle Bachelor Robinson. "Race, Women, Methods, and Access: A Journey through Cyberspace and Back." *Peitho*, vol. 19, no. 1, 2016, pp. 71–92.

Hale, Sarah Josepha. "New-Year at Home." *Godey's Lady's Book*, vol. 20, Jan. 1840, pp. 1-4.

Hall, Lydia Sears. [Adelaide] "The Wedding Day: Written on a Wedding Occasion." *Lowell Offering*, ser. 1, no. 9, Nov. 1841, p. 282.

Hallenbeck, Sarah, and Michelle Smith. "Mapping Topoi in the Rhetorical Gendering of Work." *Peitho*, vol. 17, no. 2, 2015, pp. 200–225.

Halloran, S. Michael. "The Rhetoric of Picturesque Scenery: A Nineteenth-

Century Epideictic." *Oratorical Culture in Nineteenth-Century America: Transformations in the Theory and Practice of Rhetoric*, edited by Gregory Clark and S. Michael Halloran, Southern Illinois UP, 1993, pp. 226–46.

Hamilton, Kristie. *America's Sketchbook: The Cultural Life of a Nineteenth-Century Literary Genre.* Ohio UP, 1998.

Harley, Sharon. "Northern Black Female Workers: Jacksonian Era." *The Afro-American Woman: Struggles and Images*, edited by Sharon Harley and Rosalyn Terborg-Penn, Kennikat Press, 1978, pp. 5–16.

Harley, Sharon, and the Black Women and Work Collective. "Preface: Sisters in a Circle." *Sister Circle: Black Women and Work*, edited by Sharon Harley and the Black Women and Work Collective, Rutgers UP, 2002, pp. xv–xix.

Harley, Sharon, Francille Rusan Wilson, and Shirley Wilson Logan. "Introduction: Historical Overview of Black Women and Work." *Sister Circle: Black Women and Work*, edited by Sharon Harley and the Black Women and Work Collective, Rutgers UP, 2002, pp. 1–10.

Harris, LaShawn. *Sex Workers, Psychics, and Numbers Runners: Black Women in New York City's Underground Economy.* U of Illinois P, 2016.

Hartigan, John, Jr. "Whiteness and Appalachian Studies: What's the Connection?" *Journal of Appalachian Studies*, vol. 10, nos. 1/2, 2004, pp. 58–72.

Hartman, Saidiya. *Wayward Lives, Beautiful Experiments: Intimate Histories of Social Upheaval.* W. W. Norton, 2019.

Hawhee, Debra. "Bodily Pedagogies: Rhetoric, Athletics, and the Sophists' Three Rs." *College English*, vol. 65, no. 2, 2002, 142–62.

Hawthorne, Nathaniel. "The Procession of Life." 1846. *Mosses from an Old Manse.* Vol. 1. Houghton, Osgood, and Co., 1879.

Hayasaki, Erika. "Amazon's Great Labor Awakening." *New York Times Magazine*, 18 Feb. 2021, www.nytimes.com/2021/02/18/magazine/amazon-workers-employees-covid-19.html.

Hays, Elaine. "'Be Patient, but Don't Wait!': The Activist Ethos of Student Journalism at the Colored State Normal School, Elizabeth City, North Carolina, 1892–1937." *In the Archives of Composition: Writing and Rhetoric in High Schools and Normal Schools*, edited by Lori Ostergaard and Henrietta Rix Wood, U of Pittsburgh P, 2015, pp. 149–64.

Helmerich, Nicole, Gale Raj-Reichert, and Sabrina Zajak. "Exercising Associational and Networked Power through the Use of Digital Technology by Workers in Global Value Chains." *Competition and Change*, vol. 25, no. 2, 2021, pp. 142–66.

Hersey, Heloise. "History of the Domestic Reform League." Rpt. *Federation Bulletin.* (Nov. 1903). Women's Educational and Industrial Union, Boston, MA, Papers, 1878–1919, 1927–1932, B8, Box 1, Folder 5, Schlesinger Library, Radcliffe Institute, Harvard University.

Hesford, Wendy S., and Theresa A. Kulbaga. "Labored Realisms: Geopolitical Rhetoric and Asian American and Asian (Im)migrant Women's (Auto)biography." *JAC*, vol. 23, no. 1, 2003, pp. 77–107.

Higginbotham, Evelyn Brooks. *Righteous Discontent: The Women's Movement in the Black Baptist Church, 1880–1920*. Harvard UP, 1993.

Hoffschwelle, Mary S. "'Better Homes on Better Farms': Domestic Reform in Rural Tennessee." *Frontiers: A Journal of Women Studies*, vol. 22, no. 1, 2001, pp. 51–73.

Hogg, Charlotte. "Including Conservative Women's Rhetorics in an 'Ethics of Hope and Care.'" *Rhetoric Review*, vol. 34, no. 4, 2015, pp. 391–408.

Hollis, Karyn L. *Liberating Voices: Writing at the Bryn Mawr Summer School for Women Workers*. Southern Illinois UP, 2004.

Holt, Marilyn Irvin. *Linoleum, Better Babies, and the Modern Farm Woman, 1890–1930*. U of New Mexico P, 1995.

"Housekeepers' School and What It Aims at." *Boston Herald*, Dec. 27, 1899.

Hunter, Tera W. "Domination and Resistance: The Politics of Wage Household Labor in New South Atlanta." *Labor History*, vol. 34, no. 2–3, 1993, pp. 205–20.

Hunter, Tera W. *To 'Joy My Freedom: Southern Black Women's Lives and Labors after the Civil War*. Harvard UP, 1997.

Husband, Julie. "'The White Slave of the North': Lowell Mill Women and the Reproduction of 'Free' Labor." *Legacy*, vol. 16, no. 1, 1999, pp. 11–21.

ILGWU, Appellants vs. Donnelly Garment Co., Appellees. United Circuit Court of Appeals, Eighth Circuit, No. 11,605, Civil. Filed Oct. 21, 1939. Box 6. ILGWU, Series 7, Departments and Institutes, 1884–1951, Legal Department, Donnelly Garment Company v. ILGWU. Number 5780/162. Kheel Center for Labor-Management Documentation and Archives, Cornell University Libraries.

Inscoe, John C., editor. *Appalachians and Race: The Mountain South from Slavery to Segregation*. UP of Kentucky, 2001.

International Domestic Workers Federation. "About Us." www.idwfed.org.

International Domestic Workers Federation. "My Fair Home." www.idwfed.org.

International Literacy Association. *Meeting the Challenges of Early Literacy Phonics Instruction*. Literacy Leadership Brief, 2019.

Janiewski, Dolores E. *Sisterhood Denied: Race, Gender, and Class in a New South Community*. Temple UP, 1985.

Jenkins, Eric S. "The Modes of Visual Rhetoric: Circulating Memes as Expressions." *Quarterly Journal of Speech*, vol. 100, no. 4, 2014, pp. 442–66.

Johnson, Davi. "Mapping the Meme: A Geographic Approach to Materialist Rhetorical Criticism." *Communication and Critical/Cultural Studies*, vol. 4, no. 1, 2007, pp. 27–50.

Johnson, Nan. *Gender and Rhetorical Space in American Life, 1866–1910.* Southern Illinois UP, 2002.

Johnstone, Barbara, et al. "Repetition in Discourse: A Dialogue." *Repetition in Discourse: Interdisciplinary Perspectives*, vol. 1, edited by Barbara Johnstone, Ablex, 1994, pp. 1–20.

Jones, Jacqueline. *Labor of Love, Labor of Sorrow: Black Women, Work, and the Family from Slavery to the Present.* Basic Books, 1985.

Jones, Loyal. *Appalachian Values.* Jesse Stuart Foundation, 1994.

Jones, Lu Ann. "'Work Was My Pleasure': An Oral History of Nellie Stancil Langley." *Work, Family, and Faith: Rural Southern Women in the Twentieth Century*, edited by Melissa Walker and Rebecca Sharpless, U of Missouri P, 2006, pp. 17–41.

Josephson, Hannah. *The Golden Threads: New England's Mill Girls and Magnates.* Duell, Sloan, and Pearce, 1949.

Juravich, Tom. "Constituting Challenges in Differing Arenas of Power: Worker Centers, the Fight for $15, and Union Organizing." *Labor Studies*, vol. 43, no. 2, 2018, pp. 104–17.

Karmen, Abbe L. "Putting the House in Order: Women's Cooperative Extension Work in the Early Twentieth Century." *Maine History*, vol. 32, no. 1, 1992, pp. 30–50.

Kates, Susan. *Activist Rhetorics and American Higher Education, 1885–1937.* Southern Illinois UP, 2001.

Katzman, David M. *Seven Days a Week: Women and Domestic Service in Industrializing America.* U of Illinois P, 1981.

Kellor, Frances A. *Out of Work: A Study of Employment Agencies: Their Treatment of the Unemployed, and Their Influence upon Homes and Business.* G. P. Putnam's Sons, 1904.

Kentucky Illiteracy Commission, *Kentucky Illiteracy Commission, Report 1916–1920.* Caxton, 1920.

Kessler-Harris, Alice. *In Pursuit of Equity: Women, Men, and the Quest for Economic Citizenship in 20th-Century America.* Oxford UP, 2001.

Kessler-Harris, Alice. *Out to Work: A History of Wage-Earning Women in the United States.* Oxford UP, 1982.

Kimball, Elizabeth. "Commonplace, Quakers, and the Founding of Haverford School." *Rhetoric Review*, vol. 30, no. 4, 2011, pp. 372–88.

Kitroeff, Natalie. "Fashion Nova's Secret: Underpaid Workers in Los Angeles Factories." *New York Times*, 16 Dec. 2019.

Kvidera, Peter. "Rewriting the Ghetto: Cultural Production in the Labor Narratives of Rose Schneiderman and Theresa Malkiel." *American Quarterly*, vol. 57, no. 4, 2005, pp. 1131–54.

Kynard, Carmen. *Vernacular Insurrections: Race, Black Protest, and the New Century in Composition-Literacies Studies.* State University of New York Press, 2013.

Larcom, Emeline. [Agnes] "The Love of Nature a Duty." *Lowell Offering*, ser. 1, no. 3, Feb. 1841, p. 42.

Larcom, Lucy. *A New England Girlhood*. Houghton Mifflin Company, 1889.

Laslett, John H. M. "Gender, Class, or Ethno-Cultural Struggle? The Problematic Relationship between Rose Pesotta and the Los Angeles ILGWU." *California History*, vol. 72, no. 1, 1993, pp. 20–39.

LeFlouria, Talitha L. *Chained in Silence: Black Women and Convict Labor in the New South*. U of North Carolina P, 2015.

Little, Helen. "Helen Little Oral History Interview Conducted by Rebecca Lightfoot, in Kansas City, Missouri, 1988-15-2." *Economic Development of Kansas City Oral History Project*. Kansas City Museum, Kansas City, MO.

Locklear, Erica Abrams. *Negotiating a Perilous Empowerment: Appalachian Women's Literacies*. Ohio UP, 2011.

Logan, Shirley Wilson. *"We Are Coming": The Persuasive Discourse of Nineteenth-Century Black Women*. Southern Illinois UP, 1999.

Lyman, Oliver E. "The Legal Status of Servant-Girls." *Popular Science Monthly*, vol. 22, Apr. 1883, pp. 803–15.

Mack, Kibibi Voloria C. *Parlor Ladies and Ebony Drudges: African American Women, Class, and Work in a South Carolina Community*. U of Tennessee P, 1999.

Magdol, Edward. *The Antislavery Rank and File: A Social Profile of the Abolitionists' Constituency*. Greenwood Press, 1986.

Mallinson, Christine, and Becky Childs. "The Intersection of Regional and Ethnic Identity: African American English in Appalachia." *Journal of Appalachian Studies*, vol. 10, nos. 1/2, 2004, pp. 129–42.

Martin, Louis C. "Tin Plate Towns, 1890–1910: Local Labor Movements and Workers' Responses to the Crisis in the Steel Workers' Union." *Pennsylvania History: A Journal of Mid-Atlantic Studies*, vol. 74, no. 4, 2007, pp. 492–528.

Martineau, Harriet. "Letter from Miss Martineau to the Editor, May 20, 1844." *Mind amongst the Spindles: A Selection from the Lowell Offering*, edited by Charles Knight. Charles Knight and Co., 1844, pp. xvii–xxii.

Massachusetts Bureau of Statistics of Labor. *Social Conditions in Domestic Service*. With the Women's Educational and Industrial Union. Boston: Wright and Potter, 1900.

Mattina, Anne F. "'Don't Let Them Step on You': Gender, Class, and Ethnicity in the Rhetoric of the Great Strikes, 1909–1913." *Who Says? Working-Class Rhetoric, Class Consciousness, and Community*, edited by William DeGenaro, U of Pittsburgh P, 2007, pp. 47–68.

Mattingly, Carol. *Well-Tempered Women: Nineteenth-Century Temperance Rhetoric*. Southern Illinois UP, 1998.

Matusov, Eugene, and John St. Julien. "Print Literacy as Oppression: Cases of Bureaucratic, Colonial, and Totalitarian Literacies and their Implications for Schooling." *Text*, vol. 24, no. 2, 2004, pp. 197–244.

May, Vanessa H. *Unprotected Labor: Household Workers, Politics, and Middle-Class Reform in New York, 1870–1940.* U of North Carolina P, 2011.

McCauley, Elfrieda B. *The New England Mill Girls: Feminine Influence in the Development of Public Libraries in New England 1820–1860.* Diss. Columbia University, 1971. UMI, 1974.

McKeon, Richard. "Creativity and the Commonplace." *Philosophy and Rhetoric,* vol. 6, no. 4, 1973, pp. 199–210.

McKeon, Richard. "Literary Criticism and the Concept of Imitation in Antiquity." *Modern Philology,* vol. 34, no. 1, 1936, pp. 1–35.

Miller, William L., and Benjamin F. Crabtree. "Clinical Research: A Multimethod Typology and Qualitative Roadmap." *Doing Qualitative Research,* 2nd ed., edited by Benjamin F. Crabtree and William L. Miller, Sage Publications, 1999, pp. 3–30.

Mittelhauser, Mark. "Employment Trends in Textiles and Apparel, 1973–2005." *Monthly Labor Review,* Aug. 1997, pp. 24–35.

Mohanty, Chandra Talpade. *Feminism without Borders: Decolonizing Theory, Practicing Solidarity.* Duke UP, 2003.

Montrie, Chad. "'I Think Less of the Factory Than of My Native Dell': Labor, Nature, and the Lowell 'Mill Girls.'" *Environmental History,* vol. 9, 2004, pp. 275–95.

Moonlight School Course of Study, 1918. Kentucky Illiteracy Commission, 1918.

Moretti, Franco. *Distant Reading.* Verso, 2013.

Morse, Annie Hooker. "Report of the Protective Committee." *Women's Educational and Industrial Committee, 264 Boylston St., Boston, Mass., for the Year Ending April, 1901.* Women's Educational and Industrial Union Papers, Acc#81-M237, Carton 1. Schlesinger Library, Radcliffe Institute, Harvard University.

Murolo, Priscilla. *The Common Ground of Womanhood: Class, Gender, and Working Girls' Clubs, 1884–1928.* U of Illinois P, 1997.

Mussell, James. "Cohering Knowledge in the Nineteenth Century: Form, Genre, and Periodical Studies." *Victorian Periodicals Review,* vol. 42, no. 1, 2009, pp. 93–103.

Mussell, James. "Repetition: Or, 'In Our Last.'" *Victorian Periodicals Review,* vol. 48, no. 3, 2015, pp. 343–58.

Nadasen, Premilla. *Household Workers Unite: The Untold Story of African American Women Who Built a Movement.* Beacon Press, 2015.

National Domestic Workers Alliance. www.domesticworkers.org.

Nazombe, Elmira. "Women's Labor: A Key Factor in Globalization." *Economic Justice News,* May 1999. Rpt. 20 Mar. 2000. www.globalpolicy.org/socecon/inequal/womlabor.htm.

NeCamp, Samantha. *Adult Literacy and American Identity: The Moonlight Schools and Americanization Programs.* Southern Illinois UP, 2014.

Nelms, Willie. *Cora Wilson Stewart: Crusader against Illiteracy*. MacFarland and Company, 1997.

Neth, Mary. *Preserving the Family Farm: Women, Community, and the Foundations of Agribusiness in the Midwest, 1900–1940*. Johns Hopkins UP, 1995.

O'Malley, Terence Michael. *Nelly Don: A Stitch in Time*. Covington Group, 2006.

Oakley, Seanna Sumalee. *Common Places: The Poetics of African Atlantic Postromantics*. Rodopi, 2011.

Osborn, Evanette E. "Report of the Employment Committee." *Report of the Women's Educational and Industrial Union for the Year Ending May 1, 1886*, pp. 29–31. Women's Educational and Industrial Union Papers, Acc#81-M237, Carton 1. Schlesinger Library, Radcliffe Institute, Harvard University.

"Our Domestic Affairs." *Continental Monthly*, vol. 6, no. 3, Sept. 1864, pp. 241–53.

"Our Mission." Justice for Migrant Women. www.justice4women.org.

Owen, Catherine. *Progressive Housekeeping: Keeping House without Knowing How, and Knowing How to Keep House Well*. Houghton Mifflin, 1889.

Perlstein, Meyer. Letter to David Dubinsky. 1941. Box 58, Folder 4C. ILGWU Papers, David Dubinsky, Correspondence, 5780/002. Kheel Center for Labor-Management Documentation and Archives, Cornell University Libraries.

"Permanency of the *Offering*." *Lowell Offering*, ser. 4, no. 1, Mar. 1841.

Pettingill, Lillian. *Toilers of the Home: The Record of a College Woman's Experience as a Domestic Servant*. Doubleday, 1903.

Piven, Frances Fox, and Richard A. Cloward. "Power Repertoires and Globalization." *Politics and Society*, vol. 28, no. 3, 2000, pp. 413–30.

"Plan for Mutual Relief." *Lowell Offering*, ser. 1, no. 3, Feb. 1841, p. 48.

Popp, Veronica, and Danielle Phillips-Cunningham. "Justice for All: The Womanist Labor Rhetoric of Nannie Helen Burroughs." *Peitho*, vol. 23, no. 2, 2021.

Price, Patience. "The Revolt in the Kitchen: A Lesson for Housekeepers." *Godey's Lady's Book and Magazine*, vol. 76, no. 452, Feb. 1868, pp. 142–44.

Puckett, Anita. *Seldom Ask, Never Tell: Labor and Discourse in Appalachia*. Oxford UP, 2000.

Raine, James Watt. *The Land of Saddle-Bags: A Study of the Mountain People of Appalachia*. Council of Women for Home Missions and Missionary Education Movement of the United States and Canada, 1924.

Ranta, Judith A. *The Life and Writings of Betsey Chamberlain, Native American Mill Worker*. Northeastern UP, 2003.

Ranta, Judith A. "The *Lowell Offering* Index." web.archive.org/web/20170511051409/http://library.uml.edu/clh/offering.htm.

Ratcliffe, Krista. *Rhetorical Listening: Identification, Gender, Whiteness*. Southern Illinois UP, 2005.

Redfern, Charlotte. "Report of Protective Department." *Annual Report 1879.* Women's Educational and Industrial Union Papers, Acc#81-M237, Schlesinger Library, Radcliffe Institute, Harvard University.

"Report for the Employment Committee for the Year Ending 1904." *Women's Educational and Industrial Union Report for the Year Ending April 1904*, pp. 42–46. Women's Educational and Industrial Union Papers, ACC#81-M237, Carton 1, Schlesinger Library, Radcliffe Institute, Harvard University.

Ritter, Kelly. *To Know Her Own History: Writing at the Woman's College, 1943–1963.* U of Pittsburgh P, 2012.

Rivard, Courtney. "Turning Archives into Data: Archival Rhetorics and Digital Literacy in the Composition Classroom." *College Composition and Communication*, vol. 70, no. 4, 2019, pp. 527–59.

Robbins, Sarah. *Managing Literacy, Mothering America: Women's Narratives on Reading and Writing in the Nineteenth Century.* U of Pittsburgh P, 2004.

Robinson, Harriet Hanson. 1898. *Loom and Spindle or Life among the Early Mill Girls.* Press Pacifica, 1976.

Rockwell, Geoffrey, and Stéfan Sinclair. *Hermeneutica: Computer-Assisted Interpretation in the Humanities.* MIT Press, 2016.

Roediger, David R. *The Wages of Whiteness: Race and the Making of the American Working Class.* Verso, 1991.

Rose, Mike. *The Mind at Work: Valuing the Intelligence of the American Worker.* Viking, 2004.

Rothermel. Beth Ann. "'A Home for Thought Where Learning Rules': Progressive Era Students and Teacher Identity at a Historic Normal School." *In the Archives of Composition: Writing and Rhetoric in High Schools and Normal Schools*, edited by Lori Ostergaard and Henrietta Rix Wood, U of Pittsburgh P, 2015, pp. 131–48.

Royster, Jacqueline Jones. *Traces of a Stream: Literacy and Social Change among African American Women.* U of Pittsburgh P, 2000.

Royster, Jacqueline Jones, and Gesa E. Kirsch. *Feminist Rhetorical Practices: New Horizons for Rhetoric, Composition, and Literacy Studies.* Southern Illinois UP, 2012.

Ryan, Barbara. *Love, Wages, Slavery: The Literature of Servitude in the United States.* U of Illinois P, 2006.

Ryan, Kathleen J., Nancy Myers, and Rebecca Jones. "Introduction: Identifying Feminist Ecological Ethē." *Rethinking Ethos: A Feminist Ecological Approach to Rhetoric*, edited by Kathleen J. Ryan, Nancy Myers, and Rebecca Jones, Southern Illinois UP, 2016, pp. 1–22.

S. J. H. "The Silent Expressions of Nature." *Lowell Offering*, ser. 3, no. 5, Feb. 1843, p. 102.

Salmon, Lucy Maynard. *Domestic Service.* Macmillan, 1897. Arno Press, 1972.

"Sam Walter Foss Writes the Ultimate Poem for the Common Man." New

England Historical Society. www.newenglandhistoricalsociety.com/sam-walter-foss-writes-ultimate-poem-common-man/.

Sargent, Amelia. "A Report of an Adjourned Meeting of the Improvement Circle Held in Lowell, Mass. Sept 16, 1845." *Voice of Industry*, 25 Sept. 1845.

Schilb, John. *Rhetorical Refusals: Defying Audiences' Expectations*. Southern Illinois UP, 2007.

Sharpless, Rebecca. *Cooking in Other Women's Kitchens: Domestic Workers in the South, 1865–1960*. U of North Carolina P, 2010.

Shaver, Lisa J. *Beyond the Pulpit: Women's Rhetorical Roles in the Antebellum Religious Press*. U of Pittsburgh P, 2012.

Shelfo, Helen. "Helen Shelfo Oral History Interview Conducted by Rebecca Lightfoot, in Kansas City, Missouri, 1988–4–5." *Economic Development of Kansas City Oral History Project*. Kansas City Museum, Kansas City, MO.

Simmons, Sue Carter. "Radcliffe Responses to Harvard Rhetoric: 'An Absurdly Stiff Way of Thinking.'" *Nineteenth-Century Women Learn to Write*, edited by Catherine Hobbs, U of Virginia P, 1995, pp. 264–92.

Smith, Barbara Ellen. "De-Gradations of Whiteness: Appalachia and the Complexities of Race." *Journal of Appalachian Studies*, vol. 10, nos. 1/2, 2004, pp. 38–57.

Smith, Dorothy E. "The Social Construction of Documentary Reality." *Sociological Inquiry*, vol. 44, no. 4, 1974, pp. 257–68.

Smith, Michelle C. *Utopian Genderscapes: Rhetorics of Women's Work in the Early Industrial Age*. Southern Illinois UP, 2021.

Snyder, Bob. "The Appalachian Band in the Moral Spectrum." *Appalachian Journal*, vol. 22, no. 3, 1995, pp. 250–61.

Sohn, Katherine Kelleher. "Whistlin' and Crowin' Women of Appalachia: Literacy Practices since College." *College Composition and Communication*, vol. 54, no. 3, 2003, pp. 423–52.

Solnit, Rebecca. *Hope in the Dark: Untold Histories, Wild Possibilities*. Haymarket Books, 2016.

Solomon, Martha. "Ideology as Rhetorical Constraint: The Anarchist Agitation of 'Red Emma' Goldman." *Quarterly Journal of Speech*, vol. 74, no. 2, 1988, pp. 184–200.

Sowards, Stacey K. "Rhetorical Agency as *Hacienda Caras* and Differential Consciousness through Lens of Gender, Race, Ethnicity, and Class: An Examination of Dolores Huerta's Rhetoric." *Communication Theory*, vol. 20, no. 2, 2010, pp. 223–47.

Spaulding, Mary Anne [M. A.]. "Our Improvement Circle." *Lowell Offering*, ser. 4, no. 5, Mar. 1844, pp. 114–15.

Spofford, Harriet Prescott. *The Servant Girl Question*. Houghton Mifflin, 1881. Rpt. Arno Press, 1977.

Sprague, Julia A. "Report of Protective Committee." *Report of the Women's Ed-*

ucational and Industrial Union for the Year Ending May, 1891. Women's Educational and Industrial Union Papers, Acc# 81-M237, Carton 1. Schlesinger Library, Radcliffe Institute, Harvard University.

Stake, Robert. E. "Case Studies." *Handbook of Qualitative Research*, edited by Norman K. Denzin and Yvonna S. Lincoln, Sage, 1994, pp. 236–47.

Stewart, Cora Wilson. "Address before the Kansas State Teachers Association." Nov. 1915. Cora Wilson Stewart Papers, Box 45, Folder 5. Special Collections Research Center, Margaret I. King Library, University of Kentucky.

Stewart, Cora Wilson. *Country Life Readers: First Book.* B. F. Johnson, 1915.

Stewart, Cora Wilson. *Country Life Readers: Second Book.* B. F. Johnson, 1916.

Stewart, Cora Wilson. *Country Life Readers: Third Book.* B. F. Johnson, 1917.

Stewart, Cora Wilson. *Moonlight Schools: For the Emancipation of Adult Illiterates.* E. P. Dutton, 1922.

Stump, Jacob L. "Producing Zones of Neediness in World Politics: Missionaries, Educators, and a Cultural Political Economy of Colonialism in Appalachia." *Review of International Political Economy*, vol. 28, no. 5, 2021, pp. 1119–41.

Sullivan, Dale L. "Attitudes toward Imitation: Classical Culture and the Modern Temper." *Rhetoric Review*, vol. 8, no. 1, 1989, pp. 5–21.

Sullivan, Patricia. "Inspecting Shadows of Past Classroom Practices: A Search for Students' Voices." *College Composition and Communication*, vol. 63, no. 3, 2012, pp. 365–86.

Sutherland, Daniel E. *Americans and Their Servants: Domestic Service in the United States from 1800 to 1920.* Louisiana State UP, 1981.

Swisher, Donna. "A Tough Nut to Crack: Unionization and the Donnelly Garment Company." *Kawsmouth: A Journal of Regional History*, vol. 4, no. 1, 2002, pp. 18–38.

Tambe, Ashwini. "Reckoning with the Silences of #MeToo." *Feminist Studies*, vol. 44, no. 1, 2018, pp. 197–202.

Taylor, Kathryn Trauth. "Naming Affrilachia: Toward Rhetorical Ecologies of Identity Performance in Appalachia." *Enculturation*, Issue 10, 2011.

Terrill, Robert E. "Mimesis, Duality, and Rhetorical Education." *Rhetoric Society Quarterly*, vol. 41, no. 4, 2011, pp. 295–315.

Terrill, Robert E. "Rhetorical Imitation and Civic Diversity." *Advances in the History of Rhetoric*, vol. 22, no. 2, 2019, pp. 167–78.

Thomas, Abel C. *Autobiography of Rev. Abel C. Thomas: Including Recollections of Persons, Incidents, and Places.* J. M. Usher, 1852.

Tonn, Mari Boor. "Radical Labor in a Feminine Voice: The Rhetoric of Mary Harris 'Mother' Jones and Elizabeth Gurley Flynn." *The Rhetoric of Ninteenth-Century Reform*, edited by Martha Solomon Watson and Thomas R. Burkholder, Michigan State UP, 2008, pp. 224–53.

Tórrez, Berta. "Honduras: Analysis of the Impact of the Collective of Honduran Women (CODEMUH) on Workers' Rights and Occupational Health, 2002 to 2005." Oxfam International, 2008.

Triece, Marcy E. "Appealing to the 'Intelligent Worker': Rhetorical Reconstitution and the Influence of Firsthand Experience in the Rhetoric of Leonora O'Reilly." *Rhetoric Society Quarterly*, vol. 33, no. 2, 2003, pp. 5–24.

"Turn Out at Lowell." *Boston Evening Transcript*, 17 Feb. 1934.

Turner, Abby D. [Abigail] "A Merrimack Reverie." *Lowell Offering*, ser. 1, no. 2, Dec. 1840, pp. 29–30.

UNWomen, Latin America, and the Caribbean. "'Laudelina,' an Innovative App at the Service of Domestic Workers in Brazil." 17 Aug. 2016. lac.unwomen.org.

US Census 1910. "Comparative Occupation Statistics." www2.census.gov.

Van Raaphorst, Donna L. *Union Maids Not Wanted: Organizing Domestic Workers, 1870–1940*. Praeger, 1988.

VanHaitsma, Pamela. "Between Archival Absence and Information Abundance: Reconstructing Sallie Holley's Abolitionist Rhetoric through Digital Surrogates and Metadata." *Quarterly Journal of Speech*, vol. 106, no. 1, 2020, pp. 25–47.

Vaughn, Jennie L. "Representation, Relationships, and Research: Building a Living Archive through Feminist Inquiry." *Ethics and Representation in Feminist Rhetorical Inquiry*, edited by Amy E. Dayton and Jennie L. Vaughn, U of Pittsburgh P, 2021, pp. 126–41.

Veen, Alex, Sarah Kaine, Caleb Goods, and Tom Barratt. "The 'Gigification' of Work in the 21st Century." *Contemporary Work and the Future of Employment in Developed Countries*, edited by Peter Holland and Chris Brewster. Taylor and Francis, 2020, pp. 15–32.

W. J. S. "Factory Labor." *Lowell Offering*, ser. 4, no. 9, July 1844, pp. 199–200.

Waggoner, Eric G. "Radical Rhetoric, American Iconography, and *The Autobiography of Mother Jones*." *Appalachian Journal*, vol. 32, no. 2, 2005, pp. 192–210.

Waguespack, Leslie J., Jeffry S. Babb, and David J. Yates. "Triangulating Coding Bootcamps in IS Education: Bootleg Education or Disruptive Innovation?" *Information Systems Education Journal*, vol. 16, no. 6, 2018, pp. 48–58.

Walker, Melissa. *All We Knew Was to Farm: Rural Women in the Upcountry South, 1919–1941*. Johns Hopkins UP, 2000.

Wan, Amy J. *Producing Good Citizens: Literacy Training in Anxious Times*. U of Pittsburgh P, 2014.

Wan, Amy J. "Republicanism, Religiosity, and the Rhetoric of Women's Labor Reform in Lowell, Massachusetts, 1830–1850." *Women at Work: Rhetorics of Gender and Labor*, edited by David Gold and Jessica Enoch, U of Pittsburgh P, 2019, pp. 17–30.

Ware, Caroline F. *The Early New England Cotton Manufacture: A Study in Industrial Beginnings*. Houghton Mifflin, 1931.

Webb-Sunderhaus, Sara. "Living with Literacy's Contradictions: Appalachian Students in a First-Year Writing Course." *Reclaiming the Rural: Essays on Literacy, Rhetoric, and Pedagogy*, edited by Kim Donehower, Charlotte Hogg, and Eileen E. Schell. Southern Illinois UP, 2012, pp. 207–22.

Welch, Jane Sarah. [J. S. W.] "Earth Speaks in Many Voices." *Lowell Offering*, ser. 4, no. 7, May 1844, pp. 157–58.

Welch, Jane Sarah. [J. S. W.] "The Mother and Daughter." *Lowell Offering*, ser. 4, no. 6, Apr. 1844, pp. 126–28.

Wellman, Judith. "The Seneca Falls Women's Rights Convention: A Study of Social Networks." *Journal of Women's History*, vol. 3, no. 1, 1991, pp. 9–37.

Wells, Kate Gannett. "Report from the Protective Committee." *Annual Report 1889*. Women's Educational and Industrial Union Papers, Acc#81-m237, Carton 1, Schlesinger Library, Radcliffe Institute, Harvard University.

Wells, Kate Gannett. "Report from the Protective Committee." *Report of the Women's Educational and Industrial Union for the Year Ending May 1, 1888*. Women's Educational and Industrial Union Papers, ACC#81-M237, Carton 1, Schlesinger Library, Radcliffe Institute, Harvard University.

Wells, Kate Gannett. "Report of the Protective Committee." *Report of the Women's Educational and Industrial Union for the Year Ending May 1892*. Women's Educational and Industrial Union Papers, Acc#81-m237, Carton 1, Schlesinger Library, Radcliffe Institute, Harvard University.

Wells, Kate Gannett. "The Servant Girl of the Future." *North American Review*, vol. 157, no. 445, Dec. 1893, pp. 716–21.

Welsch, Kathleen A. "Thinking Like *That*: The Ideal Nineteenth-Century Student Writer." *Local Histories: Reading the Archives of Composition*, edited by Patricia Donahue and Gretchen Flesher Moon, U of Pittsburgh P, 2007, pp. 14–37.

Whitcomb, Carrie Niles. "Training Schools for Domestic Servants." *Century Magazine*, vol. 52, no. 5, Sept. 1896, pp. 795–96.

Wilkerson, Jessica. *To Live Here, You Have to Fight: How Women Led Appalachian Movements for Social Justice*, U of Illinois P, 2019.

Wilson, Kirt H. "The Racial Politics of Imitation in the Nineteenth Century." *Quarterly Journal of Speech*, vol. 89, no. 2, 2003, pp. 89–108.

Winderman, Emily. "Anger's Volumes: Rhetorics of Amplification and Aggregation in #MeToo." *Women's Studies in Communication*, vol. 42, no. 3, 2019, pp. 327–46.

"Women Peasants Change the World." Agroecologyfund.org. 24 Sept. 2020.

Woodson, Carter G. "Freedom and Slavery in Appalachian America." *Journal of Negro History*, vol. 1, no. 2, 1916, pp. 132–50.

Yates, JoAnne. *Control through Communication: The Rise of System in American Management.* Johns Hopkins UP, 1989.

Young, Louisa C. "Report of the Committee on the School of Housekeeping for the Year Ending April 25, 1899." *Women's Educational and Industrial Union, 264 Boyleston St., Boston, Mass., for the Year Ending May, 1899*, pp. 46–49. Women's Educational and Industrial Union Papers, Acc#81–237, Carton 1, Schlesinger Library, Radcliffe Institute, Harvard University.

Young, Louisa C. "Report of the Committee on the School of Housekeeping for the Year Ending May 1898." *Women's Educational and Industrial Union, 264 Boyleston St., Boston, Mass., for the Year Ending May, 1898*, pp. 55–59. Women's Educational Industrial Union Papers, Acc#81–237, Carton 1. Schlesinger Library, Radcliffe Institute, Harvard University.

Zaeske, Susan. *Signatures of Citizenship: Petitioning, Antislavery, and Women's Political Identity.* U of North Carolina P, 2003.

Zweig, Michael. *The Working Class Majority: America's Best Kept Secret.* 2nd ed. ILR Press, 2012.

INDEX